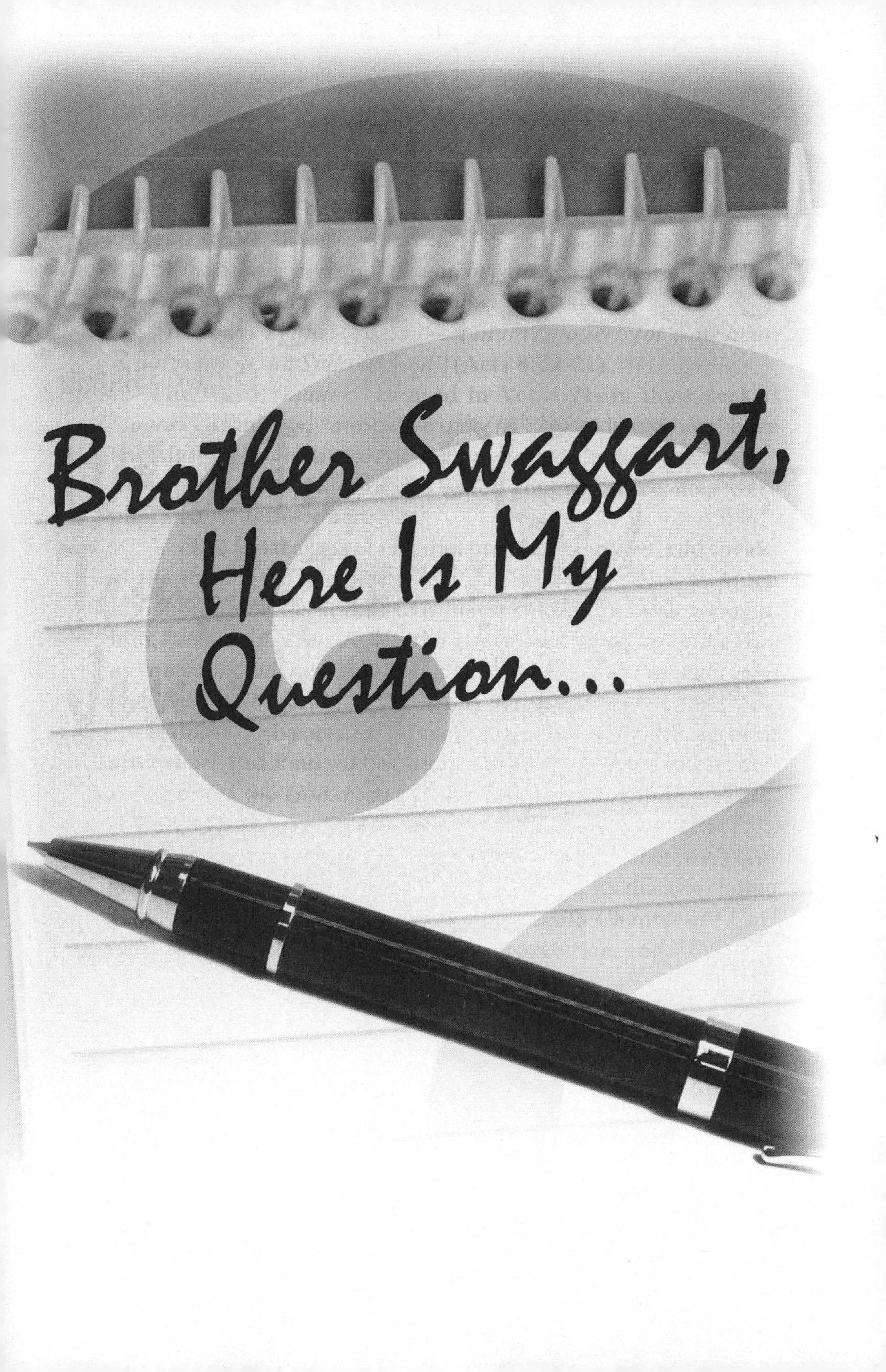
Brother Swaggart,
Here Is My
Question...

Brother Swaggart, Here Is My Question...

By Jimmy Swaggart

Jimmy Swaggart Ministries
P.O. Box 262550 • Baton Rouge, Louisiana 70826-2550
www.jsm.org

ISBN 978-1-934655-46-7
09-097
16 17 18 19 20 21 22 23 24 25 / EBM / 13 12 11 10 9 8 7 6 5 4

TABLE OF CONTENTS

INTRODUCTION

Because of preaching and teaching over Radio and Television constantly, we are at the same time constantly bombarded with questions respecting the Bible. These questions concern life and living, which, of course, are very important to all Believers and, in fact, with the answers found in the Word of God.

There isn't much that the Bible doesn't address as it regards life and living. To be sure, the Word of God is the yardstick for all answers and, in fact, is the only yardstick in the world.

The word *"Righteousness,"* actually means, *"that which is right"*; however, it is God's Definition of what is right and not man's. In fact, man has been attempting to substitute his righteousness for the Righteousness of God, from the very beginning of time. Cain was the first example, at least of which we have a record (Gen., Chpt. 4).

In this book, we are attempting to answer the questions that seem to be more prevalent among Believers, in other words, the question most asked!

THE BIBLE

We believe and teach that the Bible is the road map for life and living, the blueprint for eternity. We believe it is the only revealed Truth in the world today and, in fact, ever has been. As it regards life and living, it alone holds the answers.

I would ask you please, to look carefully at the answers we have given to particular questions. Judge what we say according to the Word of God, and not according to a personal bias or prejudice. After all, it's not what I think or you may think, but it's what the Word of God says to us.

Jesus said, *"Man shall not live by bread alone, but by every Word that proceeds out of the Mouth of God"* (Mat. 4:4).

Peter wrote as the Holy Spirit inspired him, saying:

"Grace and Peace be multiplied unto you through the knowledge of God, and of Jesus our Lord,

"According as His Divine Power has given unto us all things

that pertain unto life and Godliness, through the knowledge of Him Who has called us to Glory and virtue:

***"Whereby are given unto us exceeding great and Precious Promises: that by these you might be partakers of the Divine Nature, having escaped the corruption that is in the world through lust"* (II Pet. 1:2-4).**

As you the reader peruse these pages, you will find that we use THE EXPOSITOR'S STUDY BIBLE regarding the King James Text, and the notes.

CHAPTER ONE

Who Is Satan, And Where Do Demon Spirits Come From?

QUESTION:

WHO IS SATAN, AND WHERE DO DEMON SPIRITS COME FROM?

ANSWER:

Satan is not an evil principle, an object of the mortal mind, an influence, an abstract power, a disease germ, etc.

THE ORIGIN OF SATAN

Satan, in the beginning known as Lucifer, was created by God, along with other beings, principalities, powers, and Angels — was a sinless, perfect, beautiful, and righteous being. The name *"Lucifer,"* means *"morning star."* The name *"Satan"* which evidently was given to him after his fall, means *"adversary."*

SATAN'S REVOLUTION AGAINST GOD

We have almost no information at all concerning this particular revolution; however, we do know that it was widespread and powerful inasmuch as one third of the Angels threw in their lot with him, evidently in an effort to overthrow Jehovah. The Scripture says concerning that:

> **"And there appeared another wonder in Heaven** *(should have been translated, 'another sign')*; **and behold a great red dragon** *(denotes Satan and his murderous purpose, typified by the color of 'red')*, **having seven heads** *(refers to Empires that persecuted Israel, even until John's day; those Empires were Egypt, Assyria, Babylon, Medo-Persia, Greece, and Rome)* **and ten horns** *(represents ten nations that will be ruled by the Antichrist in the last days, and will greatly persecute Israel; actually, the seventh head is those 'ten horns'; Daniel tells us that these 'ten horns'*

representing ten nations will be in the old Roman Empire territory, which refers to the Middle East and parts of Europe [Dan. 7:7]), **and seven crowns upon his heads** *(represents the fact that Satan controlled these particular kingdoms)*.

"And his tail drew the third part of the stars of Heaven *(this goes all the way back to the original rebellion of Lucifer against God; at that time, one-third of the Angels threw in their lot with him; we know these 'stars' represent Angels, because Rev. 12:9 tells us so)*, **and did cast them to the Earth** *(is given to us more clearly in Rev. 12:7-9)* **. . ." (Rev. 12:3-4).**

John the Beloved continues to address this problem by saying:

"And there was war in Heaven *(pertains to the 'Mystery of God' being finished, which pertains to the reason that God has allowed Satan to continue this long [Rev. 10:7])*: **Michael and his Angels fought against the dragon; and the dragon fought and his Angels** *(this pertains to Satan and all the Angels who followed him being cast out of Heaven, which will take place at the midpoint of the Great Tribulation; why the Lord has allowed Satan and his minions to remain in Heaven all of this time, we aren't told; it is a 'Mystery,' but it will now be finished)*,

"And prevailed not *(Satan will then be defeated; incidentally, it is not Satan who instigates this war, but rather the Archangel Michael at the Command of God)*; **neither was their place found any more in Heaven** *(joins with the close of the Book of Revelation, where the Evil One has no more place on Earth as well, but rather the place of torment forever and ever [Rev. 20:10])*.

"And the great dragon was cast out, that old serpent, called the Devil, and Satan *(he is referred to as 'the Great Dragon' because of his propensity to 'steal, kill, and destroy' [Jn. 10:10]; he is the 'old serpent' because in his*

> *first appearance in the Bible, he chose to work through a serpent; thereby, he is what the curse caused the serpent to be, wryly subtle, and treacherous),* **which deceives the whole world** *(deception is his greatest weapon; he deceives, and is himself deceived)*: **he was cast out into the earth, and his Angels were cast out with him** *(pronounces the beginning of the end for this evil monster)*" **(Rev. 12:7-9).**

ANGELS

When God created the Angels, He created them all at the same time, all fully mature so to speak, meaning that there's never been such a thing as a baby Angel. While Angels have different ranks, they aren't of different ages. How many the Lord created, we aren't told. As well, how long it was from the time of their creation to the time of the revolution of Lucifer that we aren't told either.

Only four Angels are named in Scripture: *"Gabriel,"* who stands in the Presence of God, and who just might be the most powerful Angel of all; *"Michael,"* the only Archangel named in Scripture; *"Lucifer,"* who rebelled against God, and heads up the world of spiritual darkness; and, *"Apollyon."* Being named, he probably was one of the most powerful Angels created, and was one of the Angels that threw in his lot with Satan.

WHY DID SATAN LEAD A REVOLUTION AGAINST GOD?

All we know is the scant amount of information given to us in the Bible. I will quote directly from THE EXPOSITOR'S STUDY BIBLE:

> **"How are you fallen from Heaven, O Lucifer, son of the morning! how are you cut down to the ground, which did weaken the nations!** *(Isaiah's Prophecy now switches from the Antichrist to his unholy sponsor, Satan himself.*

"*'Lucifer' is the name of Satan. Actually, he is an Angel, originally created by God, who served the Lord in righteousness for an undetermined period of time.*

"*When he fell, he led a revolution against God, with about one-third of the Angels, it seems, throwing in their lot with him [Rev. 12:4]. Therefore, all the pain, suffering, misery, heartache, death, and deception which have ruled the nations from the very beginning can be laid at the door-step of this revolution headed up by Satan.)*

"For you have said in your heart, I will ascend into Heaven, I will exalt my throne above the stars of God: I will sit also upon the mount of the congregation, in the sides of the north:

"I will ascend above the heights of the clouds; I will be like the Most High. *(In these two Verses, we see the foment of Satan's rebellion and revolution against God. It seems that Lucifer, while true to the Lord, was given dominion of the Earth, which was before Adam. After his fall, he worked deceitfully to get other angelic rulers to follow him in his war against God.)*

"Yet you shall be brought down to Hell, to the sides of the pit. *(This will be the lot of Satan and all who seek to be like God, but in a wrong way, in effect, by making themselves God.)*" **(Isa. 14:12-15).**

A DESCRIPTION OF THE EVIL ONE

Once again, I quote directly from THE EXPOSITOR'S STUDY BIBLE:

"Moreover, the Word of the LORD came unto me, saying *(the tenor of this Chapter will now change from the earthly Monarch, the 'Prince of Tyre,' to his sponsor, Satan, of which the earthly king was a symbol)*,

"Son of man, take up a lamentation upon the king of Tyrus, and say unto him, Thus says the Lord GOD; You

seal up the sum, full of wisdom, and perfect in beauty. *(As is obvious, even though the king of Tyrus is used as a symbol, the statements made could not refer to any mere mortal. In fact, they refer to Satan.*

"The phrase, 'You seal up the sum,' means that Lucifer, when originally created by God, was the perfection of wisdom and beauty. In fact, the phrase intimates that Lucifer was the wisest and most beautiful Angel created by God, and served the Lord in Holiness and Righteousness for a given period of time.

"The phrase, 'Perfect in beauty,' means that he was the most beautiful of God's Angelic creation. The Holy Spirit even labeled his beauty as 'perfect.')

"You have been in Eden the Garden of God; every precious stone was your covering, the sardius, topaz, and the diamond, the beryl, the onyx, and the jasper, the sapphire, the emerald, and the carbuncle, and gold: the workmanship of your tabrets and of your pipes was prepared in you in the day that you were created. *(The phrase, 'You have been in Eden the Garden of God,' does not actually refer to the 'Eden' of Gen., Chpt. 3, but rather to the 'Eden' which existed on this Planet before Adam and Eve, which evidently was ruled by Lucifer before his rebellion.*

"'Every precious stone was your covering,' presents itself as very similar to the dress of the High Priest of Israel [Ex. 28:19].

"'The workmanship of your tabrets and of your pipes,' has to do with music. There is every indication that Lucifer's leadership had something to do with the worship of God. As well, he is called, 'O Lucifer, son of the morning' [Isa. 14:12]. When the Earth was originally created, the Scripture says, 'The morning stars sang together, and all the sons of God shouted for joy' [Job 38:4-7]. So, if the idiom, 'son of the morning,' can be linked to the 'morning stars,' these Passages tell us that Lucifer, at least before his fall, was greatly used in leading the Worship of God.

"*In fact, this is the reason that Satan has done everything within his power to corrupt the music of the world, and to corrupt the music of the Church above all. Inasmuch as the Book of Psalms is the longest Book in the Bible, we learn from this that music and singing are among the highest forms of worship of the Lord.)*"

THE ANOINTED CHERUB

We continue with THE EXPOSITOR'S STUDY BIBLE:

"You are the anointed Cherub who covers; and I have set you so: you were upon the Holy Mountain of God; you have walked up and down in the midst of the stones of fire. *('You are the anointed Cherub who covers,' means that Lucifer was chosen and 'anointed' by God for a particular task and service. This probably was the 'worship' to which we have just alluded.*

"'You were upon the Holy Mountain of God,' speaks of his place and position relative to the Throne [Rev. 4:2-11]. 'You have walked up and down in the midst of the stones of fire,' has reference to his nearness to the Throne [Ezek. 1:26-27]. As well, the phrase, 'Walked up and down,' seems to imply that not just any Angel would have been given such latitude.)

"You were perfect in your ways from the day that you were created, till iniquity was found in you *(pride was the form of this iniquity [Lk. 10:17-18]. The rebellion of Lucifer against God probably caused the catastrophe which occurred between the First and Second Verses of Gen., Chpt. 1)*,

"By the multitude of your merchandise they have filled the midst of you with violence, and you have sinned; therefore I will cast you as profane out of the Mountain of God: and I will destroy you, O covering Cherub, from the midst of the stones of fire. *('Violence' has been the*

earmark of Satan's rule and reign in the world of darkness [Jn. 10:10]. Lucifer being 'cast out' of the 'Mountain of God' refers to him losing his place and position, which he had held with God since his creation. It was because 'he had sinned,' which spoke of pride that caused him to lift himself up against God.)

LUCIFER SINNED AGAINST GOD

"Your heart was lifted up because of your beauty, you have corrupted your wisdom by reason of your brightness: I will cast you to the ground, I will lay you before kings, that they may behold you. *('Your heart was lifted up because of your beauty,' tells us the reason for his fall. As stated, it was pride. He took his eyes off of Christ, noticing his own beauty as it grew more and more glorious in his eyes. At some point in time, his 'heart' was changed from Christ to himself. As far as we know, this was the origin of evil in all of God's Creation.*

"'You have corrupted your wisdom by reason of your brightness,' does not refer to the loss of wisdom, but instead refers to wisdom corrupted, hence, the insidious design practiced upon the human family.

"'I will cast you to the ground,' refers to his ultimate defeat [Rev. 12:7-12].

"'I will lay you before kings, that they may behold you,' refers to him ultimately being cast into the Lake of Fire, where all the kings of the Earth who have died lost will behold him in his humiliation [Mat. 25:41; Rev. 20:10].

"You have defiled your sanctuaries by the multitude of your iniquities, by the iniquity of your traffic; therefore will I bring forth a fire from the midst of you, it shall devour you, and I will bring you to ashes upon the Earth in the sight of all them who behold you. *(When Satan at long last will be thrown into the Lake of Fire [Rev. 20:10], all the billions he has duped, who also are in Hell because of* *him, will hate him with a passion that words cannot begin to express, and a hatred which will last forever and forever.)*

"All they who know you among the people shall be astonished at you: you shall be a terror, and never shall you be any more. *(Then the prayer of Christ, 'Your Will be done in Earth, as it is in Heaven,' will finally be answered and brought to pass [Mat. 6:9-10])*" **(Ezek. 28:11-19).**

THE ACCUSER OF THE BRETHREN

We know that Satan has access to this Earth and actually roams the Earth (Job 1:7; I Pet. 5:8). We also know he has access to Heaven (Job 1:6) and to God and probably spends much time there. Above all, he is *"the accuser of the brethren"* (Rev. 12:10). In other words, he stands before God and accuses Believers day and night; however, during the Tribulation Period he will be expelled from Heaven. This will take place at approximately the midpoint of the coming Great Tribulation.

Satan has caused horrifying trouble through the ages, which is a gross understatement; however, when he is cast out of Heaven, which he will be at the time mentioned, he will come down to this Earth with a special vengeance.

OUR VICTORY

Satan is a powerful being, as should be obvious. To be frank, no earthly mortal can overcome him, at least within our own strength and power. But he can be overcome and defeated.

How?

In reality, Jesus has already defeated Satan, and has done so totally and completely. It was done at the Cross. The Scripture concerning that says:

"Blotting out the handwriting of Ordinances that was against us *(pertains to the Law of Moses, which was God's Standard of Righteousness that man could not reach)*, **which**

was contrary to us *(Law is against us, simply because we are unable to keep its precepts, no matter how hard we try)*, **and took it out of the way** *(refers to the penalty of the Law being removed)*, nailing it to His Cross *(the Law with its decrees was abolished in Christ's Death, as if Crucified with Him)*;

"*And* having spoiled principalities and powers *(Satan and all of his henchmen were defeated at the Cross by Christ Atoning for all sin; sin was the legal right Satan had to hold man in captivity; with all sin atoned, he has no more legal right to hold anyone in bondage)*, **He** *(Christ)* **made a show of them openly** *(what Jesus did at the Cross was in the face of the whole universe)*, **triumphing over them in it.** *(The triumph is complete and it was all done for us, meaning we can walk in power and perpetual victory due to the Cross)*" **(Col. 2:14-15).**

All Victory for the Believer, all overcoming strength, all, and without exception are found entirely in Christ, with the Cross serving as the Means by which this Victory is given to us. The Lord Jesus Christ is the Source of all things that we receive from God, and the Cross is the Means by which these things are given to us; all superintended by the Holy Spirit (Eph. 2:13-18).

To walk in Victory over the world, the flesh, and the Devil, the Believer, due to the fact that Victory was won at the Cross, must make the Cross of Christ the Object of his Faith, even daily (Lk. 9:23).

It is the Cross of Christ that gives the Holy Spirit the latitude to work in our hearts and lives. To be sure, He Alone can develop the Fruit of the Spirit, as well as Righteousness and Holiness and, in fact, all that we need. We cannot do it ourselves. In other words, the Believer, no matter how determined, cannot make himself what he ought to be — that lies beyond us. The Holy Spirit Alone can do such; however, the Believer must ever remember, that the Holy Spirit, Who is God, works exclusively by and through the Finished Work of Christ, meaning that the death of Christ on the Cross, where He atoned for all sin, legally

makes it possible for the Holy Spirit to work within those capacities. That's the reason the Cross of Christ is so very, very important (Rom. 8:2).

CAN SATAN FORCE A BELIEVER TO SIN AGAINST HIS WILL?

It may come as a shock and a surprise to most Christians, but Satan most definitely can force a Christian to do something wrong, even against his will, if that Christian doesn't understand God's Prescribed Order of Victory. That Prescribed Order is the Cross of Christ, and our Faith in that Finished Work.

Most Christians think that before they got Saved, that Satan could force them into certain degrees of sin and iniquity, but since they are Saved, he cannot do such. Let's be clear, even blunt:

If the Believer doesn't understand God's Prescribed Order of Victory, Satan most definitely can force the will of an individual, even one who loves God supremely.

IS SIN A CHOICE?

Yes, sin is a choice, but only in the way that we will now outline.

The choice is not, do I sin or do I not sin, but rather, do I follow God's Prescribed Order, or do I try to formulate a means of my own in order to overcome Satan?

Sin is a choice only in that capacity. If the Believer ignores the Cross, thereby placing his Faith in something else, such a Believer, in essence, has said, whether he realizes it or not, he doesn't need the Lord, and that he can overcome Satan in his own strength.

WHY DID JESUS HAVE TO COME DOWN HERE AND DIE ON THE CROSS OF CALVARY?

To be sure, if there would have been any other way for Christ

to have redeemed fallen humanity, that He would have done. He had to come down here, and for the very purpose of going to the Cross, because that was ever His destination, simply because that was the Way, and the only Way.

That means we as Believers, within our own strength, within our own ability and talents, within our own motivation and intellect, no matter how hard we try, cannot be what we ought to be in Christ, thereby, overcoming sin, unless we place our Faith exclusively in Christ and what He did at the Cross, which then gives the Holy Spirit latitude to work within our lives (Rom. 6:1-14; 8:1-2, 11; I Cor. 1:17-18, 23; 2:2; Gal., Chpt. 5; 6:14; Eph. 2:13-18; Col. 2:14-15).

All of this means that Satan can hold a Believer in bondage, making such a Believer do things he doesn't want to do, and is striving not to do, if that Believer has his faith in the wrong place, even as most do!

THE CHRISTIAN AND SIN

No true Christian wants to sin. When we come to Christ, and I speak of those who are truly Born-Again, we become new creations. Old things pass away and all things become new. Sin is abhorrent to the true Believer, so whenever the Believer sins, it's because he has tried to fight the problem by his own strength, and every time he will fail, concluding by doing exactly what he doesn't want to do. Listen to Paul:

> **"For that which I do** *(the failure)* **I allow not** *(should have been translated, 'I understand not'; these are not the words of an unsaved man, as some claim, but rather a Believer who is trying and failing)*: **for what I would, that do I not** *(refers to the obedience he wants to render to Christ, but rather fails; why? as Paul explained, the Believer is married to Christ, but is being unfaithful to Christ by spiritually cohabiting with the Law, which frustrates the Grace of God; that means the Holy Spirit will not help such*

a person, which guarantees failure [Gal. 2:21]); **but what I hate, that do I** *(refers to sin in his life which he doesn't want to do and, in fact, hates, but finds himself unable to stop; unfortunately, due to the fact of not understanding the Cross as it refers to Sanctification, this is the plight of most modern Christians)*" **(Rom. 7:15).**

The great Apostle then said:

"For the good that I would I do not *(if I depend on self, and not the Cross)*: **but the evil which I would not** *(don't want to do)*, **that I do** *(which is exactly what every Believer will do no matter how hard he tries to do otherwise, if he tries to live this life outside of the Cross [Gal. 2:20-21])*" **(Rom. 7:19).**

To be sure, when Paul wrote these words, he knew how to live in Victory, and was living in Victory. Actually, it was to Paul that the Lord gave the meaning of the New Covenant, which is the meaning of the Cross (Gal. 1:12).

Just how long that Paul lived in this state we aren't told; however, it must have been at least two or three years. Please understand the following:

THE CROSS, THE ONLY MEANS OF VICTORY

Paul had a Vision of Christ, which was on the road to Damascus. Christ spoke to him, and he also saw a Light that was so bright it blinded him. This was when he was Saved, meaning that he gave his heart to Christ.

Three days later, he was baptized with the Holy Spirit as Ananias prayed for him.

He immediately began to preach the Gospel and, in fact, was an Apostle; however, despite all of these wonderful things having happened to him, being Born-Again, baptized with the Holy Spirit, called to be an Apostle, still, he could not live a

victorious, overcoming Christian life. And if Paul couldn't do such, how do you think you can?

He couldn't live this life as he should live it, and was meant to live it, until he knew and understood the Message of the Cross. He gave that Message to us in his fourteen Epistles. That and that alone is the means by which Satan is defeated. He cannot be overcome by any other way.

CAN SATAN READ YOUR MIND?

No!

Satan is not omnipotent, meaning *"all-powerful."* He is not omniscient meaning *"all-knowing,"* or omnipresent, which means everywhere. For thousands of years, the Evil One has tried to make people believe he is all of these things. But he isn't!

Satan is a created being, and even though more powerful than a human being, still, up beside God, he is woefully limited.

As it regards reading one's mind or the lacking in such ability, we find that Satan did everything he could through king Herod, to find Baby Jesus and kill Him (Mat. 2:13-18). If Satan had been able to read the minds of individuals, there would have been no problem in finding Jesus. Baby Moses was able to be kept from the sword of Pharaoh (Ex., Chpts. 1-2); David was able to flee from the demon-possessed Saul (I Sam., Chpts. 20-22); and, Elijah was able to hide from wicked Queen Jezebel (I Ki., Chpts. 19-21). There are many such stories in the Bible of God's People escaping the hands of their enemy showing that the Devil is strangely circumscribed or limited. Satan does not have nearly the power that many people, including Christians, attribute to him. In reality, through what Jesus did at the Cross, he is a defeated foe, and on all counts.

John the Beloved wrote and said:

> **"And they overcame him by the Blood of the Lamb** *(the power to overcome and overwhelm the Kingdom of Satan is found exclusively in the Blood of the Sacrifice of*

the Son of God, and our Faith in that Finished Work [Rom. 6:3-5, 11, 14]), **and by the word of their testimony** *(the 'testimony' must pertain to the fact that the Object of our Faith is the Cross, and exclusively the Cross, which then gives the Holy Spirit latitude to work within our lives)*; **and they loved not their lives unto the death.** *(This refers to the fact that the Believer must not change his testimony regarding the Cross to something else, even if it means death.)*" **(Rev. 12:11).**

WHY HAS THE LORD ALLOWED SATAN TO CONTINUE FOR SO LONG?

To which we have already alluded in this Chapter, the Bible actually tells us that this is a *"mystery"* (Rev. 10:7). That *"mystery"* will end at approximately the midpoint of the coming Great Tribulation, when Satan will be cast out of Heaven. At the end of the Great Tribulation we are told the following:

"And I saw an Angel come down from Heaven *(continues with the idea that Angels are very prominent in the Plan and Work of God)*, **having the key of the bottomless pit** *(speaks of the same place recorded in Rev. 9:1; however, there the key is given to Satan, but this Angel of Rev. 20:11 'has the key,' implying he has had it all along; more than likely, God allows this Angel to give the key to Satan in Rev. 9:1)* **and a great chain in his hand** *(should be taken literally)*.

"And he laid hold on the dragon, that old serpent, which is the Devil, and Satan *(as a 'dragon,' he shows his power; as a 'serpent,' he shows his cunning; as the 'Devil,' he is the accuser; and as 'Satan,' he is the adversary)*, **and bound him a thousand years** *(refers to being bound by the great chain carried by the Angel)*,

"And cast him into the bottomless pit, and shut him up, and set a seal upon him *(speaks of the abyss being*

sealed to keep him there), **that he should deceive the nations no more, till the thousand years should be fulfilled: and after that he must be loosed a little season.** *(At the end of the thousand-year period, Satan will be loosed out of his prison. He will make another attempt to deceive the nations, in which he will not succeed. We aren't told how long this 'little season' will be)*" **(Rev. 20:1-3).**

And then the Scripture says:

"And when the thousand years are expired *(should have been translated, 'finished')*, **Satan shall be loosed out of his prison** *(is not meant to infer a mere arbitrary act on the part of God; He has a very valid reason for doing this)*,

"And shall go out to deceive the nations which are in the four quarters of the Earth, Gog and Magog *(the main reason the Lord allows Satan this latitude is, it seems, to rid the Earth of all who oppose Christ; George Williams says: 'The Creation Sabbath witnessed the first seduction, and the Millennial Sabbath will witness the last'; the 'Gog and Magog' spoken of by John is a Hebrew term expressive of multitude and magnitude; here it embraces all nations, 'the four quarters of the Earth')*, **to gather them together to battle: the number of whom is as the sand of the sea** *(proclaims the fact that virtually all of the population at that particular time, which did not accept Christ during the Kingdom Age, will throw in their lot with Satan)*.

"And they went up on the breadth of the earth, and compassed the camp of the Saints about, and the beloved city *(pictures Satan coming against Jerusalem with his army, which will be the last attack against that city)*: **and fire came down from God out of Heaven, and devoured them.** *(Stipulates that the Lord will make short work of this insurrection. In fact, very little information is given regarding this event, as is obvious.)*

"And the Devil who deceived them was cast into the Lake of Fire and brimstone *(marks the end of Satan regarding his influence in the world and, in fact, in any part of the Creation of God)*, **where the Beast and the False Prophet *are*** *(proclaims the fact that these two were placed in 'the Lake of Fire and Brimstone' some one thousand years earlier [Rev. 19:20])*, **and shall be tormented day and night forever and ever.** *(This signifies the Eternity of this place. It is a matter of interest to note that Satan's first act is recorded in Gen., Chpt. 3 [the third Chapter from the beginning], whereas his last act on a worldwide scale is mentioned in Rev., Chpt. 20 [the third Chapter from the end])*" **(Rev. 20:7-10).**

As to why the Lord has allowed Satan to continue for this long, perhaps the following may be of some help.

TO DEVELOP CHARACTER AND FAITH IN THE BELIEVER

James wrote: *"My Brethren, count it all joy when you fall into divers temptations; knowing this, that the trying of your Faith works patience"* (James 1:2-3).

Trials test our Salvation and Faith, and the man who stands true in his trials proves his Salvation sound and his Faith genuine. *"Tribulation works patience; and patience, experience; and experience, hope"* (Rom. 5:3-5). Peter also mentioned *"the trial of your Faith"* (I Pet. 1:7-13). It seems for this reason Satan has been allowed to continue to test man.

TO KEEP MAN HUMBLE

Paul said, *"Lest I should be exalted above measure through the abundance of the Revelations, there was given to me a thorn in the flesh, the messenger of Satan to buffet me, lest I should be exalted above measure"* (II Cor. 12:7).

We can see from this Scripture that God allows Satan to prod man to a certain extent to keep him mindful of his yet imperfect state, to keep him humble before God.

TO PROVIDE CONFLICT IN ORDER THAT SAINTS MAY BE REWARDED THROUGH THEM

John talked about overcoming the wicked one: *"I write unto you young men, because you have overcome the wicked one"* (I Jn. 2:13). Attaining victory over Satan is shown here to be a deed worthy of recognition and reward.

Further on, John differentiated between the Spirit of Truth and the spirit of error: *"We are of God: he who knows God hears us; he who is not of God hears not us. Hereby know we the Spirit of Truth, and the spirit of error"* (I Jn. 4:6).

Since the dawn of sin, there has been constant conflict between good and evil. Man has been faced continually with the decision of where to place his allegiance. Those who follow God and who possess His Spirit of Truth are made known by those with whom they choose to ally themselves with upon this Earth. Rewards await those who have undergone spiritual struggles and have chosen to serve God.

To the Seven Churches in Asia Jesus proclaimed, *"To him who overcomes will I give . . ."* (Rev., Chpts. 2-3).

TO DEMONSTRATE THE POWER OF GOD OVER THE POWER OF SATAN

Paul mentioned, in speaking of the ages to come, *"He has raised us up together, and made us sit together in Heavenly places in Christ Jesus: that in the ages to come He might show the exceeding riches of His Grace and His Kindness toward us through Christ Jesus"* (Eph. 2:6-7).

Those who know Jesus Christ as their personal Lord and Saviour have been literally given new life; they are Spiritually Reborn. Though the redeemed are still subject to undergo

battles upon this Earth, we are able to overcome by the help of God; and in the ages to come, God will further demonstrate His infinite Power through His complete defeat of Satan and through the riches He will bestow on the victorious followers of Christ.

Paul mentioned it again when he said:

***"To the intent that now unto the principalities and powers in Heavenly Places might be known by the Church the manifold Wisdom of God"* (Eph. 3:10).**

GOD USES SATAN IN AFFLICTING PEOPLE TO BRING THEM TO REPENTANCE

Paul spoke of this when he wrote of *"delivering such an one unto Satan for the destruction of the flesh that the spirit may be Saved in the day of the Lord Jesus"* (I Cor. 5:5).

God often releases men into the hands of Satan that they may, through trials, realize the hopelessness and despair of sinful living and so recommit their life to Christ. The suffering of today does not seem so great when Eternal Life is at stake.

TO PURGE MAN OF ALL POSSIBILITY OF FALLING IN THE ETERNAL FUTURE

John said: *"The nations of them who are Saved shall walk in the light of it* (the New Jerusalem)*"* (Rev. 21:24). We are also told, *"There shall in no wise enter into it anything that defiles . . . or works abomination, or makes a lie"* (Rev. 21:27).

It is necessary that conflict exists now upon the Earth that those who are truly committed to God may be revealed for the purpose of future separation of the good and the evil. God will not permit anyone who is defiled by sin to enter into the Kingdom he has prepared for His Children.

Man is presently in a probationary state. Many, if not most, fail, sad to say, but some ultimately will *"shine as the brightness of the firmament"* (Dan. 12:3).

WHERE DO DEMON SPIRITS COME FROM?

One thing is certain, the Lord did not create demon spirits as they presently are. They became that way after some type of convulsion or upheaval in the spirit world.

We know that everything that God creates is *"good"* (Gen. 1:12, 18, 21, 25). When creation was finished, the Scripture says:

> **"And God saw every thing that He had made, and, behold, it was very good** *(means that it was not simply good, but good exceedingly; it is not man alone whom God surveys, but the completed cosmos, with man as its crown and glory)***" (Gen. 1:31).**

TERRIBLE CREATURES

The Scripture tells us:

> **"And there came out of the smoke locusts upon the earth** *(these are demon locusts, even as the following Verses prove)***: and unto them was given power, as the scorpions of the earth have power** *(refers to the sting in their tails, and the pain this will cause)***.**
>
> **"And it was commanded them that they should not hurt the grass of the earth, neither any green thing, neither any tree** *(normal locusts destroy plant life; but these are not allowed to do so)***; but only those men which have not the Seal of God in their foreheads** *(refers to the 144,000 Jews who have accepted Christ as their Saviour [Rev. 7:2-8])***.**
>
> **"And to them it was given that they should not kill them, but that they should be tormented five months** *(this will be literal, yet these creatures will be invisible)***: and their torment *was* as the torment of a scorpion, when he strikes a man** *(pain and swelling)***.**
>
> **"And in those days shall men seek death, and shall not find it; and shall desire to die, and death shall flee**

from them. *(For pain to be so bad that people want to die is bad indeed! Evidently pain-killing drugs will not work. It will be interesting how medical doctors diagnose all of this, to say the least.)*

"And the shapes of the locusts *were* like unto horses prepared unto battle; and on their heads *were* as it were crowns like gold, and their faces *were* as the faces of men. *(These are demon spirits, but will be invisible. If they could be seen, this is what they would look like. We aren't told their origin in the Bible. We know they were not originally created in this manner, but evidently became this way in the revolution instigated by Lucifer against God [Isa. 14:12-20; Ezek. 28:11-19].)*

"And they had hair as the hair of women, and their teeth were as *the teeth* of lions. *(They were, no doubt, originally created by God to perform a particular function of praise and worship, even as the 'living creatures,' but they have suffered this fate due to rebellion against God.)*

"And they had breastplates, as it were breastplates of iron; and the sound of their wings *was* as the sound of chariots of many horses running to battle. *(We are given a glimpse here into the spirit world. This is the reason such foolish efforts as humanistic psychology are helpless against such foes. The only answer is Christ and the Cross.)*

"And they had tails like unto scorpions, and there were stings in their tails: and their power *was* to hurt men five months. *(This Judgment is limited to five months, which tells us Satan can only do what God allows him to do.)*

"And they had a king over them, *which is* the Angel of the bottomless pit *(gives us further insight into the spirit world of darkness)*, **whose name in the Hebrew tongue *is* Abaddon, but in the Greek tongue has *his* name Apollyon.** *(This is a powerful fallen Angel, who evidently threw in his lot with Lucifer in the great rebellion against God)*" **(Rev. 9:3-11).**

So, where did these things come from?

THE CREATION

The Scripture says:

> **"In the beginning** *(refers to the beginning of creation, or at least the creation as it refers to this universe; God, unformed, unmade, uncreated, had no beginning; He always was, always is, and always shall be)* **God** *(the phrase, 'In the beginning God,' explains the first cause of all things as it regards creation)* **created the heaven and the Earth** *(could be translated 'the heavens and the Earth' because God created the entirety of the universe)*.
>
> **"And the Earth was without form, and void; and darkness was upon the face of the deep** *(God did not originally create the Earth without form and void; it became this way after a cataclysmic happening; this happening was the revolt of Lucifer against God, which took place some time in the dateless past)*. **And the Spirit of God** *(Holy Spirit)* **moved upon the face of the waters** *(the moving of the Holy Spirit signified and signifies the beginning of life)*" **(Gen. 1:1-2).**

Inasmuch as God did not create the Earth *"without form and void, and darkness upon the face of the deep,"* it stands to reason that it became that way, as stated, after some cataclysmic happening. That happening was the revolt of Lucifer.

It also seems, that Planet Earth was the domain of Lucifer before his Fall. For him to rule this Planet before Adam and Eve, there had to be something here for him to rule. Whatever these beings were, they evidently had a physical body. They were created by God as well, but they were not created as demon spirits. They became that because they threw in their lot with Lucifer in the revolution, which distorted these beings, and left them as disembodied spirits, seeking a man or woman or even a child to inhabit, or even an animal.

These terrible things which we have just described from the Book of Revelation also became that way during the revolution.

We can see other creatures in the Book of Revelation who stayed true to God, but still are totally unlike anything that we have on this Earth.

I quote:

> **"And before the Throne *there was* a sea of glass like unto crystal** *(presents that which is perfectly transparent)***: and in the midst of the Throne, and round about the Throne, *were* four Beasts** (living creatures) **full of eyes before and behind.** *(This is introducing creatures we have no knowledge of and which are beyond comprehension, as so much in Heaven actually is.)*
>
> **"And the first Beast** *(living creature)* ***was* like a lion, and the second Beast like a calf, and the third Beast had a face as a man, and the fourth Beast *was* like a flying eagle.** *(These strange creatures are before the Throne constantly.)*
>
> **"And the four Beasts** *(living creatures)* **had each of them six wings about *him*; and *they were* full of eyes within** *(signifying the revealing of their innermost nature and being)***: and they rest not day and night** *(proclaiming that these beings are 'spirit' and not 'flesh')***, saying, Holy, Holy, Holy, Lord God Almighty, which was, and is, and is to come.** *(Using the threefold repetition calls attention to the infinite Holiness of God)***" (Rev. 4:6-8).**

We see similar creatures of this nature in the Vision that Isaiah the Prophet had. These are referred to as *"Seraphims"* (Isa. 6:1-3).

The great Prophet Ezekiel also in his Vision saw similar creatures, all which were performing the Work of God (Ezek. 1:28).

Some Bible Scholars believe that demon spirits came from the kingdom ruled by Lucifer before his revolution against God. If, in fact, that is so, they served God at that time, in Holiness

and Righteousness. But when Lucifer rebelled against God, evidently they threw in their lot with him, along with one third of the Angels.

As well, demon spirits are not fallen Angels, as some have claimed. One day soon, even to which we have already addressed ourselves, Satan along with all of his demon spirits and fallen Angels, will be placed in the bottomless pit, and ultimately in the Lake of Fire, from which they will never have access to man or any part of God's creation again.

"Long ago I planned in my passing pride,
"That today I would reign as king;
"But where is my kingdom, where is my crown?
"Is the bitter song I sing."

"What joy have I won through my evil designs?
"What peace in my soul-wrecking plan?
"I hope to conquer both Heaven and Hell,
"But have won nothing more than mere man."

"I can see above, o'er the bridgeless gulf,
"The glorified Heaven-lit strand;
"My chains make me feel the double disgrace,
"As I crouch 'neath the Infinite Hand."

"Where are my princes, my legions of dukes,
"And the millions of souls I have won?
"My pains and my chains are greater by far,
"Because of the deeds I have done."

"All my plans and my schemes in a thousand ways,
"Like bubbles are blown out of sight,
"My fancies and hopes like a passing dream,
"Are covered by shadows of night."

"Come on, all ye dupes, ye millions of men,
"Who heeded my wishes like fools;
"Take your share for aye of the galling chains,
"Under Him who in triumph rules."

"You have lived and died for my ignoble cause,
"Your souls are eternally marred;
"You shall see no more than glimpses of light,
"Of Heaven, from which you are barred."

"Then fling all your hopes, my friends, to the winds,
"As the echo of sadness replies;
"You will feel henceforth the deeper degrees,
"Of the Hell which beneath us lies."

(Author unknown)

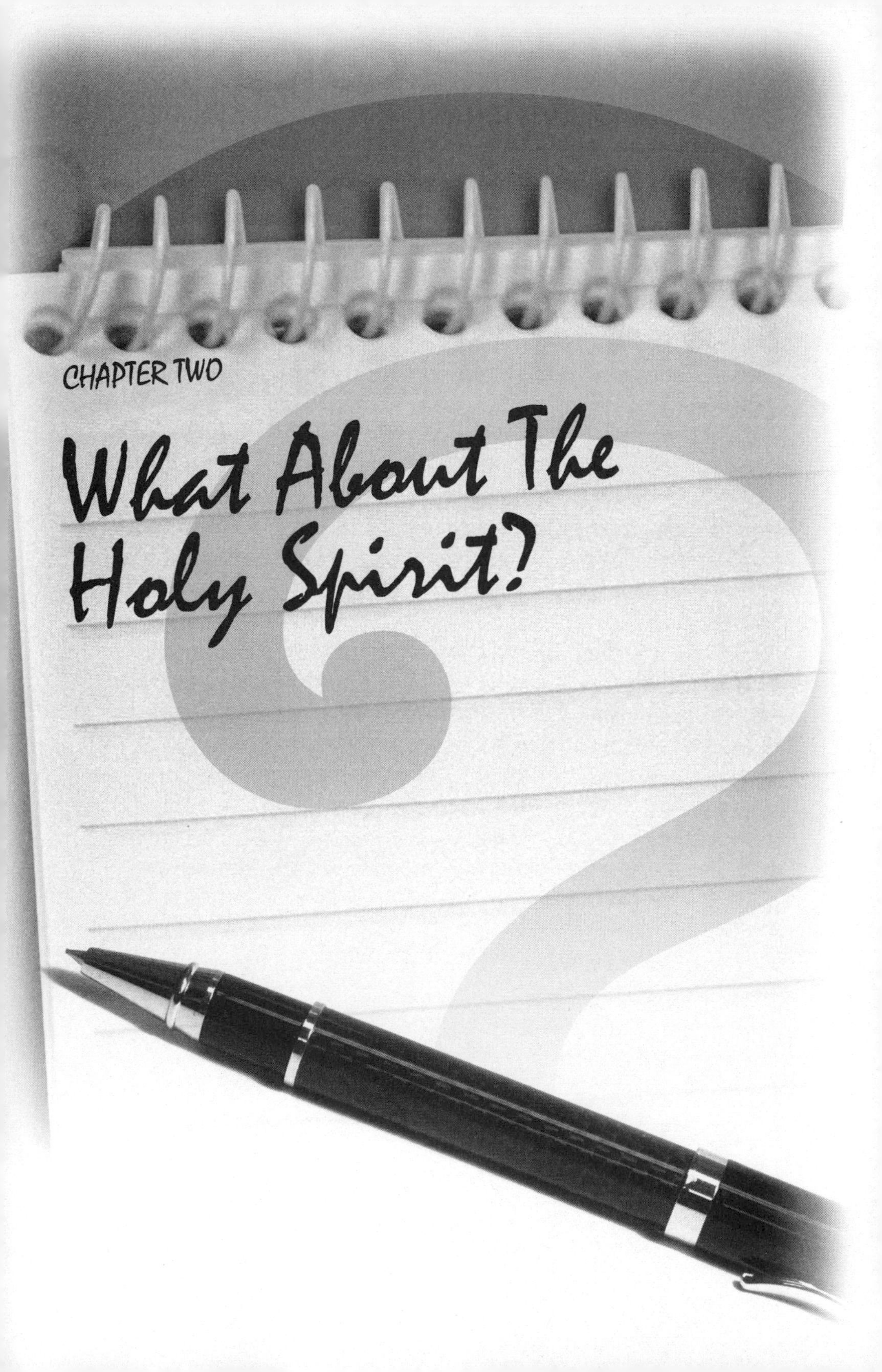

CHAPTER TWO

What About The Holy Spirit?

QUESTION:

WHAT ABOUT THE HOLY SPIRIT?

ANSWER:

Every true Believer, by intuition, knows that the Holy Spirit is extremely important, as it regards His involvement in our life and living. To be frank, every single work done on Earth by the Godhead, to date, with one exception, has been done through the Person, the Office, the Ministry, and Power of the Holy Spirit. That one exception to date is the First Advent of Christ, but even then, the Holy Spirit functioned in every capacity of our Lord's Conception, Birth, Life, Living, Miracles, Ministry, and above all, His Death at Calvary, plus the Resurrection and the Ascension. In fact, Jesus did absolutely nothing until He was guided, led, and empowered by the Spirit. He said:

> **"The Spirit of the Lord *is* upon Me** *(we learn here of the absolute necessity of the Person and Work of the Holy Spirit within our lives)*, **because He has anointed Me** *(Jesus is the ultimate Anointed One; consequently, the Anointing of the Holy Spirit actually belongs to Christ, and the Anointing we have actually comes by His Authority [Jn. 16:14])* **to preach the Gospel to the poor** *(the poor in spirit)*; **He has sent Me to heal the brokenhearted** *(sin breaks the heart, or else is responsible for it being broken; only Jesus can heal this malady)*, **to preach Deliverance to the captives** *(if it is to be noticed, He didn't say to 'deliver the captives,' but rather 'Preach Deliverance,' which refers to the Cross [Jn. 8:32])*, **and recovering of sight to the blind** *(the Gospel opens the eyes of those who are spiritually blind)*, **to set at liberty them who are bruised** *(the vicissitudes of life at times place a person in a mental or spiritual prison; the Lord Alone, and through what He did at the Cross, can open this prison door)*,

> **"To preach the acceptable Year of the Lord** *(it is believed that the day, on which Jesus delivered this Message was the first day of the year of Jubilee)***" (Lk. 4:18-19).**

As God, Jesus did not need any anointing; however, as the Man Christ Jesus, He most definitely did need the Anointing of the Spirit.

WHO IS THE HOLY SPIRIT?

The Holy Spirit is God. Jesus said:

"Go ye therefore, and teach all nations, baptizing them in the Name of the Father, and of the Son, and of the Holy Spirit" **(Mat. 28:19).**

Over and over again, Jesus used personal pronouns regarding the Holy Spirit, proving that He is not merely an emanation from the Father, etc. He said:

> **"Howbeit when He, the Spirit of Truth, is come** *(which He did on the Day of Pentecost)***, He will guide you into all Truth** *(if our Faith is properly placed in Christ and the Cross, the Holy Spirit can then bring forth Truth to us; He doesn't guide into some truth, but rather 'all Truth')***: for He shall not speak of Himself** *(tells us not only What He does, but Whom He represents)***; but whatsoever He shall hear, that shall He speak** *(doesn't refer to lack of knowledge, for the Holy Spirit is God, but rather He will proclaim the Work of Christ only)***: and He will show you things to come** *(pertains to the New Covenant, which would shortly be given)***" (Jn. 16:13).**

DOES THE HOLY SPIRIT HAVE A SPIRIT BODY?

I believe that God the Father has a Spirit Body, meaning that if you saw Him, and quite a number of people have, He would look in appearance somewhat like a man. Yet, His Body

is not physical but rather Spirit. The Scripture says:

***"And I saw in the Right Hand of Him Who sat on the Throne a Book written within and on the back side, sealed with Seven Seals."* The Scripture then says, *"He* (the Lord Jesus Christ, proving that our Saviour is different from God the Father, although they are One in essence) *came and took the Book out of the Right Hand of Him Who sat on the Throne"* (Rev. 5:1-7).**

The Lord Jesus Christ presently has a physical body, albeit glorified. The Scripture says:

"But they were terrified and affrighted, and supposed that they had seen a spirit.

"And He said unto them, Why are you troubled? and why do thoughts arise in your hearts?

"Behold My Hands and My Feet, that it is I Myself: handle Me, and see; for a spirit has not flesh and bones as you see Me have.

***"And when He had thus spoken, He showed them His Hands and His Feet"* (Lk. 24:37-40).**

The Holy Spirit, I personally believe, has as well a Spirit Body.

Luke wrote of the Water Baptism of Christ by saying, *"And the Holy Spirit descended in a bodily shape like a Dove upon Him, and a Voice came from Heaven, which said, You are My Beloved Son; in You I am well pleased"* (Lk. 3:22).

This statement did not mean that the Holy Spirit looked like a dove, but rather refers to the gentleness of the Holy Spirit.

The Scripture mentions the *"bodily shape,"* and I would deduce from that, that the Holy Spirit does have a Spirit Body.

WHAT DOES IT MEAN TO BE BORN OF THE SPIRIT?

It means that the believing sinner must be Born-Again, which speaks of a Spiritual Birth, and which is work carried out by the Holy Spirit (Jn. 3:3-6).

Jesus further said to Nicodemus:

> **"Marvel not that I said unto you, You must be born again** *(evidently addresses itself to the surprise, which must*

have been registered on the countenance of Nicodemus).

"The wind blows where it listeth, and you hear the sound thereof, but cannot tell from where it comes, and whither it goes *(presents the way in which Jesus explains the 'Born-Again' experience; He likens it to the wind which comes and goes, but is impossible to tell exactly how)*: **so is everyone who is born of the Spirit** *(it is a Spiritual Birth, so it cannot be explained intellectually)*" **(Jn. 3:7-8).**

For the sinner to be Saved, the Holy Spirit has to first place such a person under conviction, which He does by the Word in some manner being given to them. The Scripture says:

"And when He *(the Holy Spirit)* **is come, He will reprove** *(convict)* **the world of sin** *(the supreme sin of rejecting Christ)*, **and of Righteousness, and of Judgment:**

"Of sin, because they believe not on Me;

"Of Righteousness, because I go to My Father, and you see me no more;

"Of Judgment, because the Prince of this world is judged" (Jn. 16:8-11).

When the believing sinner is placed under conviction, the Holy Spirit then gives Faith to that individual. It says:

"According as God has dealt to every man the measure of Faith" **(Rom. 12:3).**

At this juncture, the believing sinner can say *"yes"* or *"no"* to Christ. The Lord will never violate the free moral agency of an individual. If the person says *"yes"* to Christ, at that moment, at least in the Mind of God, the believing sinner is baptized into Christ by the Holy Spirit.

The Scripture says:

"Know you not, that so many of us as were baptized into Jesus Christ *(plainly says that this Baptism is into Christ and not water [I Cor. 1:17; 12:13; Gal. 3:27; Eph. 4:5;*

Col. 2:11-13]) **were baptized into His Death?** *(When Christ died on the Cross, in the Mind of God, we died with Him; in other words, He became our Substitute, and our identification with Him in His Death gives us all the benefits for which He died; the idea is that He did it all for us!)*

"Therefore we are buried with Him by baptism into death *(not only did we die with Him, but we were buried with Him as well, which means that all the sin and transgression of the past were buried; when they put Him in the Tomb, they put all of our sins into that Tomb as well)***: that like as Christ was raised up from the dead by the Glory of the Father, even so we also should walk in newness of life** *(we died with Him, we were buried with Him, and His Resurrection was our Resurrection to a 'Newness of Life')***.**

"For if we have been planted together *(with Christ)* **in the likeness of His Death** *(Paul proclaims the Cross as the instrument through which all Blessings come; consequently, the Cross must ever be the Object of our Faith, which gives the Holy Spirit latitude to work within our lives)***, we shall be also *in the likeness* of *His* Resurrection** *(we can have the 'likeness of His Resurrection,' i.e., 'live this Resurrection Life,' only as long as we understand the 'likeness of His Death,' which refers to the Cross as the means by which all of this is done)***" (Rom. 6:3-5).**

Of course, all of this was done strictly by us evidencing Faith in Christ. But in the Mind of God, it was very real, and is very real, which pertains to the moment we were *"Born-Again."* In other words, all of this is what happened in the spirit world, which then has a direct affect on our hearts and lives. So much so that Paul said:

"Therefore if any man *be* in Christ *(Saved by the Blood)***, *he is* a new creature** *(a new creation)***: old things are passed away** *(what we were before Salvation)***; behold, all things are become new.** *(The old is no longer useable,* *with everything given to us now by Christ as 'new.')"* **(II Cor. 5:17).**

That is what it means to be *"born of the Spirit."*

WHAT IS THE BAPTISM WITH THE HOLY SPIRIT?

Someone has said, and rightly so, that at Salvation, the Holy Spirit baptizes us into Christ, which is done by our Faith in Christ and what He did for us at the Cross. As stated, it has nothing to do with Water Baptism. Regarding the Baptism with the Holy Spirit, it is Jesus Who baptizes us into the Third Person of the Godhead, i.e., *"the Holy Spirit."* John the Baptist said of Christ:

***"I indeed baptize you with water unto Repentance: but He* (Christ) *Who comes after me is mightier than I, Whose Shoes I am not worthy to bear: He shall Baptize you with the Holy Spirit, and with fire"* (Mat. 3:11).**

WHAT IS THE DIFFERENCE IN *"BORN OF THE SPIRIT"* AND *"BAPTIZED WITH THE SPIRIT"*?

As is obvious, the Holy Spirit is very much involved in both situations. The first refers to Salvation, which pertains to the individual being Born-Again, as we've already explained. The second pertains to the Believer being equipped for Service, with all the help that the Holy Spirit provides. Jesus said:

"But you shall receive power *(Miracle-working Power)*, **after that the Holy Spirit is come upon you** *(specifically states that this 'Power' is inherent in the Holy Spirit, and solely in His Domain)*: **and you shall be witnesses** *(doesn't mean witnessing to souls, but rather to one giving one's all in every capacity for Christ, even to the laying down of one's life)* **unto Me** *(without the Baptism with the Holy Spirit, one cannot really know Jesus as one should)* **both in Jerusalem, and in all Judaea, and in Samaria,**

and unto the uttermost part of the Earth *(proclaims the Work of God as being worldwide)*" **(Acts 1:8).**

Jesus also said that the Baptism with the Spirit would afford the following:

- ***"He will guide you into all Truth."***
- ***"He will show you things to come."***
- ***"He shall glorify Christ."***
- ***"He shall receive of Mine and shall show it unto you"*** **(Jn. 16:13-15).**

To sum it up, one might say the Baptism with the Holy Spirit does the following for the Believer, which cannot be done otherwise:

A. Gives the Believer power (Acts 1:8).

B. Gives the Holy Spirit access to the Believer as it refers to the Believer's Sanctification (Jn. 14:16-18).

C. Gives the Believer access to the Holy Spirit, which is the most important of all (Jn. 16:13-15).

DOES ONE RECEIVE THE HOLY SPIRIT AT CONVERSION?

Yes! As we've already stated, the Holy Spirit is the very One Who effects Salvation for the Believer, actually baptizing the Believer into Christ, which is all done by Faith on the part of the Believer (Eph. 2:8-9). However, and as we have already explained, there is a vast difference in being *"born of the Spirit,"* and being *"baptized with the Spirit."*

Even though the Holy Spirit most definitely comes into the heart and life of the Believer at conversion, still, that is not the Spirit Baptism, which the Believer cannot receive until he is Born-Again. Jesus said:

"And I will pray the Father, and He shall give you another Comforter, that He may abide with you forever; even the Spirit of Truth; Whom the world cannot receive . . ." **(Jn. 14:16-17).**

Due to what Jesus said, and which should be obvious, it's

not even possible for a Believing sinner to be baptized with the Holy Spirit in the Salvation process. Salvation has to be effected first, and then the Believer can receive. They may receive, in fact, seconds after being Saved, even as did Cornelius and those with him, or it may be a period of several years, but it's always after Salvation.

At Salvation, one is Washed, Sanctified, and Justified (I Cor. 6:11).

Sanctification makes one clean, while Justification, being a legal Work, declares one clean. The person is then a fit subject for the Baptism with the Spirit, but not before then.

The Baptism with the Holy Spirit is a separate and distinct Work, apart from Salvation, meaning that it follows Salvation, meaning that it is given to those who ask for it (Lk. 11:13).

THE RECORD OF THE BOOK OF ACTS

Five different experiences of Believers being baptized with the Holy Spirit are given to us in the Book of Acts. Of course, there were many, many more, even thousands, no doubt, but the Holy Spirit saw fit to give us five accounts. They are as follows:

1. In Acts, Chapter 2, we have the initial outpouring of the Spirit, which took place on the Day of Pentecost (Acts 2:1-4). We have to admit, that all of those who were baptized with the Spirit that day, were already Saved. This was not a Salvation experience, that already having taken place some time before, but was the advent of the Holy Spirit in a brand-new Dispensation. Jesus had effected the Work at Calvary, now making it possible for the Holy Spirit to come into the hearts and lives of Believers and to abide permanently. Jesus said:

> **"And I will pray the Father, and He shall give you another Comforter, that He may abide with you forever** *(before the Cross, the Holy Spirit could only help a few individuals, and then only for a period of time; since the Cross, He lives in the hearts and lives of Believers, and does*

so forever)" **(Jn. 14:16).**

It is the Cross of Christ that made all of this possible.

2. The second account is found in Acts 8:14-17. Phillip had gone to a city in Samaria and has preached Jesus to them, with many being Saved; however, none at that time were baptized with the Holy Spirit; consequently, *"when the Apostles which were at Jerusalem heard that Samaria had received the Word of God, they sent unto them Peter and John: who, when they were come down, prayed for them, that they might receive the Holy Spirit"* (Acts 8:14-15).

Now, if Believers automatically are baptized with the Holy Spirit at conversion, as some teach, what in the world were Peter and John doing by going back to Samaria and laying hands on these Samaritans that they might be baptized with the Holy Spirit, which they were? Once again, this proves that Believers are not automatically baptized with the Holy Spirit at conversion.

3. The third account is found in Acts 9:10-18. It's the account of the Apostle Paul.

The great Apostle was Saved on the road to Damascus, and then some three days later baptized with the Holy Spirit. Ananias said to him:

> **"Brother Saul** *(he addressed Paul in this manner because Paul was already Saved, and had been so for the last three days and nights)*, **the Lord, *even* Jesus, Who appeared unto you in the way as you came, has sent me, that you might receive your sight, and be filled with the Holy Spirit" (Acts 9:17).**

Once again, this proves that the Baptism with the Spirit is not an automatic thing at conversion. If it was, what was Ananias doing going some three days later to pray for Paul to be filled with the Spirit?

4. The fourth account is found in Acts, Chapter 10, which pertained to Cornelius and his household, who was the first

Gentile to be Saved and baptized with the Spirit.

Cornelius was Saved, along with those with him, as Peter preached the Gospel unto them, and then baptized with the Holy Spirit, it seems, moments later.

5. The last account is found in Acts 19:1-7.

The Apostle Paul came in contact with *"certain Disciples,"* at Ephesus:

> **"And said unto them, Have you received the Holy Spirit since you believed?** *(In the Greek, this is literally, 'having believed, did you receive?' We know these men were already Saved because every time the word 'Disciples' is used in the Book of Acts, it refers to individuals who have accepted Christ. Paul could tell that these individuals, although Saved, had not yet been baptized with the Holy Spirit.)* **And they said unto him, We have not so much as heard whether there be any Holy Spirit** *(doesn't mean that they didn't know of the existence of the Holy Spirit, but they were not aware that the Age of the Spirit had come, and that Believers could literally be baptized with Him; at Salvation, the Holy Spirit baptizes Believing sinners into Christ; at the Spirit Baptism, Jesus Baptizes Believers into the Holy Spirit)*"
>
> **"And when Paul had laid *his* hands upon them, the Holy Spirit came on them; and they spoke with Tongues, and prophesied" (Acts 19:2, 6).**

From the Word of God it is conclusively proved that the Baptism with the Holy Spirit, as stated, is an experience separate and apart from Salvation, and is available to all Believers.

WHAT IS THE INITIAL PHYSICAL EVIDENCE THAT ONE HAS BEEN BAPTIZED WITH THE HOLY SPIRIT?

Even though there are many evidences, still, the initial physical evidence that one has been baptized with the Spirit,

is *"speaking with other Tongues as the Spirit of God gives the utterance."* There are no exceptions to this. And once again, we will prove from the Word of God that this is the case.

Some people have claimed that some can be baptized with the Spirit without speaking with other Tongues. There's nothing in the Word of God that substantiates such thinking. And please understand, it's not what denominations might say, or particular preachers, etc., but rather what the Word of God gives us. Unequivocally, it proclaims speaking with other Tongues as the initial physical evidence. Once again, we go to the five accounts given us in the Book of Acts and, as well, we will briefly address the Fourteenth Chapter of I Corinthians.

1. Acts 2:4 plainly says, *"And they were all filled with the Holy Spirit, and began to speak with other Tongues, as the Spirit gave them utterance."*

Some have foolishly claimed that speaking with other Tongues is no more than incoherent babble, or gibberish. The Word of God says different. In fact, Tongues are always a language known somewhere in the world, but not by the speaker.

For instance, on the Day of Pentecost the Scripture tells us that on this Feast Day, which characterized all the Feast Days in Jerusalem, Jews had come in from all over the Roman Empire. In fact, this happened three times every year, the times of the various Jewish Feasts.

When the Holy Spirit fell in the Temple, for that's where they were on this particular day, the Bible says:

> **"The multitude came together** *(what was happening attracted a multitude)*, **and was confounded, because that every man heard them speak in his own language** *(means that these on-looking Jews heard these people speaking in many different languages, in fact, languages of the nations of their residence, wherever that might have been, proving that this was not gibberish or babble as some claim).*
>
> **"And they were all amazed and marveled** *(mostly centered upon this speaking with other tongues)*, **saying one**

to another, Behold, are not all these which speak Galileans? *(This means that the Galilean accent was peculiar and well-known [Mk. 14:70; Lk. 22:59].)*

"And how hear we every man in our own tongue, wherein we were born? *(This proves once again that this was not babble, mere chatter, or gibberish, but rather a language known somewhere in the world, but not by the speaker.)*

"Parthians, and Medes, and Elamites, and the dwellers in Mesopotamia, and in Judaea, and Cappadocia, in Pontus, and Asia,

"Phrygia, and Pamphylia, in Egypt, and in the parts of Libya about Cyrene, and strangers of Rome, Jews and proselytes,

"Cretes and Arabians, we do hear them speak in our tongues the wonderful Works of God *(this tells us what speaking in Tongues actually is, a recitation of the 'Wonderful Works of God')*" **(Acts 2:6-11).**

All of these Jews from various parts of the Roman Empire who were present in the Temple that day, and who, in fact, spoke several languages, no doubt, Hebrew, Greek, and the dialect of the country of their domicile, all of these heard these Galileans speaking in their languages, and they knew that these Galileans did not know these languages themselves.

The Holy Spirit orchestrated this entire event, so it would be crystal clear as to what the initial physical evidence of the Baptism with the Holy Spirit would be, which is speaking with other Tongues.

2. In Acts, Chapter 8 we have the second account. When Peter and John came to Samaria and preached to these Samaritans about the Baptism with the Holy Spirit, and then laid hands on them that they might receive, this they did; however, nothing is mentioned about tongues.

But then we have the account of Simon the Sorcerer.

He observed Peter and John praying for these people, and them receiving the Holy Spirit. He then foolishly offered Peter

and John money that they would tell him how he, as well, could have this gift. Peter said to him:

"Your money perish with you, because you have thought that the Gift of God may be purchased with money.

***"You have neither part nor lot in this matter: for your heart is not right in the Sight of God"* (Acts 8:20-21).**

The word *"matter"* as used in Verse 21, in the Greek is *"logos."* It means, *"a word or speech."* So it should have been translated, *"you have neither part nor lot in this utterance,"* proving that they spoke with other Tongues when they were baptized with the Spirit.

3. The third account is found in Acts, Chapter 9, and speaks of the infilling of the Spirit by Paul. It doesn't give us much information in this account. It just speaks of Ananias saying to him, *"the Lord, even Jesus, Who appeared unto you in the way as you came, has sent me, that you might receive your sight, and be filled with the Holy Spirit"* (Acts 9:17).

It doesn't give us any information concerning this account after that. But Paul said as it regards his personal experience:

***"I thank my God, I speak with Tongues more than you all"* (I Cor. 14:18).**

Paul wasn't speaking of any linguistic ability concerning languages that he learned as a child or in school. As the associating Texts bear out, the entirety of this Fourteenth Chapter of I Corinthians is dealing with Tongues, Interpretation, and Prophecy.

Paul was speaking about his worshipping the Lord in Tongues, which he, no doubt, did constantly. One can do this, as I personally do myself and constantly, doing so in my spirit, which is actually done silently. That is what Paul was addressing.

4. The next account is Acts, Chapter 10 where Cornelius and his household were Saved and baptized with the Holy Spirit. The Scripture says:

> **"While Peter yet spoke these words** *(concerning Believing in Him)*, **the Holy Spirit fell on all them which heard the Word** *(even though we are given very little*

information here, this is the moment when Cornelius and his household accepted Christ, and were Saved).

"And they of the Circumcision *(Jews)* **which believed** *(believed in Christ)* **were astonished** *(at what they saw the Lord doing, which could not be denied)*, **as many as came with Peter, because that on the Gentiles also was poured out the Gift of the Holy Spirit** *(Cornelius and his household were Saved, and then moments later Baptized with the Holy Spirit; it was quite a meeting!)*.

"For they heard them speak with Tongues *(this is the initial, physical evidence that one has been Baptized with the Holy Spirit; it always and without exception accompanies the Spirit Baptism)*, **and magnify God** *(means that some of them would stop speaking in Tongues momentarily, and then begin to praise God in their natural language, magnifying His Name)*" **(Acts 10:44-46).**

5. The last account is found in Acts, Chapter 19. Paul, in speaking to certain Believers, evidently ascertained that they had not yet been baptized with the Holy Spirit. So he asked them the question, *"Have you received the Holy Spirit since you believed?"* (Acts 19:2).

They pleaded ignorance regarding his question, then he explained the Baptism with the Spirit to them, laid hands on them, and the Scripture says, *"The Holy Spirit came on them; and they spoke with Tongues, and prophesied"* (Acts 19:6).

6. And then we have in the Fourteenth Chapter of I Corinthians all the teaching that the Apostle gave as it regards how Tongues are to be used in the public assembly. If something of this nature didn't exist, I hardly think that the Apostle would have given over this much space to such a subject.

DOES ONE HAVE TO SPEAK IN TONGUES TO BE SAVED?

No!

Speaking with other Tongues has absolutely nothing to do with one's Salvation. One is Saved by believing in Christ, in other words, accepting Him as one's Saviour and Lord, which can be done in a moment's time, and anywhere.

Concerning one experience, the Scripture tells us of the jailer in Philippi who having come through the earthquake, *"fell down before Paul and Silas . . . and said, Sirs, what must I do to be Saved? And they said, Believe on the Lord Jesus Christ, and you shall be Saved, and your house"* (Acts 16:29-31).

When one comes to Christ, one is fully justified, for there is no such thing as a partial Justification. This means that when one is baptized with the Holy Spirit with the evidence of speaking with other Tongues, it does not make one more Saved. That's not its purpose. Its purpose is, as we have stated, that you the Believer might have power to carry forth the Work of the Lord, among other things.

WHAT GOOD ARE TONGUES?

The Scripture is abundantly clear on that subject. Some of the *"good"* is as follows:

1. Anything that the Lord gives is good. Concerning speaking with other Tongues, the Scripture says, *"As the Spirit gave them utterance."* I don't think I would want to speak disparagingly of something that's given by the Holy Spirit. Anything He does is *"good."*

2. When one speaks in Tongues, one is declaring *"the wonderful Works of God"* (Acts 2:11).

3. The great Prophet Isaiah said some 750 years before Christ, *"For with stammering lips and another Tongue will He speak to this people.*

***"To whom He said, This is the rest wherewith you may cause the weary to rest; and this is the refreshing: yet they would not hear"* (Isa. 28:11-12).**

These two Verses tell us that speaking with other Tongues brings about a *"rest"* from the tiredness of the journey of life.

As well, speaking with other Tongues brings about a *"refreshing,"* which rejuvenates the person. In fact, the Apostle Paul quoted part of these Verses in I Corinthians 14:21-22.

4. The person who speaks in Tongues speaks unto God (I Cor. 14:2). Anything that's spoken directly to God is good.

5. Speaking in other Tongues edifies the Believer, which we all need (I Cor. 14:4). This is the Lord's answer for stress, emotional disturbances, nervous disorders, the pressures of life in general, etc.

6. When one prays in an unknown Tongue, one's spirit prays, which means that one prays exactly as the Holy Spirit desires the prayer to be given (I Cor. 14:14).

7. Tongues are for a sign to unbelievers (I Cor. 14:22). Even though most unsaved do not know this, and would not understand it if it was told to them; still, in essence, it means that this latter day outpouring proclaims the fact that we're living in the last of the last days. It is a sign in this respect to the unbelieving world.

DOESN'T THE BIBLE TEACH THAT TONGUES SHALL CEASE WHEN LOVE PREVAILS?

No!

The Scripture says:

> **"Love never fails** *(because love cannot fail)*: **but whether *there be* Prophecies, they shall fail; whether *there be* Tongues, they shall cease; whether *there be* Knowledge, it shall vanish away.** *(This refers to the fact that the Gifts of the Spirit will not be needed in the coming Resurrection, as well as many other things we could name.)***"**
> **(I Cor. 13:8).**

Those who talk about Tongues ceasing, never mention knowledge ceasing. When Jesus comes back, and we speak of the Second Coming, there will be many changes made, as should be obvious.

WHEN THE BIBLE WAS COMPLETED, DIDN'T ALL THESE THINGS CEASE?

No!

The Scripture says:

> **"For we know in part** *(pertains to the 'Word of Knowledge,' which is just part Knowledge)*, **and we Prophesy in part** *(falls into the same category)*.
>
> **"But when that which is perfect is come** *(refers to the Rapture of the Church, i.e., the Resurrection)*, **then that which is in part shall be done away** *(as should be obvious)*" **(I Cor. 13:9-10).**

This is not speaking of the Canon of Scripture being completed, but rather, the coming Resurrection, which, as stated, will bring about many changes.

ISN'T IT TRUE THAT ONLY IMMATURE CHRISTIANS SPEAK IN TONGUES?

Again, no!

Paul continues, *"When I was a child, I spoke as a child, I understood as a child, I thought as a child: but when I became a man, I put away childish things"* (I Cor. 13:11).

The Apostle is comparing our present state, *"as a child,"* to that which is coming, symbolized by a mature adult. That is the difference between the present state and the coming Resurrection.

So, if one wants to know what the coming Kingdom Age is going to be like, well then the Holy Spirit gives us here that information.

It is the difference in my little two year old great granddaughter, Sam, who most definitely knows some things, but still in no way compares to the knowledge and maturity of her parents. There is quite a difference in the two, as there is quite a difference

in our present state and that which is to come.

THE WORK OF THE HOLY SPIRIT

There are two particulars that should be noted in the Word of God as it regards this all-important subject. They are:

1. Jesus, before beginning His public Ministry, was baptized with the Holy Spirit (Lk. 3:21-22).

2. Jesus was the Son of God, in effect, God manifest in the flesh. He was Perfect in every respect, never having failed or sinned even one time in thought, word, or deed. But yet, as He began His public Ministry, He first of all was baptized with the Holy Spirit. So the great question is:

If Jesus, who was the Son of God, needed the Baptism with the Holy Spirit in order to carry out His Ministry, where does that leave us?

Jesus was very God and very Man. This means that He wasn't half God and half Man, but rather fully God and fully Man; however, He never performed any of His Miracles, or did anything by the Power of His Deity, which He always possessed. He did everything as a man, filled with the Holy Spirit. Surely we would understand if Jesus, the Son of the Living God, needed the Holy Spirit to carry out His Work and Ministry, don't you think that we need such as well? I can assure you, that we do!

THE COMMAND OF CHRIST

The Scripture says as it concerns Christ:

> **"And, being assembled together with *them*** *(speaks of the time He ascended back to the Father; this was probably the time 'He was seen of above five hundred Brethren' [I Cor. 15:6]),* **Commanded them** *(not a suggestion)* **that they should not depart from Jerusalem** *(the site of the Temple where the Holy Spirit would descend),* **but wait for the Promise of the Father** *(spoke of the Holy Spirit Who*

> *had been promised by the Father [Lk. 24:49; Joel, Chpt. 2])*, **which, said** ***He,*** **you have heard of Me** *(you have also heard Me say these things [Jn. 7:37-39; 14:12-17, 26; 15:26; 16:7-15])*.
>
> **"For John truly baptized with water** *(merely symbolized the very best Baptism Believers could receive before the Day of Pentecost)*; **but you shall be baptized with the Holy Spirit not many days hence** *(spoke of the coming Day of Pentecost, although Jesus did not use that term at that time)*" **(Acts 1:4-5).**

In essence, our Lord told His Followers, ***"Don't go preach the Gospel, don't go sing the Gospel, don't go witness for Me, until you first are baptized with the Holy Spirit."***

IS THIS COMMAND INCUMBENT UPON BELIEVERS PRESENTLY?

Most definitely it is, with two exceptions:

1. They were told to ***"wait for the Promise of the Father."*** **We do not now have to wait because the Holy Spirit has already come. At this time He had not yet come and, in fact, would come on the Day of Pentecost. From that day until now, because of what Jesus did at the Cross, the Holy Spirit continues to function now exactly as He did then.**

2. They were told to wait in Jerusalem because this is where the Holy Spirit would make His Entrance in His new Dimension. In the other accounts given of people being baptized with the Spirit, we see that the next place was Samaria, and then Damascus where the Apostle Paul was filled, and then Caesarea where Cornelius and his household were filled, and then Ephesus recorded in Acts, Chapter 19.

Peter also said:

> **"Repent, and be baptized every one of you in the Name of Jesus Christ for the Remission of sins** *(should*

have been translated, 'because of remission of sins'), **and you shall receive the Gift of the Holy Spirit.**

"For the Promise is unto you, and to your children, and to all who are afar off, ***even*** **as many as the Lord our God shall call** *(that 'Call' is 'whosoever will' [Jn. 7:37-39; Rev. 22:17])*" **(Acts 2:38-39).**

The ***"Command,"*** **remains, as it regards the necessity of the Baptism with the Holy Spirit.**

According to the Word of God, very little is going to be done by Believers who aren't baptized with the Holy Spirit. While there may be big crowds involved, and even with much money taken in, the truth is, without the preacher, and the people being baptized with the Holy Spirit, precious few people are going to truly be Saved, lives changed, the sick healed, with the powers of darkness defeated. The Holy Spirit is needed and, in fact, is demanded, in every aspect of our life and living.

And yet, we must understand, while the Holy Spirit is Perfect, we who have had the privilege of being baptized with the Spirit, are very imperfect. So that means that He has imperfect vessels to work through. That means that we sometimes make mistakes, and sometimes do things very wrong; however, that is not the fault of the Spirit, but rather our fault.

I would strongly caution those who claim that this of which we speak is of the Devil. That's coming perilously close to blaspheming the Holy Spirit. In fact, if the Baptism with the Holy Spirit with the evidence of speaking with other Tongues is of the Devil, it's the only thing the Devil has that makes people love Jesus supremely, makes them love God's Word, makes them desire to tell others about Jesus, makes them take this Gospel, the greatest Story ever told, to the far ends of the Earth.

Jesus said, and the Promise still holds:

"If any man thirsts, let him come unto Me, and drink.

"He who believes on Me as the Scripture has said out of his belly shall flow rivers of Living Water.

"But this spoke He of the Spirit . . ." **(Jn. 7:37-39).**

CHAPTER THREE

What Is Blaspheming The Holy Spirit?

QUESTION:

WHAT IS BLASPHEMING THE HOLY SPIRIT?

ANSWER:

We will address the following questions from the Word of God:

- **What is blaspheming the Holy Spirit?**
- **Can a person blaspheme the Holy Spirit and not know that he has?**
- **Is it possible for a person to desire to be Saved, and they cannot, because they have blasphemed the Holy Spirit?**
- **Who can blaspheme the Holy Spirit?**
- **Can one through discerning of spirits know if someone else has blasphemed the Holy Spirit?**

Regarding this subject, we will quote from THE EXPOSITOR'S STUDY BIBLE:

> **"And the Scribes which came down from Jerusalem said** *(evidently sent by the Sanhedrin in order to find something in which they could undermine His Influence)*, **He has Beelzebub, and by the prince of the devils casteth He out devils** *(they blasphemed the Holy Spirit when they accused Christ of casting out devils by the power of Satan)*.
>
> **"And He called them *unto Him*** *(the Scribes)*, **and said unto them in Parables, How can Satan cast out Satan?** *(Why would Satan undo what he had done?)*
>
> **"And if a kingdom be divided against itself, that kingdom cannot stand.**
>
> **"And if a house be divided against itself, that house cannot stand** *(internal fighting respecting a family will ultimately lead to the destruction of that family)*.
>
> **"And if Satan rise up against himself, and be divided, he cannot stand, but has an end** *(would wreck his kingdom of darkness)*.

"No man can enter into a strong man's house *(in this case the house of Satan)*, **and spoil his goods, except he will first bind the strong man** *(Jesus overthrew Satan)*; **and then he will spoil his house** *(Christ defeated Satan at the Cross, by atoning for all sin [Col. 2:14-15])*.

"Verily I say unto you *(speaking to all, but more directly to the Scribes)*, **All sins shall be forgiven unto the sons of men, and blasphemies wherewith soever they shall blaspheme** *(providing forgiveness is asked of the Lord; this is a wonderful Promise, and has been upheld in the hearts and lives of untold millions)*:

"But he who shall blaspheme against the Holy Spirit hath never forgiveness *(only a Believer who has ceased to believe, in other words, ceases to evidence Faith in Christ, and a professor of religion, such as these Pharisees, etc., can blaspheme the Holy Spirit; an unsaved person, who has made no profession of faith, cannot blaspheme the Spirit; and when one does blaspheme the Holy Spirit, there will not be any desire to serve Christ, as there was no desire by the Pharisees, etc., to serve Christ)*, **but is in danger of eternal damnation** *(refers to those who would attribute the Power of God to Satan, as the Pharisees had done; to label anything which is actually of God, as being of Satan is a serious offense indeed!)*:

"Because they said, He has an unclean spirit *(most serious)*.**" (Mk. 3:22-30).**

WHAT IS BLASPHEMING THE HOLY SPIRIT?

In the case of Christ, and the reason that He gave this dissertation, is because the Pharisees accused him of casting out demons and healing the sick, etc., by the power of Satan. Jesus answered them, as we have stated, by saying, *"How can Satan cast out Satan?"* In essence, those who did this thing blasphemed the Holy Spirit, which means they could not be Saved. In other words, from that moment their fate was sealed. When they died

they would go to an eternal Hell, thereby being there forever and forever.

The Pharisees were the fundamentalists of Jesus' Day. Being a *"fundamentalist,"* means that they claimed to believe all of the Bible. Their Bible at that time consisted of Genesis through Malachi. Most of them were bitter enemies of Christ.

Why did they hate Him so?

It was their self-righteousness that hated Him. In fact, there is nothing more evil, I think, than self-righteousness. That's what nailed Christ to the Cross. And let us say this quickly:

If the Believer presently, doesn't have his Faith exclusively in Christ and the Cross, and maintain his Faith exclusively in Christ and the Cross, self-righteousness will always, and without exception, be the result. While there may be degrees of self-righteousness, the fact of that terrible blight will not be in question. It is either Faith in Christ and the Cross, which will produce the Righteousness of God, and is the only kind that God will accept, or it is self-righteousness.

As well, blaspheming the Holy Spirit is an insulting remark regarding the Holy Spirit, made by a professor of religion. This is an unforgivable sin when it is done maliciously and knowingly. It is unpardonable because it is a willful rejection of Light (Jn. 3:19). As such, it is a deliberate insult to the last and the only Instrument of God held out to man for the purpose of bringing about the remission of sin.

When professors of religion reject and spurn God's only agent for Redemption — and His only avenue for forgiveness — there is no one else to plead their case before God! The Holy Spirit is the Person of the Godhead Who presents the case of the individual before God. Those who willfully and blatantly reject this representation are, therefore, left with no further recourse. They have mindlessly rejected their last resort.

The reason this sin is so uniquely appalling is because of Whom it is directed against. God the Father made this world and governs it whether or not men like the things He does. Likewise, Jesus Christ came down from Heaven and went to

the Cross at Calvary regardless of man's desires, preferences, or anything that they might have tried to do to prevent Him. The Holy Spirit, however, is totally different. He responds to the wishes — to the reception or rejection — of men. He never imposes His Will on anyone. The Holy Spirit always operates *"as gently as a dove,"* thus, to reject Him is to cut off all hope.

CAN A PERSON BLASPHEME THE HOLY SPIRIT AND NOT KNOW THAT HE HAS?

Yes, he can! In fact, virtually all people who blaspheme the Holy Spirit do so without knowing it; however, for this question to be fully answered, one would have to read carefully our answer to the question as to who can blaspheme the Holy Spirit!

To be sure, these Pharisees who blasphemed the Holy Spirit, meaning they could never be Saved and despite all their religiosity, did not agree at all with Jesus when He, in essence, told them that they had blasphemed the Holy Spirit. They did not know they had, did not believe they had, and, no doubt, remained in that frame of mind until the day they died — and I might quickly add, died eternally lost. In fact, their anger against Him grew in intensity, until it culminated with Him being nailed to the Cross, and because they demanded His Crucifixion.

But, to answer the question, *"Can a person blaspheme the Holy Spirit and not know that he has,"* in another direction, it is imperative that we say the following:

It is not possible for an unsaved person, who is not a professor of religion, even though he may have made some slight remark about the Holy Spirit, and did so in ignorance, for such a person to blaspheme the Holy Spirit. They need not worry that they had done so in ignorance.

Paul said of himself: *"Who was before a blasphemer, and a persecutor, and injurious; but I obtained Mercy, because I did it ignorantly in unbelief"* (I Tim. 1:13). Here Paul specifically states that he was a blasphemer, but that he didn't know any better. There is nothing in the Word of God that suggests saying

something negative about the Holy Spirit as being unforgivable by those who have never had an opportunity to understand God's Mercy and God's Grace. To be sure, these people are lost; however, any moment they choose, they may, by the Grace of God, come to the Lord Jesus Christ, regardless of what they may have done in the past. Their sins can be forgiven, and they can be cleansed and washed in the Blood, becoming new creations in Christ Jesus. The choice is theirs!

IS IT POSSIBLE FOR A PERSON TO DESIRE TO BE SAVED, AND THEY CANNOT BECAUSE THEY HAVE BLASPHEMED THE HOLY SPIRIT?

No!

If a person wants to be Saved it is the Holy Spirit Who has placed, and is placing that desire in such a heart. He would not place such a desire in such a person, and then refuse to save that person, that is if they want to be Saved. Anyone who wants to be Saved, and I mean anyone, can be Saved. All they have to do is believe that Jesus Christ is the Son of God, and that He died on the Cross of Calvary for their sins and, thereby, accept Him as their Saviour and their Lord. Doing that, they will be instantly Born-Again, and that is guaranteed.

Jesus said, *"No man can come to Me, except the Father Who has sent Me draw him"* (Jn. 6:44).

If the Holy Spirit draws an unsaved person to Christ, all that remains is for that person to say *"yes"* to Christ, and they will be Saved. So, the idea that a person would desire to be Saved, and they cannot be Saved, because they think they've blasphemed the Holy Spirit, is not Scriptural, or plausible.

Unfortunately, Satan has used this ploy on many people, trying to make them believe, that despite the desire to be Saved, that they simply cannot be Saved, because of something they did or said in the past. As long as he can get them to believe that lie, he will have succeeded in his purpose, and they will die eternally lost, if they continue in that vein. But the moment they believe,

and that capacity is theirs, they will be instantly Saved.

WHO CAN BLASPHEME THE HOLY SPIRIT?

Now that's the great question!

First of all, let's see who cannot blaspheme the Holy Spirit.

It is not possible for an unsaved person, and I'm speaking of those who are not professors of religion, to blaspheme the Holy Spirit. No matter what such a person may say or do, whatever it is they do that's extremely negative toward the Lord, or even toward the Holy Spirit, is done in acute ignorance. In other words, they don't even really know what they're doing. It might be said, they don't know enough about the Holy Spirit to blaspheme the Holy Spirit. Once again, it doesn't matter how evil, how wicked, how sinful, how reprobate that a person is, if that person wants to be Saved, the very desire that is in their heart, has been placed there, as stated, by the Holy Spirit, and to be sure, that person can be Saved. There are millions of people all over the world, and down through the ages of time, who have done some terrible things as it regards sin and iniquity, but there came an hour that they gave their heart and life to Jesus Christ. And when they did, every sin was cleansed, every iniquity was purged. Jesus said:

***"Come unto Me, all you who labor and are heavy laden, and I will give you rest"* (Mat. 11:28).**

He didn't put a limit on this invitation! In fact, He said *"all."*

The only kind of individual who can blaspheme the Holy Spirit, is one who has truly been Saved, and then has turned his back upon the Lord, and ceased to believe, or else a professor of religion who, in fact, has never been Saved, but who like the Pharisees profess great things. These are the only ones who can blaspheme the Holy Spirit, and when they do such, they won't even know it. In fact, they won't believe it, even as stated, like the Pharisees of old.

I remember once hearing a preacher, with whom I was not acquainted, over the Radio, making some terrible, blasphemous

statements as it regards the Holy Spirit and speaking with other Tongues.

He mimicked those who speak with Tongues, actually barking like a dog, and claiming that they sounded like dogs, etc.

For the few moments I listened to him, as I heard him making these statements, I grew cold all over. Did he blaspheme the Holy Spirit?

I'll have to leave that up to the Lord. I cannot answer; however, this one thing I will say, if he didn't do such, and I pray that he didn't, he came perilously close to sealing his doom.

Sometime back, I read a statement given in a publication put out by a so-called Christian College. The President of that particular school, with whom I was acquainted, made the following statement, and I paraphrase:

"Anyone who speaks with Tongues is either mentally deranged or demon possessed. And if anyone practices such in this school, and it is found out, they will be summarily dismissed."

Did this preacher blaspheme the Holy Spirit by linking speaking with other Tongues with demon powers?

Once again, I cannot answer that. I'll have to leave it with the Lord. But one thing is certain, he was most definitely skating on very thin ice.

As it regards anyone who doesn't believe in the Baptism with the Holy Spirit with the evidence of speaking with other Tongues, I would strongly advise such a person to just say, *"I don't see it that way,"* and let it go at that. To make such statements as we have quoted, is attributing the Work of God to the powers of darkness. That's what caused the Pharisees to blaspheme the Holy Spirit, and it is quite possible, and, no doubt, is the same presently with some people.

CAN ONE THROUGH *"DISCERNING OF SPIRITS,"* KNOW IF SOMEONE ELSE HAS BLASPHEMED THE HOLY SPIRIT?

One of the Nine Gifts of the Spirit described as *"discerning*

of spirits," **refers to human spirits, evil spirits, or the Spirit of God.**

I would not say that the Holy Spirit through an individual, who is used in this manner has never done such, but I would say if such has happened, that it's been very rare.

As we have stated, it seems from the Word of God, that the only individuals who can blaspheme the Holy Spirit and thus commit the unpardonable sin are those who have once known God — or at least made a conscious profession of knowing Him — who then willfully turn their backs on that knowledge, thereby making extremely derogatory remarks about the Holy Spirit. They thus sin against Light; consequently, they blaspheme the Holy Spirit thereby committing the unpardonable sin.

In conclusion, God will forgive any sin, no matter how despicable. In fact, any person who comes to Him, He will in no wise cast him out (Jn. 6:37). But if professors of religion willfully sin against Light and turn their backs upon God and put Christ to an open shame by denying His Precious Blood; if they willfully, with eyes wide open, ascribe the Works of the Holy Spirit to the Devil; and if they willfully and knowingly apostatize, then there is no way for them to be Saved. As stated, the truth is, they won't even desire the things of the Lord, at least that which is legitimate. They have blasphemed the Holy Spirit; they have committed the unpardonable sin.

CHAPTER FOUR

What Is The Error Of The "Jesus Only" Doctrine?

QUESTION:

WHAT IS THE ERROR OF THE "JESUS ONLY" DOCTRINE?

ANSWER:

This doctrine began, as far as we know, about 1914. It was at this time that the Assemblies of God was formed. A preacher in that particular Movement claimed that the Lord gave him a Revelation as it regards the Name of Jesus and other particulars. Again, as far as we know, in the beginning stages, all the preachers who believed this *"new revelation,"* came out of the Assemblies of God. We quickly must state, this so-called revelation was rejected by the Assemblies of God.

This *"new revelation"* came to be referred to as the *"Jesus Only People"* or *"Oneness"* with their major denomination referred to as *"United Pentecostals"*. Their basic doctrines are:

- **They claim there is only One Person in the Godhead Who is Jesus Christ.**
- **They are vehemently opposed to the Doctrine of the Trinity, claiming it is of human origin.**
- **They teach that in order to be Saved one has to be baptized in water and, as well, baptized according to a certain formula, which is a formula of their own devisings.**
- **They also teach that in order to be Saved, one has to speak with other Tongues.**

The two basic Scriptures which address themselves to this controversy are:

***"And Jesus came and spoke unto them, saying . . . go you therefore, and teach all nations, baptizing them in the Name of the Father, and of the Son, and of the Holy Spirit"* (Mat. 28:18-19).**

***"Then Peter said unto them, Repent, and be baptized every one of you in the Name of Jesus Christ for the Remission of sins . . ."* (Acts 2:38).**

THREE GODS OR ONE?

We teach there is One God manifest in Three Persons: God the Father, God the Son, and God the Holy Spirit. The *"Jesus Only People"* teach that Christ is the Father, He is the Son, and He is the Holy Spirit, hence, the name, *"Jesus Only"*.

I believe we can provide proper evidence from the Word of God that this is not the case and that the teaching advanced by these people is erroneous and does not accord proper due and honor to the Godhead.

The Scripture does state that there is *"One God."* But the word *"one"* relates to unity as well as number.

John the Beloved wrote, and we quote from THE EXPOSITOR'S STUDY BIBLE:

***"For there are Three Who bear record in Heaven, the Father, the Word, and the Holy Spirit: and these Three are One"* (I Jn. 5:7).**

Jesus said: *"That they all may be One; as You, Father are in Me, and I in You, that they also may be One in Us: that the world may believe that You have sent Me.*

***"And the glory which You gave Me, I have given them; that they may be one, even as We are One"* (Jn. 17:21-22). And yet, there are Three distinct Persons: the Father, the Son, and the Holy Spirit. The Three are spoken of as One in number and yet treated individually in Scripture. There is one God the Father, one Lord Jesus Christ, and one Holy Spirit.**

***"But to us there is but One God, the Father of Whom are all things and we in Him; and One Lord Jesus Christ, by Whom are all things, and we by Him"* (I Cor. 8:6).**

And then the Apostle said: *"Endeavoring to keep the unity of the Spirit in the bond of peace.*

"There is one body and one Spirit, even as you are called in one hope of your calling;

"One Lord, one Faith, one Baptism,

***"One God and Father of all, Who is above all, and through all, and in you all"* (Eph. 4:3-6). Thus, there are three separate**

Persons in Divine individuality and Divine plurality. The Father is called God, with the Scripture just quoted (I Cor. 8:6). The Son is called God.

"For unto us a Child is born, unto us a Son is given: and the Government shall be upon His Shoulder: and His Name shall be called Wonderful, Counselor, The Mighty God, The Everlasting Father, The Prince of Peace.

***"Of the increase of His Government and peace there shall be no end, upon the throne of David, and upon His Kingdom, to order it, and to establish it with judgment and with justice from henceforth even forever. The zeal of the LORD of Hosts will perform this"* (Isa. 9:6-7).**

And then: *"But unto the Son He said, Your Throne, O God, is for ever and ever: a scepter of Righteousness is the scepter of Your Kingdom"* (Heb. 1:8).

And finally: *"In the beginning was the Word, and the Word was with God, and the Word was God.*

***"The same was in the beginning with God"* (Jn. 1:1-2).**

As well, the Holy Spirit is called God but Peter said, *"Ananias, why has Satan filled your heart to lie to the Holy Spirit, and to keep back part of the price of the land?*

***"While it remained, was it not your own? and after it was sold, was it not in your own power? why have you conceived this thing in your heart? you have not lied unto men, but unto God"* (Acts 5:3-4). Individually, each is God; collectively, they can be spoken of as One God because of their Perfect Unity and Essence.**

The word *"God"* can be used either in the singular or in the plural, like sheep. Everything that could pertain to God collectively could also apply equally to each Member of the Godhead as individuals; however, there are some particulars which relate to each individual Person of the Deity as to position, office, and work that could not be attributed to either of the other Members of the Godhead. For instance, the Father is the Head of Christ.

"But I would have you know, that the Head of every man is

Christ; and the Head of the woman is the man; and the Head of Christ is God" **(I Cor. 11:3). The Son is the Only Begotten of the Father.** *"Grace be with you, Mercy, and Peace, from God the Father, and from the Lord Jesus Christ, the Son of the Father, in Truth and Love"* **(II Jn. 1:3).**

The Holy Spirit proceeds from both the Father and the Son.

"And I will pray the Father and He shall give you another Comforter, that He may abide with you forever" **(Jn. 14:16).**

And then: *"And there appeared unto them cloven tongues like as of fire, and it sat upon each of them.*

"And they were all filled with the Holy Spirit, and began to speak with other Tongues, as the Spirit gave them utterance" **(Acts. 2:3-4).**

ELOHIM

The Names of God prove plurality of Persons. The Hebrew word *"Elohim,"* **translated** *"God"* **in Genesis 1:1 and also in more than 2,700 other places in the Old Testament, is a uniplural noun, which means,** *"more than one."* **Had the sacred writer been led to use the singular** *"El," then there would have been no indication of a Divine plurality. But in this initial reference to God, he was led of the Holy Spirit to pen the word "Elohim."*

"In the beginning God **(Elohim)** *created the heaven and the Earth"* **(Gen. 1:1).**

Also when one considers that the word *"Elohim"* **is used about ten to one over the word** *"El,"* **we would have to conclude that the preference for the plural over the singular indicates a definite sign of plurality in the Godhead.**

PLURALITY IN SCRIPTURES

In Genesis 3:22 it says, *"The man has become one of Us,"* **which proves plurality of Persons by the use of the pronoun** *"Us."*

Two Lords are mentioned in Genesis, Chapter 19.

"Then the LORD rained upon Sodom and upon Gomorrah

brimstone and fire from the LORD out of heaven" **(Gen. 19:24). We have here one Lord on Earth and another in Heaven.**

Two Lords sit side by side in Psalm 110:

"The LORD said unto my Lord, Sit You at My Right Hand, until I make Your Enemies Your Footstool.

"The LORD shall send the rod of Your Strength out of Zion: rule You in the midst of Your Enemies.

"Your People shall be willing in the day of Your Power, in the beauties of holiness from the womb of the morning: You have the dew of Your Youth.

"The LORD has sworn, and will not repent, You are a Priest forever after the order of Melchizedek.

"The Lord at Your Right Hand shall strike through kings in the day of His Wrath" **(Ps. 110:1-5).**

And then: ***"The LORD said unto My Lord, sit You on My Right Hand, till I make Your Enemies Your Footstool?"*** **(Mat. 22:44).**

And finally: ***"Therefore being by the Right Hand of God exalted and having received of the Father the Promise of the Holy Spirit, He has shed forth this, which you now see and hear.***

"For David is not ascended into the Heavens: but he said himself, the LORD said unto My Lord, sit You on My Right Hand,

"Until I make Your Foes Your Footstool.

"Therefore let all the house of Israel know assuredly, that God has made that same Jesus, Whom you have Crucified, both Lord and Christ" **(Acts 2:33-36).**

As well, Two and Three Persons are mentioned in the introductions to many New Testament Books: Romans, James, I Corinthians, I Peter, etc., to name a few.

JESUS IS NOT THE FATHER

Only one Scripture in the Word of God states that Jesus is the Father. This is found in Isaiah.

"For unto us a Child is born, unto us a Son is given: and the Government shall be upon His Shoulder: and His Name shall be called Wonderful, Counselor, The Mighty God, The Everlasting

Father, The Prince of Peace" **(Isa. 9:6). And this is a Hebrew idiom concerning the terminology of the Jews. And we know from the Word of God that while Jesus was on Earth the Father was in Heaven.**

"That you may be the Children of your Father Who is in Heaven: for He makes His Sun to rise on the evil and on the good, and sends rain on the just and on the unjust" **(Mat. 5:45).**

We also know from Scripture that Christ now sits at the Right Hand of the Father. Jesus said He would confess men before His Father Who was in Heaven, proving He (Jesus) is not Himself the Father.

"Whosoever therefore shall confess Me before men, him will I confess also before My Father Who is in Heaven" **(Mat. 10:32).**

And then: ***"He who overcomes, the same shall be clothed in white raiment; and I will not blot out his name out of the Book of Life, but I will confess his name before My Father, and before His Angels"*** **(Rev. 3:5).**

Jesus always prayed to the Father as a separate Person: ***"At that time Jesus answered and said, I thank You, O Father, Lord of Heaven and Earth, because You have hid these things from the wise and prudent, and have revealed them unto babes.***

"Even so, Father: for so it seemed good in Your Sight" **(Mat. 11:25-26). Both Jesus and Satan refer to God apart:**

"Then the Devil took Him up into the Holy City, and sat Him on a pinnacle of the Temple,

"And said unto Him, If You be the Son of God, cast Yourself down: for it is written, He shall give His Angels charge concerning You: and in their hands they shall bear You up, lest at any time You dash Your Foot against a stone.

"Jesus said unto him, It is written again, you shall not tempt the Lord your God.

"Again, the Devil took Him up into an exceeding high mountain, and showed Him all the kingdoms of the world, and the glory of them;

"And said unto Him, All these things will I give You, if You will fall down and worship me.

"Then said Jesus unto him, Get thee hence, Satan: for it is written, you shall worship the Lord your God, and Him only shall you serve" **(Mat. 4:5-10).**

Jesus was the Only Begotten Son of the Father. Hence, Jesus could not be the Father, nor could He beget Himself. ***"And the Word was made flesh, and dwelt among us, (and we beheld His Glory, the Glory as of the Only Begotten of the Father,) full of Grace and Truth"*** **(Jn. 1:14). Over 80 times in the Word of God Jesus affirmed that He was not the Father, nor was He the only Person in the Godhead.**

Admittedly, we do not understand everything about the Trinity; however, it does become somewhat less confusing and mysterious if we don't try to force two or more separate Persons into becoming only one Person, simply because we choose not to recognize that the true meaning of the word ***"one"*** **actually refers to unity. So what we have is, only one Scripture (easily explained) in the Old Testament stating that Jesus is the Father, and so very, very many confirming that He is not the Father.**

The way the word ***"Father"*** **is used in Isaiah 9:6, is that Jesus is the Father of Redemption, the Resurrection, etc.**

Paul said: ***"For whom He did foreknow, He also did predestinate to be conformed to the Image of His Son, that He might be the firstborn among many Brethren"*** **(Rom. 8:29).**

This doesn't mean that Jesus was ***"Born-Again"*** **as some teach, but rather that He is the Father of the Salvation Plan, having paid the price on the Cross, which made it all possible.**

Paul also said: ***"Who is the Image of the invisible God, the Firstborn of every creature"*** **(Col. 1:15).**

Once again, this doesn't mean that Jesus as God is a created being. It actually means that He is the Creator of all things, the Father of Creation.

The Apostle also said: ***"And He is the Head of the Body, the Church: Who is the beginning, the firstborn from the dead"*** **(Col. 1:18).**

Once again, this does not mean that Jesus was Born-Again, but rather that He was the first to be raised from the dead as it

regards the Resurrection, and never to die again, meaning that He is the Father of the Resurrection.

THE GREEK WORD *"PROTOKOS"*

The word *"firstborn"* is the nearest English word that can be interpreted from the Greek word *"protokos."* It means *"the beginning of,"* or *"the father of."* So, to try to force Jesus as being also the Father from Isaiah 9:6, presents a complete misunderstanding of the Text.

THE HOLY SPIRIT IS NOT JESUS OR THE FATHER

The Holy Spirit is Another and He is from both the Father and the Son.

"And I will pray the Father and He shall give you another Comforter that He may abide with you forever;

***"Even the Spirit of Truth; Whom the world cannot receive, because it sees Him not, neither knows Him: but you know Him; for He dwells with you, and shall be in you"* (Jn. 14:16-17). So that the Holy Spirit could come, it was necessary that Jesus go away.**

***"Nevertheless I tell you the truth; It is expedient for you that I go away: for if I go not away, the Comforter will not come unto you; but if I depart, I will send Him unto you"* (Jn. 16:7). Even then, He could not be sent from God until Christ was glorified. But at that time He would be sent from both the Father and the Son.**

"In the last day, that great day of the Feast, Jesus stood and cried, saying, If any man thirst, let him come unto Me, and drink.

"He who believes on Me, as the Scripture has said, out of his belly shall flow rivers of Living Water.

***"But this spoke He of the Spirit, which they who believe on Him should receive: for the Holy Spirit was not yet given; because that Jesus was not yet glorified"* (Jn. 7:37-39). The Holy Spirit was sent from the Father to endue Jesus with Power. This clearly requires three Persons — the One Who sent Him, and the One being sent, and the One Who received Him!**

A clear distinction is made between the Son Who prays, the Father to Whom He prays, and the Holy Spirit for which He prays (Jn. 14:16).

The descent of the Holy Spirit acknowledged the arrival of Jesus in Heaven to sit at the Right Hand of God, thus proving three separate and distinct Persons.

"Therefore being by the Right Hand of God exalted, and having received of the Father the Promise of the Holy Spirit, He has shed forth this, which you now see and hear.

***"For David is not ascended into the Heavens: but he said himself, the LORD said unto my Lord, Sit You on My Right Hand"* (Acts 2:33-34).**

So, what do we have? Jesus is God, the Holy Spirit is God, and the Father is God. But Jesus is not the Holy Spirit and Jesus is not the Father. Neither is the Father the Lord Jesus Christ nor is the Father the Holy Spirit.

The Scriptural Passages which provide the basis for the Trinitarian Doctrine cannot be reconciled to the *"Jesus Only"* position without totally disregarding the meaning of language and without totally ignoring many contrary Scriptures. On the other hand, the favorite *"Jesus Only"* Passages cannot be reconciled without strain or contradiction to the Trinitarian position.

"Holy, Holy, Holy! Lord God Almighty!
"Early in the morning our song shall rise to Thee;
"Holy, Holy, Holy, Merciful and Mighty!
"God in Three Persons, Blessed Trinity!"

"Holy, Holy, Holy! All the Saints adore Thee,
"Casting down their golden crowns around the glassy sea;
"Cherubim and Seraphim, falling down before Thee,
"Who was, and is, and evermore shall be."

THE FORMULA FOR WATER BAPTISM

The Trinitarians baptize according to Matthew 28:19, using

the Words of the Lord Jesus Christ where He said that we should baptize in the Name of the Father, and of the Son, and of the Holy Spirit. We do this for many reasons, and I will go into some of the details concerning the differences between the two baptismal formulas.

"Go you therefore, and teach all nations, baptizing them in the Name of the Father, and of the Son, and of the Holy Spirit" **(Mat. 28:19).**

The *"Jesus Only People"* affirm that the Matthew 28:19 method is not once found in the Book of Acts, and was unknown in the Early Church, but was introduced centuries later by apostates in total disregard of apostolic practice. Trinitarians are, therefore, they say, admonished to conform to the Scriptural pattern, and to follow the example of those who have the true *"revelation"* of the Name. This is taken to mean that unless one is baptized in the Name of Jesus Christ, they cannot be forgiven their sins, etc. (This is the sum total of the *"Jesus Only"* doctrine concerning the method of Water Baptism.)

NAMES

The *"Jesus Only People"* claim that the words *"Father"* and *"Son"* do not constitute names. We maintain they do. We believe that Matthew 28:19 definitely confirms that *"Father"* is a Name, that *"Son"* is a Name, that *"Holy Spirit"* is a Name, simply because we are not generalizing just any father or just any son. We are talking about God the Father and God the Son; and most anyone in Christendom today would readily recognize and know Who is being spoken of.

In Isaiah 9:6, which we have already quoted, the Bible says, *"His Name shall be called Wonderful, Counselor, The Mighty God, The Everlasting Father, The Prince of Peace."* Each one of these appellations would be labeled a title by *"Jesus Only"* interpreters, but Isaiah's Text calls each one a *"Name."* This is also the one Verse of Scripture in the entirety of God's Word, where Jesus Christ is called the Father, which we have already

addressed; but still, somehow, these people are blinded to the fact that this Verse actually disproves their theory concerning titles and names, simply because it gives the name of *"Father"* to Jesus.

So I simply ask a question. According to Isaiah, isn't *"Wonderful"* a name? Isn't *"Prince of Peace"* a name? Isaiah uses five different names here and yet, under Divine Inspiration, he specifically chose the singular when he said, *"And His 'Name' shall be called . . ."* so what more needs to be said in answer to this strange insistence that if *"Father, Son, and Holy Spirit"* are names (plural), then Matthew 28:19 should read, they say, *"In the names of"*? The writers, under Divine Inspiration, used the singular instead of the plural. They did it for a Divine reason.

THE BOOK OF ACTS AND THE BAPTISMAL FORMULA

There is not a single incident in the Book of Acts where any particular baptismal method is given. There is no record of the dialogue of the baptizer while standing in the water with the convert. You will look in vain for any Scripture which would state, *"I baptize you in the Name of Jesus Christ"* (or any other variation of the precious Name of our Lord). If one would produce such an explicit procedure, I would be thrilled to admit that we have a Scriptural right to baptize thusly, but it cannot be produced. It doesn't exist.

On a personal basis, I really have no preference as to what the Bible teaches. I only want to know what it teaches, and then to do my best to obey what is given to us.

The *"Jesus Only People"* read into the record what is not there. They have taken the words of Peter, assumed that they were the properly expressed formula, and place them onto the lips of those who baptized in water — without a shred of evidence to support their action. The *"Jesus Only"* proponents proclaim that Acts 2:38 is the baptismal formula.

"Then Peter said unto them, Repent, and be baptized every

***one of you in the Name of Jesus Christ for the remission of sins, and you shall receive the Gift of the Holy Spirit"* (Acts 2:38).**

And yet Acts 8:16 and Acts 19:5 simply state they were baptized in the Name of the Lord Jesus.

***"For as yet He was fallen upon none of them: only they were baptized in the Name of the Lord Jesus"* (Acts 8:16).**

And then: *"When they heard this, they were baptized in the Name of the Lord Jesus"* (Acts 19:5).

And if you will notice, in these two latter Verses, the word *"Christ"* was omitted altogether.

If Peter, on the Day of Pentecost, received a baptism *"revelation"* which the *"Jesus Only"* proponents claim is *"in the Name of Jesus Christ,"* why, we ask, is the later variation produced which we have just quoted? You see, there is no fixed wording to follow, and there is no regular or prescribed usage of certain words. So the question has to be asked, should we baptize in the Name of Jesus Christ, or in Christ Jesus, or in the Lord, or in the Lord Jesus, or in the Lord Jesus Christ? Which would be correct? Was Peter right? or Philip? or Paul?

***"Jesus Only"* exponents say they are sticklers (fanatics) for the exact words of Scripture, and that they use the identical words of the Apostles; yet, their demands are not accompanied by quotations from God's Word, or the words themselves. Even in those Passages where their purported words are found, their full formula is lacking. One of their chief proponents some years ago stated that the following formula should be used: *"I baptize you in the Name of the Lord Jesus Christ, which is the Name of the Father, and of the Son, and of the Holy Spirit."* When this particular brother was asked to cite Chapter and Verse for this formula, he was speechless. Apparently, it had not ever occurred to him that the formula he had conjured up had no Scriptural connotation whatsoever.**

BAPTISMAL FORMULA?

So, the question still must be asked. Which is the right way

to baptize and what was the meaning of Peter's or Paul's words in the Book of Acts?

There is no way one can take the Passages in the Book of Acts to be intended as a baptismal formula. The words should be regarded as a compendious description of the entire Rite. In Acts 2:38, 8:16, 10:48, and 19:5, the details of the baptismal ceremony are not set forth. What is set forth is a condensed, brief, abridged reference to the sacred experience. The words describe the sphere, the foundation, or ground of baptism, rather than the prescribed words of the formula.

Every Trinitarian using the Matthew 28:19 formula refers to Water Baptism as *"Christian Baptism"* and this is as it should be, for Christ is assuredly the central figure in Water Baptism. Jesus Christ is the One Who died and rose again; not the Father and not the Holy Spirit. It is into His Death that we are symbolically buried, and in the likeness of His Resurrection we are raised to walk in Newness of Life; therefore, belief in, and confession of the Lord Jesus Christ, and what He did for us at the Cross, is a central part of our baptismal ceremony.

THE REASON WE ACCEPT THE MATTHEW 28:19 BAPTISMAL FORMULA

- **Both the Minister and the Believer render obedience to the Master's Own explicit command whenever the words are used, *"In the Name of the Father, and of the Son, and of the Holy Spirit."***
- **Matthew 28:19 fits the definition of a formula. It is an orderly statement of Faith and Doctrine. It is the prescribed words of a ceremony or rite. The words of the Lord Himself are all contained in one concise declaration. It is not necessary, as in the *"Jesus Only"* formula, to combine it with other Scriptures in order to get the complete Name. It is complete within itself.**
- **Matthew 28:19 incorporates an orderly statement of Faith. It summarizes the scattered and unsystemized thought and language of the entire New Testament concerning the nature**

of the Godhead. He Who spoke these words desired their use as the formula, for they were purposely designed to set forth the Doctrine of the Trinity in this initiatory Christian Rite. The Master's Own Baptism by John was a vivid precedent for associating the Trinity with Baptism. Jesus was there in Person, God spoke from Heaven, and the Holy Spirit descended like a Dove upon Him.

• Matthew 28:19 is the only command in the entire Bible given specifically to those performing the Rite of Baptism. If you will examine all the Passages in Acts dealing with Baptism, you will discover that the commands there are to the Believers themselves and not to the Baptizer or the Minister. Matthew 28:19 is a direct order to those who administer the Ordinance informing them to baptize *"in the Name of the Father, and of the Son, and of the Holy Spirit."*

• It is unthinkable that the Disciples disobeyed the express Command of their Lord. The only logical and Scriptural conclusion is that the Apostles and other leaders not only obeyed His Command to baptize but also obeyed His Command to *"baptize in the Name of the Father, and of the Son, and of the Holy Spirit."*

• The Matthew 28:19 baptismal formula is abundantly confirmed by the earliest Christian writings while the *"Jesus Only"* formula has no historical support at all. Justin's first apology was written in A.D. 153, about ninety years after the death of Peter and Paul. It was about sixty years after the death of John the Apostle. Justin was a contemporary of Polycarp, who was a Disciple of John himself, and he stated that Matthew 28:19 was the correct formula.

THE DIDACHE

There is another book called, *"The Teaching Of The Twelve Apostles"* and it is the oldest book outside the New Testament. It is also known as the *"Didache"* and is dated by most authorities between years A.D. 70 and A.D. 100. Although the author of

the book is unknown, it is a compilation of the teachings of the Apostles, which he had apparently learned either by personal instruction, oral tradition, or through their (the Apostle's) own writings, or other New Testament writings then in circulation. While it does not possess the inspiration of the Scriptures, the *"Didache"* is an authentic record of primitive Christianity. It includes as instructions for baptizing that we ought to baptize in the Name of the Father, and of the Son, and of the Holy Spirit, and also that we ought to baptize in running or living water. There again, the Matthew 28:19 formula is used. And, lest we forget, I would remind you that there is not a single recorded incident in the Bible or any other genuine First Century book where any other formula was ever used in the first 100 years of the Christian Era.

• Matthew 28:19 can be used as the formula and the baptism still be in the Name of Jesus Christ because the Son is Jesus Christ. Jesus Christ is the sphere, the foundation, and the ground for Trinitarian Baptism. Belief in, and confession of, Christ is the very heart of our baptism. Consequently, the word spoken by most Ministers of the Gospel, baptizing according to Matthew 28:19, follow this pattern: *"On the confession of your Faith in the Lord Jesus Christ, I baptize you in the Name of the Father, and of the Son, and of the Holy Spirit."*

DOES THE WATER SAVE?

The *"Jesus Only"* proponents basically teach baptismal regeneration. In other words, the water saves. This teaching, plus the implication that if one is not baptized in the Name of Jesus Only (or similar expressions), is a most effective means of frightening people into accepting the *"Jesus Only"* doctrine. The people are taught that if they are not baptized in this manner, their sins cannot be forgiven and they will be lost and will burn in Hell eternally. In fact, fear is the motivating factor in this particular doctrine.

Most Trinitarians believe Water Baptism to be a simple step

of obedience to the Lord. We believe in emersion, seeing the meaning of the word *"baptize"* as being a symbol of the death, burial, and the Resurrection of Jesus Christ. We believe that Water Baptism is not so much as some would make it, or so little as others would make it. The Lord Himself defined its purpose: to fulfill all Righteousness.

It is our Christian duty to be baptized. It is also our joyous privilege to testify publicly by the act of baptism that Jesus Christ is our Saviour and Lord. Nevertheless, we cannot attach the same importance to Water Baptism that some legalists such as the *"Jesus Only"* advocates do.

SAVED?

We would not attempt to exclude from the Kingdom all those who have not been baptized in the precise manner in which we deem Scriptural. The pages of Church history are filled with the names of men whose baptism in water we may regard as incorrect, but whose lives and ministries testify to an unquestionable experience with God. Yet, many *"Jesus Only"* adherents state and believe if individuals have not been baptized according to the *"Jesus Only"* formula, they are not even considered Saved. Some would make the statement that they are not *"fully Saved."* Of course, it is difficult to understand at all how a person can be partially Saved, i.e., *"partially justified."* We maintain, apart from the definite Spiritual and Scriptural relationship with the Lord, there is no virtue in the waters of baptism; or in the bread and wine, for that matter, of the Lord's Supper. In Acts 22:16, if when Paul used the words *"wash away your sins"* and this means the water would actually save a person; it would seem strange that Paul would say:

"I thank God that I baptized none of you, but Crispus and Gaius" (I Cor. 1:14).

Actually, when Paul used the term, *"Arise, and be baptized, and wash away your sins"* (Acts 22:16), it could be translated, *"Arise, and be baptized, and because your sins have been washed away."*

The statement refers to a present action being done because of a past action. He was being baptized in water because his sins had already been washed away by the Blood of Jesus.

No, Baptism is a symbol of what it represents, namely the Death, Burial, and Resurrection of our Lord.

THE BLOOD OF JESUS CHRIST

What is it that washes away sins? *"The Blood of Jesus Christ, His Son, cleanses us from all sin"* (I Jn. 1:7). Sin is, basically, an inner state which may or may not express itself outwardly. It stands to reason that mere outward work like Water Baptism cannot remove that which is inward. Also, water is a Scriptural Symbol for the Word (used in Eph. 5:26; Ps. 119:9; Jn. 15:3). As well, when Jesus spoke to Nicodemus saying:

"Verily, verily, I say unto you, except a man be born of water and of the Spirit, he cannot enter into the Kingdom of God" **(Jn. 3:5), by using the phrase *"born of water,"* He was not speaking of Water Baptism, but rather the natural birth of a baby, which is proven in Verse 6.**

As well, if water saves, what type of water should be used — tap water, running water, still water, deep water, shallow water, river water, or what type of water? What would happen if there was no water in which to administer the sacred Rite? Would that mean a person would be consigned to Hell forever, even though he had believed in and on the Lord Jesus Christ, if there was no water in which baptism could be applied, and the individual is dying?

THE THIEF ON THE CROSS

What happened to the thief on the Cross when Jesus turned to him and said, *"This day you shall be with Me in Paradise"*? There was no way for him to be baptized. Did he die and go to Hell? Certainly not. Water has never begotten anyone. Water is water, whether it's flowing water, still water, baptismal water,

or so-called holy water. Only believing in the Lord Jesus Christ makes one born of God.

***"For by Grace are you Saved through Faith . . . it is not of works, lest any man should boast"* (Eph. 2:8-9).**

SPEAKING WITH OTHER TONGUES

We teach and preach that the Baptism with the Holy Spirit is an experience subsequent to Salvation. And we believe when one is baptized with the Holy Spirit according to Acts 2:4 that he speaks with other Tongues as the Spirit of God gives the utterance.

However, while we cherish the Baptism with the Spirit, we must reject the insistence of the *"Jesus Only People"* that the experience is necessary for Salvation. We cannot accept the view that *"born of the Spirit"* in John 3:5 refers to the experience depicted in Matthew 3:11.

"I indeed baptize you with water unto Repentance but He Who comes after Me is mightier than I, Whose Shoes I am not worthy to bear: He shall baptize you with the Holy Spirit and with fire"* (Mat. 3:11). The only Baptism that John could give anyone was the *"Baptism unto Repentance."* He states here that Jesus would Baptize *"With the Holy Spirit, and with fire."

Incidentally, there are three Baptisms in which the Believer should engage.

THREE BAPTISMS

1. The Baptism into Christ, which is done by Faith, and speaks of the Crucifixion of Christ, and we are symbolically crucified with Him, buried with Him, and raised with Him in Newness of Life. It has nothing to do with water (Rom. 6:3-5).

2. Water Baptism (Mat. 28:19).

3. Baptism with the Holy Spirit (Mat. 3:11; Acts 2:4).

We believe and teach that the Baptism with the Holy Spirit is available to any and every Believer, and is a product of our

Salvation; however, it cannot be labeled as a requisite for Salvation itself. There is a great difference between that which we must do in order to be Saved, which is to trust Christ, and those Blessings that come to us because we are already Saved.

I will admit that non-Pentecostal Christians have for years made the mistake of confusing the Ministry of the Spirit at the New Birth, the Ministry of Regeneration, with the Baptism with the Spirit after the New Birth. There is a vast difference between being Born of the Spirit, and baptized with the Spirit. They have attempted to make these two separate experiences one in the same; however, I feel the Word of God makes it unquestionably clear that the Baptism with the Holy Spirit is a gift received subsequent to Salvation. The Baptism with the Holy Spirit is not given to us as a cause of Salvation, but as a consequence of Salvation.

For instance, in Acts 11:17 Cornelius and his fellow Gentiles were *"saved"* by believing the words told them by Peter, and then God poured out the Holy Spirit upon them. There is not a single Scripture, which states that one must be baptized with the Holy Spirit and speak with other Tongues in order to be Saved.

The Disciples and followers of Christ were not commanded to *"tarry in Jerusalem"* until they received an enduement of power which would save them, but to tarry for an enduement of Power which would enable them to be witnesses.

Any teaching that states you have to be baptized according to the Acts 2:38 experience and also speak in Tongues in order to be Saved, would not only bar from Heaven many of the Christians in the world today, but also the countless millions of Christians, Believers, who lived prior to the present-day outpouring of the Holy Spirit, not to mention all the host of non-Pentecostal Christians in the world today whose Salvation is as genuine and scripturally correct as my own.

I remember speaking on the radio with one of the adherents of the *"Jesus Only"* doctrine once. I asked him this question, What about men like D. L. Moody, Charles Spurgeon, Charles Finney, and several others I could name? These were great

men of God, who stirred the world and caused untold tens of thousands to come to the Lord Jesus Christ. These people were not baptized according to Acts 2:38. Neither did they speak in Tongues. Are you telling me they did not go to Heaven?

The man was very knowledgeable in his beliefs, but he hedged strongly. He tried repeatedly to change the subject. I kept pulling him back to it. Finally, he stated that God would have to take care of that, he just didn't know.

Of course, that answer is ridiculous because there are not several ways to be Saved. There is only one way and, in fact, there has ever been only one way and that is to believe on the Lord Jesus Christ. And if the *"Jesus Only People"* are correct, then basically no one was Saved up until 1914, and the only ones Saved in the world today are those who adhere to their particular Acts 2:38 formula and other peculiarities of their doctrine. When one begins to look at this, one can see how ridiculous it is. But, of course, maybe their answer would be that these people were partially Saved and not fully Saved. I will let you, the reader, form your own conclusions respecting that final statement.

IN CONCLUSION

Paul said:

"For by Grace are you Saved through Faith, and that not of yourselves: it is the Gift of God:

***"Not of works, lest any man should boast"* (Eph. 2:8-9).**

In view of what Paul said, are the *"Jesus Only"* adherents Saved?

They are basing their Salvation on their faith in Water Baptism and speaking with other Tongues; however, God cannot honor a salvation by works, only by Faith in Christ, and what Christ has done for us at the Cross. Paul also said:

"That if you shall confess with your mouth the Lord Jesus, and shall believe in your heart that God has raised Him from the dead, you shall be Saved.

***"For with the heart man believes unto Righteousness; and with the mouth confession is made unto Salvation"* (Rom. 10:9-10).**

Not one time here does Paul mention Water Baptism or speaking with other Tongues, or anything else for that matter, only *"confessing"* and *"believing."* So, in view of all of that, we ask again the question, *"Are the 'Jesus Only' adherents Saved?"*

Some are and some aren't!

If one's faith is in Water Baptism or speaking in other Tongues, or anything other than Christ and what Christ has done for us at the Cross, pure and simple, it is a belief system consisting of *"works."* God cannot accept that, He can only accept His Son and what He did for us at Calvary, and our Faith in that Finished Work.

I want it said, however, that we must ever exalt with ever-increasing fervor and devotion, the Precious Name of Jesus; however, I feel it is heretical to apply the Name of Jesus to the Father and the Holy Spirit. Nevertheless, it is my earnest prayer that our souls will be set aflame with the true glory of the wondrous Name of the Son, the Lord Jesus Christ. I would pray daily that we would receive a fresh Revelation of the Beauty and Power of that Name, the Blessed Name, *"Jesus."*

***"Jesus, O, how sweet the Name!
"Jesus, everyday the same;
"Jesus, let all Saints proclaim,
"It's worthy praise forever."***

(I owe a debt of gratitude to Carl Brumback for information gleaned from his book, *"God In Three Persons"*.)

CHAPTER FIVE

Did Jesus Have Brothers And Sisters Or Was He The Only Child Of Mary?

QUESTION:

DID JESUS HAVE BROTHERS AND SISTERS OR WAS HE THE ONLY CHILD OF MARY?

ANSWER:

To answer your question; yes, Jesus had brothers and sisters. They were His half-brothers and half-sisters, we might say, since Joseph was not Jesus' biological father. Of course, it goes without saying that Jesus had no earthly father; he was begotten of God. Now I will qualify my answer from Scripture.

1. The Word of God says, *"Is not this the carpenter's son? is not His Mother called Mary? and His Brethren, James, and Joses, and Simon and Judas? And His Sisters, are they not all with us?"* (Mat. 13:55-56; Mk. 6:3). In reply, Jesus Himself referred to them as *"His Own House"* and *"His Own Kin"* (Mat. 13:57; Mk. 6:4).

2. The Lord is called Mary's *"Firstborn"* (Mat. 1:25; Lk. 2:7). The natural inference here, of course, is that she did have other children. The Greek word *"prototokos"* is used in these two Scriptures, as well as in Romans 8:29; Colossians 1:15, 18; Hebrews 1:6; 11:28; 12:23, meaning, among others, *"the first of many others."*

If Jesus had been her only son, the Greek word would have been *"monogenes,"* which occurs in Luke 7:12; 8:42; 9:38; etc. (referring to human parentage of an *"only son," "only daughter,"* or *"only child"*) and in John 1:14; I John 4:9; (referring to the Lord Jesus as *"the Only Begotten of the Father" and "His Only Begotten Son"*).

Thus, we see clearly that Jesus was the Only Begotten Son of God (monogenes), but the firstborn son of Mary (prototokos).

FOR THE PROOF

3. It was predicted through the Psalmists that Mary would

have other children and that the Messiah would have brothers: *"I am become a stranger to My Brethren, and an alien unto My Mother's Children"* (Ps. 69:8).

4. *"His Mother and His Brethren"* are mentioned as following Him to Capernaum and seeking to hinder His Work (Mat. 12:46-50; Mk. 3:31-35; Lk. 8:19-21; Jn. 2:12). The English *"brethren"* in these Passages is the Greek *"adelphos,"* meaning *"brother"*; technically, *"one of the same womb." "Cousins"* may have gone along, certainly, but people who knew them (as the writers of Holy Scripture knew Jesus and Mary) would not have referred to them as brothers. Jesus' Brothers, along with His Mother, were following Him on His way to Capernaum. The Bible is clear on the subject, and we can be as well.

5. *"His Brethren"* are mentioned as not believing on Him until after the Resurrection. John 7:3-10 records the account of their unbelief; note, in particular, *"for neither did His Brethren believe in Him"* (Vs. 5).

6. Acts 1:14 records their presence in the Upper Room, along with Jesus' Disciples, awaiting the advent of the Holy Spirit — *"These all continued with one accord in prayer and supplication, with the women, and Mary the Mother of Jesus, and with His Brethren."*

7. James, the leader of the Early Church, is called *"the Lord's Brother"* (Gal. 1:19).

PAGAN CORRUPTION

This question would never have been raised except that the Catholic Church became steeped in pagan corruption and began to take portions of Scripture and use them to suit their own peculiar *"revelations."* This particular Passage, *"Is not this the carpenter's son? is not His Mother called Mary? and His Brethren, James, and Joses, and Simon, and Judas? And His Sisters, are they not all with us?,"* came into dispute when they sought to raise Mary from just a *"handmaid of the Lord"* (Lk. 1:38) to the Mother of God — thus, investing her with Divine power as

a goddess. By raising Mary to this status (which, incidentally, is not Scriptural) the way was cleared to identify her with other goddesses of paganism. These goddesses were supposedly mothers of divine sons and yet virgins. Such a goddess is known in Egypt as Isis, the mother of Horus; in India as Isi; in Asia as Cybele; in Rome as Fortuna; in Greece as Ceres; in China as Shing Moo; and, in other lands by different names, but always with a son in arms.

APOSTASY

So it is said that Mary had no other children and that Jesus' brethren were cousins by another Mary and her husband, Cleophas (Jn. 19:25). It is also said that Joseph was too old to have children by Mary, or that he had children by a former marriage. None of this is true, naturally, if it were, Scripture or history (or both) would bear it out.

If Joseph did have children before Jesus was born, then Jesus could not be the legal heir to David's throne, which by law went to the firstborn.

So, in summing it up, let me say it again; yes, Jesus was Mary's firstborn, but not her only-born. Joseph was the foster father of Jesus. Our Lord did have half-brothers and half-sisters, as is plainly stated in the Scriptures, the written Word of God.

CHAPTER SIX

What Type Of Temptations Did Jesus Suffer?

QUESTION:

WHAT TYPE OF TEMPTATIONS DID JESUS SUFFER?

ANSWER:

***"For we have not an High Priest Who cannot be touched with the feeling of our infirmities; but was in all points tempted like as we are, yet without sin"* (Heb. 4:15).**

Concerning and considering this Verse, many Believers ask the question, *"Was Jesus tempted to steal? tempted to commit adultery? tempted to lie?"*, etc.

No!

Most definitely, our Lord was tempted, and without a doubt to a far greater degree even than we are tempted, but it was not to do the things mentioned above.

JESUS WAS TEMPTED TO STEP OUTSIDE OF THE REVEALED WILL OF GOD

The account given in Matthew portrays the type of temptation which He suffered, and if we understand it as we should, it's the type of temptation that we suffer as well, of which we will address momentarily.

I'm going to quote from THE EXPOSITOR'S STUDY BIBLE the account of our Lord's temptations. I think it will shed some light on the subject.

> **"THEN** *(immediately after the descent of the Holy Spirit upon Him)* **was Jesus led up** *(urgently led)* **of the Spirit** *(Holy Spirit)* **into the wilderness** *(probably close to Jericho)* **to be tempted of the Devil** *(as the Last Adam, He would be tempted in all points like as we are [Heb. 4:15; I Cor. 15:21-22, 45, 47]).*
>
> **"And when He had fasted forty days and forty nights, He was afterward hungry** *(other than Christ,*

three men in the Bible fasted forty days and forty nights: Moses [Deut. 9:9, 18, 25; 10:10], Joshua [Ex. 24:13-18; 32:15-17], and Elijah [I Ki. 19:7-8]).

"And when the tempter *(Satan)* **came to Him, he said, If You be the Son of God** *(since You are the Son of God)*, **command that these stones be made bread** *(Christ was tempted to use His Power for His Own benefit, which He was to never do).*

"But He answered and said, It is written, Man shall not live by bread alone, but by every Word that proceeds out of the Mouth of God *([Deut. 8:3]; man is a Spiritual Being as well as a physical being; therefore, dependent on God).*

"Then the Devil took Him up *(a powerful force)* **into the Holy City** *(Jerusalem)*, **and set Him on a pinnacle of the Temple** *(its highest point, which Josephus stated, was about 700 feet from the ravine below)*,

"And said unto Him, If You be the Son of God *(since You are the Son of God)*, **cast Yourself down** *(literally spoken)*: **for it is written, He shall give His Angels charge concerning You: and in *their* hands they shall bear You up, lest at any time You dash Your foot against a stone** *(derived from Ps. 91:11-12).*

"Jesus said unto him, It is written again, you shall not tempt the Lord your God *([Deut. 6:16]; to tempt God is to question His Word, which casts doubt on His ability to do what He has promised).*

"Again *(the third temptation)*, **the Devil took Him up into an exceeding high mountain** *(not definitely known, but probably Nebo)*, **and showed Him all the kingdoms of the world, and the glory of them** *(showed them to Him, not in a physical sense, but rather in a spiritual sense)*;

"And said unto Him, All these things will I give You, if You will fall down and worship me *(the temptation was that Christ abrogate the Cross, through which He would regain all things).*

"Then said Jesus unto him, Get thee hence, Satan *(presents Christ for the first time Personally addressing Satan)*: **for it is written, you shall worship the Lord your God, and Him only shall you serve** *(Satan desires that mankind worship and serve him; we are to worship and serve the Lord Alone)*.

"Then the Devil left Him *('departed from Him for a season,' meaning that there would be other temptations [Lk. 4:13])*, **and, behold, Angels came and ministered unto Him** *(in what manner they ministered, we aren't told)*" **(Mat. 4:1-11).**

JESUS DID NOTHING BUT THE FATHER'S WILL

"Jesus said unto them, My meat is to do the Will of Him Who sent Me, and to finish His Work **(Jn. 4:34).**

"Then answered Jesus and said unto them, Verily, verily, I say unto you, The Son can do nothing of Himself, but what He sees the Father do: for what things soever He does, these also do the Son likewise" **(Jn. 5:19).**

As is obvious from these Texts, the mission of our Lord was to do exactly what the Father wanted Him to do, no more, no less! So this is where Satan's temptations centered on as it regards Christ. It was to endeavor to get Him to step outside of the revealed Will of God, and to use His Power for His Own benefit, or to do anything, which was not sanctioned by the Father. That was His temptation!

Actually, this was a type of the very First Temptation leveled at Eve in the Garden of Eden. Once again, allow me to quote from THE EXPOSITOR'S STUDY BIBLE.

THE FALL OF MAN

"And the LORD God planted a Garden eastward in Eden *(it was actually planted before Adam was created; the area is believed by some Scholars to be the site where the* *city of Babylon would ultimately be built)*; **and there He put the man whom He had formed** *(the Garden of Eden was to be the home place of man)*.

"And out of the ground made the LORD God to grow every tree that is pleasant to the sight *(beautiful trees)*, **and good for food** *(every fruit tree imaginable, even those which bear nuts)*; **the Tree of Life also in the midst of the Garden** *(evidently contained a type of fruit; 3:22 says as much! the Tree of Life had the power of so renewing man's physical energies that his body, though formed of the dust of the ground and, therefore, naturally mortal, would, by its continual use, live on forever; Christ is now to us the 'Tree of Life' [Rev. 2:7; 22:2]; and the 'Bread of Life' [Jn. 6:48, 51])*, **and the Tree of Knowledge of Good and Evil** *(presents the tree of death)*" **(Gen. 2:8-9).**

"And the LORD God took the man, and put him into the Garden of Eden to dress it and to keep it.

"And the LORD God commanded the man, saying, Of every tree of the Garden you may freely eat *(as stated, before the Fall, man was vegetarian)*:

"But of the Tree of the Knowledge of Good and Evil, you shall not eat of it *(as for the 'evil,' that was obvious; however, it is the 'good' on this tree that deceives much of the world; the 'good' speaks of religion; the definition of religion pertains to a system devised by men in order to bring about Salvation, to reach God, or to better oneself in some way; because it is devised by man, it is unacceptable to God; God's answer to the dilemma of the human race is 'Jesus Christ and Him Crucified' [I Cor. 1:23])*: **for in the day that you eat thereof you shall surely die** *(speaks of spiritual death, which is separation from God; let it be understood that the Tree of the Knowledge of Good and Evil was not the cause of Adam's Fall; it was a failure to heed and obey the Word of God, which is the cause of every single failure; spiritual death ultimately brought on physical death, and has, in fact, filled the world with death, all* *because of the Fall)*" **(Gen. 2:15-17).**

THE TEMPTATION

"Now the serpent was more subtle than any beast of the field which the LORD God had made *(the word 'subtle,' as used here, is not negative, but rather positive; everything that God made before the Fall was positive; it describes qualities such as quickness of sight, swiftness of motion, activity of self-preservation, and seemingly intelligent adaptation to its surroundings)*. **And he said unto the woman** *(not a fable; the serpent before the Fall had the ability of limited speech; Eve did not seem surprised when he spoke to her!)*, **Yes, has God said, You shall not eat of every tree of the Garden?** *(The serpent evidently lent its faculties to Satan, even though the Evil One is not mentioned. That being the case, Satan spoke through the serpent, and questioned the Word of God.)*

"And the woman said unto the serpent *(proclaims Satan leveling his attack against Eve, instead of Adam; his use of Eve was only a means to get to Adam)*, **We may eat of the fruit of the trees of the Garden** *(the trial of our First Parents was ordained by God, because probation was essential to their Spiritual Development and self-determination; but as He did not desire that they should be tempted to their Fall, He would not suffer Satan to tempt them in a way that would surpass their human capacity; the tempted might, therefore, have resisted the tempter)*:

"But of the fruit of the tree which is in the midst of the Garden, God has said, You shall not eat of it, neither shall you touch it, lest you die *(Eve quoted what the Lord had said about the prohibition, but then added, 'neither shall you touch it')*.

"And the serpent said unto the woman, You shall not surely die *(proclaims an outright denial of the Word of God; as God had preached to Adam, Satan now preaches* *to Eve; Jesus called Satan a liar, which probably refers to this very moment [Jn. 8:44])*:

"For God does know that in the day you eat thereof, then your eyes shall be opened *(suggests the attainment of higher wisdom)*, **and you shall be as gods, knowing good and evil.** *(In effect, says, 'You shall be Elohim.' It was a promise of Divinity. God is Omniscient, meaning that His Knowledge of evil is thorough, but not by personal experience. By His very Nature, He is totally separate from all that is evil. The knowledge of evil that Adam and Eve would learn would be by moral degradation, which would bring wreckage. While it was proper to desire to be like God, it is proper only if done in the right way, and that is through Faith in Christ and what He has done for us at the Cross.)*

"And when the woman saw that the tree was good for food *(presents the lust of the eyes)*, **and that it was pleasant to the eyes** *(the lust of the flesh)*, **and a tree to be desired to make one wise** *(the pride of life)*, **she took of the fruit thereof, and did eat** *(constitutes the Fall)*, **and gave also unto her husband with her; and he did eat** *(refers to the fact that evidently Adam was an observer to all these proceedings; some claim that he ate of the forbidden fruit which she offered him out of love for her; however, no one ever sins out of love; Eve submitted to the temptation out of deception, but 'Adam was not deceived' [I Tim. 2:14]; he fell because of unbelief; he simply didn't believe what God had said about the situation; contrast Verse 6 with Lk. 4:1-13; both present the three temptations, 'the lust of the flesh,' 'the lust of the eyes,' and 'the pride of life'; the first man falls, the Second Man conquers)*.

"And the eyes of them both were opened *(refers to the consciousness of guilt as a result of their sin)*, **and they knew that they were naked** *(refers to the fact that they had lost the enswathing light of purity, which previously had clothed their bodies)*; **and they sewed fig leaves together,**

and made themselves aprons *(sinners clothe themselves with morality, sacraments, and religious ceremonies; they are as worthless as Adam's apron of fig leaves)*" **(Gen. 3:1-7).**

As it regards Eve, it was not the fruit that was the temptation, but rather to step outside of the revealed Will of God. In effect, even though Adam was not tempted, still, he did the same identical thing, which was to disobey the Word of the Lord, i.e., ***"to step outside of the revealed Will of God."*** **In fact, every single temptation that man has experienced began with this temptation, which is to ignore the Word of God, or to register unbelief as it regards the Word of God.**

TEMPTATIONS WHICH CHRISTIANS FACE

The temptation by Satan as it regards every Child of God falls into the same category. The first temptation, and one can say always, is to step outside of God's Word. In other words, to contradict the Word, to violate the Word, or to ignore the Word.

We may think that the temptation is to lie, to commit adultery, to steal, to cheat, or whatever it might be in that capacity, but it all begins with a temptation to step outside of the revealed Will of God. While Satan may use other things, his primary purpose is to get me and you to disobey the Word.

When the Believer mentions that he was tempted to do something wrong in the realm of stealing, adultery, or cheating, etc., the truth is, first of all, he is tempted to disobey the Word of God. That's where the real temptation is. Whatever it is that Satan uses is for but one purpose, and that is that the Believer will step outside of the revealed Word of God, which guarantees destruction. Let us say it again.

No!

The temptation of Christ was to disobey the Word, i.e., ***"disobey His Father."*** **Never once considering such a thing, even though He was sorely tempted, the means by which Satan would do this, held no attraction.**

THE INGREDIENTS OF THE TEMPTATION

After Jesus had fasted forty days and forty nights, the Scripture says, *"He was afterward hungry."* So, at that time, Satan tries to get Him to use His Power to make the stones into bread. The ingredients were all there:

- **He was very much hungry;**
- **He had the power; and,**
- **The stones were available.**

The reasoning would have been, why not? What harm would it do? He was hungry, so this was a means of providing for Himself.

However, His Father had not told Him to do such a thing. So to use His Power solely for His Own benefit would have been sin. It would have been sin because He would have stepped outside of the revealed Will of God.

Christians are fond of asking, *"Is it sin?"* and whatever it might be!

However, that really is the wrong question. The correct question is, *"Does it bring Glory to God?"*

Under Law it was, *"Is it sin?"* Under Grace, *"Does it bring Glory to God?"*

DID JESUS EVER GET SICK?

No, in His earthly sojourn of some thirty-three and a half years, He never got sick in any capacity. That means that He never had a cold, never had a headache, never had a backache, etc.

Sickness stems from sin, and we speak of original sin, the Fall of Adam and Eve. Jesus was not a product of man per se, therefore, not a product of the Fall, being Virgin Born; consequently, He not only never got sick, the truth is, had He not purposely laid down His Life, which, in effect, He came to do, He would never have died. He said:

"Therefore does My Father love Me, because I lay down My Life, that I might take it again.

***"No man takes it from Me, but I lay it down of Myself. I have power to lay it down, and I have power to take it again. This Commandment have I received of My Father"* (Jn. 10:17-18).**

I think it could be said and without reservation, that Jesus was as is sometimes commonly used, *"a man's man."* As a boy He was trained as a carpenter, and functioned as such until He began His Ministry. Josephus, the great Jewish historian, says that Jesus primarily made plow yokes. This was heavy, hard, even back-bending work. No doubt, the citizens of Nazareth, for that was His boyhood home, observed Him repeatedly bringing sizeable tree trunks loaded on His Shoulder. As a boy, some might ask, did He ever get splinters in His Hands, or scrape His Knuckles, etc.

Of course, we have no way of knowing, but I'm sure He did.

Again, as it regards sickness, even though He was never sick in His Life and Living, there is evidence that He became sick on the Cross. The Scripture says:

***"He is despised and rejected of men; a man of sorrows, and acquainted with grief* (Isa. 53:3).**

***"Acquainted with grief,"* actually refers to diseases and sicknesses, for that's what the word *"grief"* in the Hebrew actually means.**

The statement refers to Christ healing the sick, which He did constantly and, in fact, all manner of diseases. As well, there is some evidence in the Text, that in some way He, as stated, became sick on the Cross. The Scripture says, even as the word *"griefs"* is used again, *"Surely He has borne our griefs, and carried our sorrows: yet we did esteem Him stricken, smitten of God, and afflicted"* (Isa. 53:4).

VICARIOUS

Concerning this Verse, twelve times within the space of nine Verses in this Fifty-third Chapter of Isaiah the Prophet asserts, with a most emphatic reiteration, that all the Servant's Sufferings were vicarious; i.e., *"borne for man to save him from the*

consequences of his sins, to enable him to escape punishment." **In other words, Jesus did this all for us.**

"Yet we did esteem Him stricken, smitten of God, and afflicted," **proclaims the fact that because He died on a Cross, Israel assumed that He died under the curse of God, because Moses had said, *"For he who is hanged is accursed of God"* (Deut. 21:23).**

What they did not understand was that He was not a curse; neither in Himself was cursed, but, in fact, was *"made a curse for us."*

Israel assumed He was *"smitten of God,"* and, in a sense, He was. He suffered in our stead, actually as our Substitute, which means that the blow that should have come to us, instead, went to Him. But yet, it was not for His sins, because He had none, but instead was for our sins. He was *"afflicted"* for us. As stated, He was our Substitute.

CHAPTER SEVEN

Did Our Lord Die Spiritually On The Cross As Well As Physically?

QUESTION:

DID OUR LORD DIE SPIRITUALLY ON THE CROSS AS WELL AS PHYSICALLY?

ANSWER:

No!

The essence of this question is, *"Did Jesus become a sinner on the Cross and thereby experience spiritual death, as some teach?"*

Or was He rather a Sin Offering?

We teach and believe that Jesus was a Sin Offering. We also teach that He was Holy and Pure, just as the Old Testament Offerings foreshadowed. Isaiah said:

***"Yet it pleased the LORD to bruise Him; He has put Him to grief: when You shall make His Soul an Offering for sin, He shall see His Seed, He shall prolong His Days, and the pleasure of the LORD shall prosper in His Hand"* (Isa. 53:10).**

NOTES FROM THE EXPOSITOR'S STUDY BIBLE ON VERSE TEN

***"'Yet it pleased the LORD to bruise Him,'* refers to the sufferings of Christ, which proceeded from the *'determinate counsel and foreknowledge of God'* (Acts 2:23), and which, being permitted by Him, were in some way His doing. It *'pleased Him'* moreover that they should be undergone, for the Father saw with satisfaction the Son's self-sacrifice, and He witnessed with joy man's Redemption and Deliverance affected thereby.**

***"'He has put Him to grief,'* actually says *'He has put Him to sicknesses'* or *'He has made Him sick.'* This spoke of the time He was on the Cross bearing our sins and *'sicknesses'* (Mat. 8:16-17; I Pet. 2:24). And yet, while all sin and sickness were atoned at the Cross, the total effects of such will not be completely dissipated until the coming Resurrection (Rom. 8:23).**

***"'When You shall make His Soul an Offering for sin,'* is**

powerful indeed! The word *'Offering'* in the Hebrew is *'Asham,'* and means *'a Trespass Offering,'* an *'Offering for sin.'*

"Offerings for sin, or *'guilt offerings,'* were distinct from *'Sin Offerings.'* The object of the former was *'satisfaction'*; of the latter, *'expiation.'* The Servant of Jehovah was, however, to be both. He was both the *'Sin Offering'* and the *'Guilt Offering.'*

"This completely destroys the idea that Jesus died spiritually on the Cross, meaning that He became a sinner on the Cross, and died and went to Hell as all sinners, and was born again in Hell after three days and nights of suffering, etc. None of that is in the Word of God. While Jesus definitely was a *'Sin Offering,'* He was not a sinner, and did not become a sinner on the Cross. To have done so would have destroyed His Perfection of Sacrifice, which was demanded by God. In other words, the Sacrifice had to be perfect, and He was Perfect in every respect.

"*'He shall see His Seed,'* refers to all His *'true followers,'* which include all who have ever been Born-Again.

"*'He shall prolong His Days,'* refers to His Resurrection.

"*'And the pleasure of the LORD shall prosper in His Hand,'* refers to the great victory that He would win at Calvary, which would ultimately restore everything that Adam lost."

IT IS FINISHED

Jesus did not go to the burning side of Hell for three days to redeem mankind from the terrible ravages of sin. Rather, He preached to the spirits which were in prison in Hell and, as well, He went to Paradise to deliver every person who had gone there for the past 4,000 years.

The Scripture says:

> **"By which also He went** *(between the time of His Death and Resurrection)* **and preached** *(announced something)* ***unto the spirits in prison*** *(does not refer to humans, but rather to fallen Angels; humans in the Bible are never referred to in this particular manner; these were probably*

the fallen Angels who tried to corrupt the human race by cohabiting with women [II Pet. 2:4; Jude, Vss. 6-7]; these fallen Angels are still locked up in this underworld prison)" **(I Pet. 3:19).**

And then Jesus went into Paradise. The Scripture says:

> **"Wherefore He said** *(Ps. 68:18)*, **When He ascended up on high** *(the Ascension)*, **He led captivity captive** *(liberated the souls in Paradise; before the Cross, despite being Believers, they were still held captive by Satan because the blood of bulls and goats could not take away the sin debt; but when Jesus died on the Cross, the sin debt was paid, and now He makes all of these His Captives)*, **and gave Gifts unto men.** *(These 'Gifts' include all the Attributes of Christ, all made possible by the Cross.)*
>
> **"(Now that He ascended** *(mission completed)*, **what is it but that He also descended first into the lower parts of the earth?** *(Immediately before His Ascension to Glory, which would be done in total triumph, He first went down into Paradise to deliver all the believing souls in that region, which He did!)*
>
> **"He Who descended is the same also Who ascended** *(this is a portrayal of Jesus as Deliverer and Mediator)* **up far above all Heavens** *(presents His present location, never again having to descend into the nether world)*, **that He might fill all things.)** *(He has always been the Creator, but now He is also the Saviour.)"* **(Eph. 4:8-10).**

THE LAST WORDS

Even though the Bible does not tell us exactly which words were the last spoken by Christ on the Cross before He died; however, it is believed that it was in this order: ***"It is Finished, Father, into Your Hands I commend My Spirit"*** **(Lk. 23:46; Jn. 19:30).**

What was finished?

The Work Christ came to do. As of that moment, man's Salvation was complete. Nothing else was needed. Nothing else could be done that could add to His Finished Work at Calvary. It must be remembered, that while the Resurrection was of extreme significance, as should be obvious, still, the Resurrection, the Ascension, and the Exaltation of Christ were a result of the Cross. In fact, had one sin been left unatoned, due to the fact that the wages of sin is death, Christ could not have risen from the dead (Rom. 6:23). The fact of His Resurrection portrays the glaring truth that all was completed at Calvary. Actually, nothing else could be done that could add to His Finished Work. So these three words, *"It is finished,"* stand as a permanent rebuke to the doctrine that Jesus had to go to Hell and die spiritually to redeem man.

DIED AS A LOST SINNER ON THE CROSS?

This false doctrine of Jesus dying spiritually, also teaches that the sinless Son of God became unregenerate and died as a lost sinner at Calvary and that He had to be born again and justified from sin. The pitiful thing about this whole line of thinking is that He, they claim, was somehow born again in, of all places, Hell!

Now if perchance this were true, it would have been necessary for someone to die for the Lord Jesus Christ to redeem Him from His unregenerate state and provide for His Justification. Of course, we know this is all utter foolishness, because Jesus did not become unregenerate, and He did not die a lost sinner.

THE BLOOD?

Some time ago one of the leading proponents of this heresy, and heresy it is, stated, *"When His Blood was poured out, it did not atone. It simply did away with the handwriting of the Ordinances that were against us."*

He went on to say that Jesus redeemed man, not on the Cross but in Hell. Hopefully, the proponents of this doctrine do not realize what they are doing, for they are actually denying the Blood Atonement of Jesus Christ, and that is a very serious thing! It seems they do not understand that they have negated the power of Jesus' Blood to cleanse from sin, by their teaching that Jesus became an unholy sacrifice on the Cross. This is heresy, and it is dangerous.

HERESY

This heresy appears to teach that Jesus identified with the sinner on the Cross, while it ignores the fact that Jesus became a substitute for sinners — confusing the identification of Jesus with the human race at His Birth with His Substitution for sinners on the Cross.

If Jesus had become literal sin and had become lost and unregenerate while He hung on the Cross of Calvary, then He would have been an unacceptable sacrificial offering to God for the sins of others. Whereas if He indeed remained Pure and Holy as the Scriptures assert, then God could accept Him as a Substitute on behalf of sinners. It was only in this way that He could fulfill the Old Testament Type where the animal for the Sin Offering had to be spotless and *"without blemish"* (Lev. 4:2-3). If you remember, the Sin Offering was regarded as most holy even after its death.

Concerning our Lord, Peter also said:

> **"For even hereunto were you called** *(called to act Christlike, irrespective)***: because Christ also suffered for us** *(Peter reminds these slaves that Christ also suffered unjustly, for He the Just One died on behalf of unjust ones)***, leaving us an example, that we should follow His Steps** *(we are to reproduce Christ in our lives, which we can only do by the Help, Guidance, Leading, and Power of the Holy Spirit [Jn. 16:7-16])***:**

"Who did no sin *(Christ was the only sinless human being Who ever lived)*, **neither was guile found in His Mouth** *(He never sinned by speaking hypocritically or falsely, not even one time)*:

"Who, when He was reviled, reviled not again *(He did not respond in kind)*; **when He suffered, He threatened not** *(when He suffered unjustly, He did not call down wrath from Heaven, which He definitely could have done)*; **but committed *Himself* to Him Who Judges Righteously** *(He committed His defense to God, which we as well should do)*:

"Who His Own Self bear our sins in His Own Body on the tree *(gave Himself in Sacrifice on the Cross, taking the full penalty for our sins, which was physical death; it was not Christ's suffering that redeemed us, although that definitely was a part of what happened, but rather the price He paid by the giving of Himself)*, **that we, being dead to sins, should live unto Righteousness** *(we are 'dead to sins' by virtue of us being 'in Christ' when He died on the Cross, which is done by our exhibiting Faith in Christ [Rom. 6:3-5]; and we were raised with Him in 'newness of life,' which guarantees us a perfect, spotless Righteousness)*: **by Whose stripes you were healed.** *(This refers to the healing of our souls, and the healing of our physical body as well. The Atonement included everything man lost in the Fall, but we only have the Firstfruits now, with the balance coming at the Resurrection [Rom. 8:23].)*" **(I Pet. 2:21-24).**

THE JUST!

Peter also said:

"For Christ also has once suffered for sins *(the suffering of Christ on the Cross was but for one purpose, and that was 'for sins'; while we as Believers might suffer for sins as well, such is never in the realm of Atonement; the price has been fully paid, which means there is nothing left owing)*,

the just for the unjust *(Christ was the Perfect Sacrifice, the One Who was born without original sin, and Who lived a Perfect Life, never failing even in one point; He Alone was the 'Just')*, **that He might bring us to God** *(refers to the way being opened for sinful man to come into the very Presence of God)*, **being put to death in the flesh** *(refers to the fact that Jesus died physically in order to serve as a Sacrifice, which means He didn't die spiritually, as some claim!)*, **but quickened by the Spirit** *(raised from the dead by the Holy Spirit [Rom. 8:11])*" **(I Pet. 3:18).**

The Scripture in this Passage plainly says that Jesus, while suffering for our sins was *"just."* So if He was just, while He was on the Cross suffering for our sins, how could He at the same time be unjust? The unjust as given here in this Passage, could not redeem the unjust. Such thinking is ludicrous to say the least! But, if Jesus became a sinner on the Cross as the Word of Faith people claim, how could He at the same time be *"just"*?

WHAT DIFFERENCE DOES IT MAKE?

Someone may ask the question, *"What difference does all of this make?"* The answer is, *"It makes all the difference in the world,"* because according to the Word of God our eternal Salvation rests upon what we personally believe concerning the Blood Atonement of Jesus Christ. It is here, at the Cross that a person's Salvation either stands or falls. The doctrine of Jesus dying spiritually on the Cross and going to Hell, and Him having to be *"born again"* as a sinner, is heresy of the most serious kind — its seriousness stemming from the fact that if a person believes this perverted doctrine, he will find that in the end he has been robbed of the truth of the Blood Atonement.

The Bible is emphatic on this matter: one sinner cannot redeem another sinner. Only one who is guiltless could ever act as a substitute and suffer the punishment for the guilty party, thereby saving the guilty party. Even Jesus, although the Son of

God could not have done this if He had become guilty Himself, as this particular doctrine contends. The central thrust of the entire Old Testament Sacrificial System is that Jesus was the guiltless Substitute, Who, like the Old Testament Type, remained Pure and Holy both on the Cross and after His Death.

There is nothing more important than the Atonement. If we are wrong about that, then we are wrong about our Salvation.

Using the physical body as an example, if we have a hangnail, that's one thing; however, if we have a problem with our heart that's something else altogether. The hangnail won't kill you, the heart will! The Atonement is the heart of the Gospel, so to speak, and millions are in Hell today, and millions are on their way to Hell, to put it bluntly, simply because they believed a false way of Salvation. Nothing is worse than that!

THE JESUS DIED SPIRITUALLY DOCTRINE

According to the proponents of this heresy, and heresy it is, Jesus became sin on the Cross when He yielded Himself to Satan. He swallowed up the evil nature of Satan, thus becoming one in nature with the adversary, taking upon Himself the diabolical nature of Satan. At that time He became a lost man, they say, crying, *"My God, My God, why have You forsaken Me?"* (Mat. 27:46; Ps. 22:1). These teachers, therefore, conclude that Jesus at that time died spiritually, i.e., became a lost sinner.

He was then taken to the pit of Hell, they say, and we speak of the burning side of Hell, where He was chained with the fetters of sin, wickedness, disease, and all other evils of Satan. The Devil stood before the darkness, crying, *"We have conquered the Son of God."* There followed, they continue, a gala celebration down in the Pit. Satan believed he had finally triumphed over God.

Jesus consequently suffered agonies beyond description in the Pit for three days as all the hosts of Hell were upon Him. But then suddenly, they say, Jesus was justified. From His Throne in Heaven, Almighty God arose and put His Hands to His Mouth and screamed, *"It is Finished; it is enough."* Jesus was now, they say, *"born again"* and made spiritually alive once more.

Hell itself then was shaken, they say. Jesus shook off His Chains of sin, sickness, and evil. He walked over to the Devil, grabbed him, and threw him to the ground. As the Devil cowered and trembled on the floor of the Pit, Jesus put His Foot on top of him and took the keys of death, Hell, and the grave from Satan.

At this time, according to these teachers, the Holy Spirit kicked open the gates of Hell and raised Jesus from death. He then ascended to the Father and announced, *"I have paid the price. The prison is now opened."* He was now a born again man who had defeated Satan. Jesus was the firstborn from the spiritually dead. Thus, it was at the time Jesus was made alive down in the Pit that the Believer was also made alive. The Church, they continue, had its origin in the pit of Hell when Jesus was begotten from the dead as the *"firstborn among many brethren"* (Rom. 8:29).

At first glance, this doctrine appears to be a glorious cause for rejoicing; however, if you think about it for a moment, you quickly realize that you have never read anything of this nature on the pages of your Bible. Why? Because it's not in the Bible! It is fictitious from beginning to end.

THE TRUTH

The truth is, *"He blotted out the handwriting of Ordinances that was against us, which was contrary to us, and took it out of the way, nailing it to His Cross; and having spoiled principalities and powers, He made a show of them openly, triumphing over them in it"* (Col. 2:14-15). The words, *"Nailing it to His Cross . . . triumphing over them in it"* means that Jesus' great victory was won on the Cross, and on the Cross exclusively.

THE OLD TESTAMENT SACRIFICES

The Old Testament animal sacrifice (a Type of Jesus), which was to die as a substitute for the sinner, had to be without spot or blemish. The Scripture says:

"If the Priest that is anointed do sin according to the sin of the people; then let him bring for his sin, which he has sinned, a young bullock without blemish unto the LORD for a Sin Offering. *(In the 'Burnt Offering,' the sinlessness of the victim was transferred to the worshipper. In the 'Sin Offering,' the sinfulness of the sinner was transferred to the victim.)***"** **(Lev. 4:3).**

And then:

"And if any one of the common people sin through ignorance, while he does somewhat against any of the Commandments of the LORD concerning things which ought not to be done, and be guilty;

"Or if his sin, which he has sinned, come to his knowledge: then he shall bring his Offering, a kid of the goats, a female without blemish, for his sin which he has sinned. *(As is obvious here, in the Eyes of God, sin is sin, irrespective as to who commits it. It must be addressed and, in essence, addressed the same way, even if it's a 'common person,' or a 'ruler,' or a 'Priest,' or even the entirety of the Nation of Israel. The only answer is the Cross.)*

"And he shall lay his hand upon the head of the Sin Offering, and slay the Sin Offering in the place of the Burnt Offering *(Jesus became a Sin Offering on the Cross [Isa. 53:10])***.**

"And the Priest shall take of the blood thereof with his finger and put it upon the horns of the Altar of Burnt Offering, and shall pour out all the blood thereof at the bottom of the Altar. *(If it is to be noticed, the solution for all, with some minor variations, is the same. So, why the constant repetition? It is that we might know the seriousness of the matter, as it regards the horror of sin, and its only solution, which is the shed Blood of Jesus Christ [Eph. 2:13-18])***"** **(Lev. 4:27-30).**

And then:

***"And if there be any blemish therein, as if it be lame, or blind, or have any ill blemish, you shall not sacrifice it unto the LORD your God"* (Deut. 15:21).**

All of this was to teach Israel (and the Church) that a substitute acceptable to God had to be Holy and guiltless in order to bear the punishment for the guilt of the sinner.

This ritual, carried out again and again in the Old Testament, was fully and finally realized in Jesus Christ as the Lamb of God, Who *"offered Himself without spot to God."*

I quote from THE EXPOSITOR'S STUDY BIBLE:

"How much more shall the Blood of Christ *(while the Sacrifice of animals could cleanse from ceremonial defilement, only the Blood of Christ could cleanse from actual sin; so that throws out every proposed solution other than the Cross)*, **Who through the Eternal Spirit offered Himself without spot to God** *(in this phrase, we learn Christ did not die until the Holy Spirit told Him to die; in fact, no man took His Life from Him; He laid it down freely [Jn. 10:17-18]; as well, the fact that Jesus 'offered Himself without spot to God' shoots down the unscriptural doctrine that 'Jesus died Spiritually' on the Cross; had He died Spiritually, meaning He became a sinner on the Cross, He could not have offered Himself without spot to God, as should be obvious; God could only accept a perfect Sacrifice; when He died on the Cross, He took upon Himself the sin penalty of the human race, which was physical death; inasmuch as His Offering of Himself was Perfect, God accepted it as payment in full for all sin — past, present, and future, at least for those who will believe [Jn. 3:16])*, **purge your conscience from dead works to serve the Living God?** *('Dead works' are anything other than simple Faith in the Cross of Christ, i.e., 'the Blood of Christ')***" (Heb. 9:14).**

When these false teachers claim that Jesus literally became sin with the inherent need to become *"born again,"* they expose the basic flaw in their doctrine, which stems from apparent ignorance of the nature of the Old Testament Sacrifices, especially the Sin Offering. They conveniently forget (if indeed they ever really knew) that the Old Testament clearly teaches that at no point does the Sin Offering become an unholy sacrifice, either before or after its death.

THE HEBREW MEANING OF SIN

The Apostle Paul said: *"For He has made Him to be sin for us, Who knew no sin"* (II Cor. 5:21).

In the Hebrew language the term *"chetta't"* is the same word used for *"sin"* and *"Sin Offering."* A single Hebrew term translates both words. *"Sin"* and *"Sin Offering,"* then, are one and the same. It was the context in which the term was used that expressed whether a person was speaking of *"Sin Offering"* or *"sin."*

For example, if it was a matter concerning sacrifices, *"chetta't"* was understood to mean a *"Sin Offering."* If the matter was one of offense, the same word would be used, but the people involved would understand the meaning by the usage, and the context in which it was used.

No Jewish Christian would ever confuse *"sin"* with the *"Sin Offering,"* even though the two thoughts are both expressed by the same Hebrew term. It is the same with the terms *"trespass"* and *"Trespass Offering."* The same Hebrew word is used, *"asham,"* meaning that Jesus' death on the Cross is to be regarded as a Trespass Offering for sinners and not that He Himself became a *"trespass"* or *"sin."*

THE SERPENT ON THE POLE

The idea of Christ becoming sin hinges on an interpretation of Numbers, Chapter 21 (which presents the account of the lifting up of the brazen serpent in the wilderness for the healing

of those bitten) that Jesus was also lifted up as a serpent when He was made sin on the Cross, and at that time took on the evil nature of Satan. The teachers espousing this doctrine quote, *"And as Moses lifted up the serpent in the wilderness, even so must the Son of Man be lifted up"* (Jn. 3:14). From this they conclude that Jesus became one with the serpent, Satan, and died spiritually.

However, the account in Numbers, Chapter 21 does not support this fantasy. God did send fiery serpents as punishment against the rebellious Israelites. As a result of the intercession of Moses, God directed him to make a figure of a serpent in copper, to be elevated on a pole so that it could be seen from all quarters of the camp. All who looked in Faith in its direction were healed. Naturally, we understand that the copper serpent did not produce healing; it was merely an emblem of their sin and signified the nature of Divine Judgment. The idea is, Satan is the cause of sin, sickness, and death, and the Cross of Christ would defeat him, by atoning for all sin, past, present, and future, at least for all who would believe (Jn. 3:16), which would remove the legal right that Satan had to hold mankind in bondage. But, let it never be forgotten, it was the Cross of Christ that effected this great victory, and as far as man is concerned, Satan could not be defeated any other way. It took the Cross, which proclaims Christ offering up Himself as a Perfect Sacrifice for sin, and it was for sin, which He Alone could do. In essence, our Lord paid the ransom to God, for it was to God that man owed this monstrous debt, for which we could not pay. So, when Jesus died on the Cross, He paid the debt, and in doing so, He at the same time atoned for all sin, which was the occasion of Satan's defeat. Paul said:

THE DEFEAT OF SATAN

"Buried with Him in Baptism *(does not refer to Water Baptism, but rather to the Believer baptized into the Death of Christ, which refers to the Crucifixion and Christ as our Substitute [Rom. 6:3-4])*, **wherein also you are risen with**

Him **through the Faith of the Operation of God, Who has raised Him from the dead.** *(This does not refer to our future physical Resurrection, but to that Spiritual Resurrection from a sinful state into Divine Life. We died with Him, we are buried with Him, and we rose with Him [Rom. 6:3-5], and herein lies the secret to all Spiritual Victory.)*

"And you, being dead in your sins and the uncircumcision of your flesh *(speaks of spiritual death [i.e., 'separation from God'], which sin does!)***, has He quickened together with Him** *(refers to being made Spiritually Alive, which is done through being 'Born-Again')***, having forgiven you all trespasses** *(the Cross made it possible for all manner of sins to be forgiven and taken away)***;**

"Blotting out the handwriting of Ordinances that was against us *(pertains to the Law of Moses, which was God's Standard of Righteousness that man could not reach)***, which was contrary to us** *(Law is against us, simply because we are unable to keep its precepts, no matter how hard we try)***, and took it out of the way** *(refers to the penalty of the Law being removed)***, nailing it to His Cross** *(the Law with its decrees was abolished in Christ's Death, as if Crucified with Him)***;**

"*And* having spoiled principalities and powers *(Satan and all of his henchmen were defeated at the Cross by Christ Atoning for all sin; sin was the legal right Satan had to hold man in captivity; with all sin atoned, he has no more legal right to hold anyone in bondage)***, He** *(Christ)* **made a show of them openly** *(what Jesus did at the Cross was in the face of the whole universe)***, triumphing over them in it.** *(The triumph is complete and it was all done for us, meaning we can walk in power and perpetual victory due to the Cross)***" (Col. 2:12-15).**

THE WORDS OF OUR LORD

Jesus alluded to this when He said to Nicodemus:

> **"And as Moses lifted up the serpent in the wilderness** *(refers to Num. 21:5-9; the 'serpent' represents Satan who is the originator of sin)***, even so must the Son of Man be lifted up** *(refers to Christ being lifted up on the Cross, which alone could defeat Satan and sin)***:**
>
> **"That whosoever** *(destroys the erroneous hyper-Calvinistic explanation of predestination that some are predestined to be Saved, while all others are predestined to be lost; the word 'whosoever' means that none are excluded from being lost, and none are excluded from being Saved)* ***believes* in Him** *(believes in Christ and what He did at the Cross; otherwise, one would perish)* **should not perish, but have Eternal Life** *(the Life of God, the Ever-Living One, Who has life in Himself, and Alone has immortality)***" (Jn. 3:14-15).**

It is obvious from the statement of Christ, that He is not referring to Himself becoming a sinner on the Cross, but rather the very opposite. He is exhorting, even demanding that people believe in Him, which refers to belief in what He did to redeem humanity by giving Himself as a Perfect Sacrifice on the Cross, Who was accepted by God as payment in full, and Who totally and completely defeated Satan, symbolized by the copper serpent on the pole.

As the dying Israelites at the time of Moses were told to look at that copper serpent and they would be healed, all of this symbolized Satan's total and complete defeat, which was by and through Jesus offering Himself, as stated, as a Perfect Sacrifice on the Cross. The serpent symbolized Satan who would be defeated, and defeated by what Christ did at the Cross.

That's the whole purpose of this great symbol in the wilderness. It was to portray the fact that it would take the Cross, and it would be by the Cross that Satan would have the stranglehold he held over humanity broken.

Approximately 400 years earlier the Lord had shown Abraham the manner of Salvation; it would be through the death of

an innocent victim, namely the Son of God (Jn. 8:36). It was to Moses, however, that the Lord proclaimed the way that the Son of God would die; it would be by the Cross, symbolized by the serpent on the pole. That Sacrifice would totally and completely defeat Satan (Num. 21:8-9).

To look upon an inanimate object (in this case, a serpent of copper) in itself could never produce healing, but Faith in Christ and what He would do there, and which Jesus stressed in His statement to Nicodemus, most definitely could bring about Spiritual Healing for the soul and, in fact, is the only thing that can.

By analogy, if Jesus became a serpent in nature, as this erroneous teaching contends, then healing was provided by Satan, the serpent, not God. What was being spoken of here was the manner in which Jesus would die, not a change in His Nature. As that serpent was lifted up on a pole, Jesus would also be lifted up on a pole — the Cross, which would defeat the serpent.

We know that all men are the children of wrath (Rom. 3:9; 5:12; Eph. 2:3). But we also know that Jesus lived without committing any act of sin (Jn. 14:30; II Cor. 5:21; Heb. 4:15). The teachers of this erroneous doctrine say that Jesus did not personally sin, but that He was made a sinner by God, thereby taking upon Himself the sinfulness of the human race and became evil with Satan's nature.

THE SINNER

Of course, this is impossible. Sin is a personal act of disobedience to the Will of God, and Jesus never once disobeyed His Father, and certainly not while He hung on the Cross.

Sin is not something tangible like a coat of black paint that God could drape over His Son, nor is it some type of inoculation of germs that scientists could inject into the blood stream. Sin is an act (whether deed, word, or thought) that a person must personally commit. This fact alone rules out any possibility that Jesus could be made sin.

In the study of Biblical theology, the Scriptural doctrine of *"imputation"* shows that sin or righteousness can be imputed or charged to another's account in a legal sense. Applied to Jesus and His Sacrifice as a Sin Offering, this indicates that He did not become sin, at least as it regards a sinner, but remained sinless that He might be able to bear the punishment for our guilt that was imputed to Him. In other words, Jesus did not bear the wickedness and the filth of our sinful nature, but He did bear the terrible punishment that should have been poured out on us. On the Cross He became a *"Sin Offering."*

Our punishment was imputed to Him. Our sins, in regard to their moral character, are our own. They could not by imputation become someone else's. However, Jesus Christ could take upon Himself the punishment for the guilt of our sins, which has reference to the legal liabilities that Christ assumed on our behalf.

So the transfer of our sins to Jesus Christ was not a transfer of the actual transgressions themselves — that is not possible — but Christ made Himself liable to endure the penalty for our sins. On that Cross and in His Death, Christ was a Holy, spotless Sin Offering. To have been anything otherwise would have violated the Old Testament Type and would have disqualified Him as an acceptable Substitute to God.

JUSTIFIED!

Paul said about Christ:

> **"And without controversy great is the mystery of Godliness** *(refers to the Truth of the Cross previously hidden, but now fully revealed)***: God was manifest in the flesh** *(refers to the Incarnation of Christ)***, justified in the Spirit** *(vindicated, endorsed, proved, and pronounced by the Holy Spirit)***, seen of Angels** *(refers to the fact that Angels witnessed every capacity of His Birth, Life, Passion, Resurrection, and Ascension)***, Preached unto the Gentiles**

(would have been better translated, 'Preached unto the Nations'; His Atonement was for the entirety of mankind, which Message is to be proclaimed to the entirety of the world), **believed on in the world** *(accepted by many)*, **received up into Glory.** *(His Mission was accomplished, finished, and accepted in totality by God.)*" **(I Tim. 3:16).**

The teachers of the *"Jesus died spiritually doctrine"* conclude from the phrase, *"justified in the Spirit"* that Jesus Himself had to be justified, and had to be made sin, and possess an evil, satanic nature. Thus, they say, He had to be made righteous once more, justified, and born again. But, according to the Greek, even as we have already stated, *"to justify"* as it is used here is *"to declare righteous"* or *"to show to be righteous."* Jesus was *"evinced to be righteous as to His Spiritual Nature."*

The Bible, in this Passage, is not saying that Jesus was being made righteous, but that His Righteousness was being announced. Jesus never ceased to be righteous; He never ceased to be just. But as a Man, the Man Christ Jesus, the Holy Spirit, in essence, is saying that Christ is just as righteous now as He was before the Incarnation.

Therefore, without any Scriptural support whatsoever, these teachers declare, *"suddenly God justified Jesus in the Pit and He was born again."*

There is no Scriptural basis whatsoever for the doctrine that says that God arbitrarily waved His Hand over Christ and said, *"be Thou cleansed,"* and suddenly Jesus was justified (made righteous), born again, and restored to Sonship with the Father.

THE GODHEAD

Was Jesus abandoned by God at Calvary, as these teachers claim?

No!

Jesus was God's Own Sacrifice, chosen by Him (Isa., Chpt. 53;

Jn. 1:29; 3:16) and never out of Divine Favor for one moment. He was called *"an Offering and a Sacrifice to God for a sweetsmelling savor"* (Eph. 5:2). This is in perfect harmony with the Old Testament teaching that the Sin Offering was "*most holy*" to God (Lev., Chpt. 6).

First of all, it is impossible to separate the Godhead — Father, Son, and Holy Spirit. *"For in Him dwells all the fullness of the Godhead bodily"* (Col. 2:9). If Jesus had died spiritually, then at the Cross — by Him being lost — He would have divided the Godhead, or at least had made the entire Godhead sinful and in need of the new birth. The idea of dividing up the Godhead for three days by sending the Son of God to Hell as a lost sinner, totally abandoned by God the Father and God the Holy Spirit, is totally ridiculous. This spurious teaching even goes so far as to say that God was no longer the Father of Jesus while He was in Hell.

THE WORDS OF JESUS ON THE CROSS

When Jesus uttered the words on the Cross, *"My God, My God, why have You forsaken Me?"* Jesus was quoting from a Prophetic Passage, Psalms 22:1. He also said, *"I thirst"* (Jn. 19:28). An utterance based upon another Old Testament Prophecy, Psalms 69:21. When He uttered these words, *"My God, My God,"* the religious leaders and the people of His day misinterpreted them saying, *"This man calls for Elijah"* (Mat. 27:47).

With these words Jesus consciously identified Himself as the One of Whom the Old Testament Prophecy spoke. Someone has even supposed that Jesus recited all of Psalm 22 as well as other Prophecies concerning Him while He hung on the Cross for several hours. We do know, of course, that not everything Jesus did was recorded. Only a small portion was, in fact, recorded (Jn. 21:25).

Was Jesus forsaken by God?

No, He was not.

God had temporally *"turned a deaf ear,"* in that, instead

of delivering His Son from death, which He did do on several occasions, the Father delivered Him up unto death when He became a Sin Offering for others; but this was not abandonment. Jesus Himself said, *"Behold, the hour comes, yes, is now come, that you shall be scattered, every man to his own, and shall leave Me alone: and yet I am not alone, because the Father is with Me"* (Jn. 16:32). He could say this because *"God was in Christ, reconciling the world unto Himself"* (II Cor. 5:19).

PHYSICAL DEATH

The Bible states again and again that Jesus offered up His Body as a Sacrifice for our sins, that He was put to death in the flesh. In other words, Jesus died physically but not spiritually. Nowhere in the Word of God does it tell us that Jesus died in His Spirit. However, it does say . . .

- *"Christ . . . His Own Self bear our sins in His Own Body on the tree"* (I Pet. 2:21-24).
- *"Christ . . . was put to death in the flesh, but quickened by the Spirit"* (I Pet. 3:18).
- *"Christ has suffered for us in the flesh"* (I Pet. 4:1).
- *"He reconciled us in the Body of His Flesh through death"* (Col. 1:21-22).
- *"We are Sanctified through the Offering of the Body of Jesus Christ once for all"* (Heb. 10:10).
- *"He abolished in His Flesh the enmity, even the Law of Commandments"* (Eph. 2:15).

So, while Scriptures repeatedly stress that Jesus offered up His Body and His Flesh as a Sacrifice for sin, not once do they say He died in His Spirit.

God could not die spiritually. Why would the Son of God need a body of flesh? He took on flesh so that He could die physically on behalf of sinners as had the Old Testament Type.

The erroneous teaching, it seems, is that the shedding of Jesus' Blood was insignificant. The following are some of the ridiculous theories of this doctrine.

FALSE ASSERTIONS OF THIS UNSCRIPTURAL DOCTRINE

- When His Blood was poured out, it did not atone.
- Jesus bled only a few drops, and when people sing about the Blood of Jesus, they do not know what they are talking about.

To comment on this would be a waste of time. The efficacy of the Atonement did not depend on how much blood was shed on the Cross, or how much time was involved in the process of dying. The Atonement's validity depended on the fact that the Son of God shed His spotless Blood and died on our behalf. This false teaching claims that . . .

FALSE TEACHING

- Jesus was *"born again"* in the pit of Hell as the first man to be regenerated under the New Covenant. The proponents of this doctrine apparently are referring to the Verse that says, *"God . . . has raised up Jesus again; as it is also written in the Second Psalm, 'You are My Son, this day have I begotten You'"* (Acts 13:33).
- He was the first begotten from spiritual death, citing, *"Jesus Christ, Who is the faithful Witness, and the first begotten of the dead"* (Rev. 1:5).
- Jesus started the Church in Hell when He was *"born again"* in the Pit, citing, *"Jesus became the Firstborn among many brethren"* (Rom. 8:29).
- He was righteous while on Earth, but while on the Cross He became unrighteous, and went to Hell, and then in the Pit was made righteous once more. That seems strange when the Bible says that He is unchangeable (Mal. 3:6; Heb. 13:8).

The first thing we must make clear is that two different English terms were used by the King James translators to translate the same Greek word. *"Firstborn and Firstbegotten"* both translate *"prototokos." "Firstbegotten"* (Heb. 1:6; Rev. 1:5) is *"firstborn." "Begotten"* (Acts 13:33), a different Greek word

altogether, refers to the physical Resurrection of Jesus and completely rules out the fanciful notion that Jesus was born again in Hell.

In the preceding Verses (Acts 13:16-32) Paul spoke of Christ's physical Death and the burial of His Body in a sepulcher. Verses 30 through 33 speak of His physical Resurrection from the dead. The Resurrection of Jesus in the Bible always has reference to the Resurrection of His Body and not of His Spirit, since His Spirit did not die (Lk. 24:36-46; I Cor. 15:20-23).

The term *"firstborn"* in Scripture is used not only to refer to the physical birth of the first child in a family, but also to speak of position and inheritance rights. So, the term refers not merely to birth, but also to birthright as well as to position or status. The firstborn always held a special position in God's Sight, possessing special rights and privileges. In this same sense, Jesus Christ is called the *"firstborn"* (Rom. 8:29; Col. 1:15; Heb. 1:6).

In Romans 8:29, it refers to Jesus as being the Father of the Salvation Plan.

In Colossians 1:15, it refers to Jesus being the Creator of all things.

In Hebrews 1:6, it refers to Jesus being born of the Virgin Mary.

In Colossians 1:18, it refers to Jesus being the first to be raised from the dead as it regards the Resurrection, never to die again. In other words, Jesus is the Father of Creation, the Father of Salvation, and the Father of the Resurrection. That is what the word *"firstborn,"* means. In fact, the Greek Scholars tell us, that the word *"firstborn"* is as near in English that can be obtained from the Greek word *"prototokos,"* but doesn't quite give it the full meaning.

FROM THE CROSS TO THE RESURRECTION

After His Death on Calvary, Jesus did go down into Paradise, which, in effect, was a part of Hell, even as our Lord outlined it in Luke, Chapter 16, where the righteous souls — such as Abraham,

Isaac, Jacob, David, and other Old Testament Saints — were kept, and one might say, against their will. Actually, they were captives of Satan, even though he could not harm them, with our Lord saying that they were comforted (Lk. 16:25).

All of this means that when the Old Testament Saints died, they could not be taken to Heaven, but were rather taken down into Paradise, sometimes referred to as *"Abraham's bosom"* (Lk. 16:23). There was a reason that they could not be taken to Heaven at that time.

Jesus had not yet gone to the Cross, and Paul plainly stated, *"For it is not possible that the blood of bulls and goats should take away sins"* (Heb. 10:4). While these Old Testament Saints most definitely were Saved, their Salvation to be sure, was predicated totally and solely upon the Redemption that would be afforded upon Christ going to the Cross. In other words, everything hinged on the Cross. It was there that every sin was atoned, which included all the Old Testament Saints.

The animal blood being insufficient to remove the sin debt, this means that the terrible realization of such, was forever with the Old Testament Saints. Concerning this, Paul also said:

> **"The Holy Spirit this signifying** *(the Holy Spirit was both the Divine Author of the Levitical system of worship, and its Interpreter)*, **that the way into the Holiest of all was not yet made manifest** *(proclaims the fact [and by the Holy Spirit, at that] that access to God was blocked while the Law was enforced, except in the most limited way)*, **while as the First Tabernacle was yet standing** *(show the limitations of the Levitical system)*:
>
> **"Which *was* a figure for the time then present** *(refers to the Tabernacle being a representation of Heavenly realities)*, **in which were offered both Gifts and Sacrifices, that could not make him who did the service perfect, as pertaining to the conscience** *(portrays the weakness of the First Covenant, in that it was based on animal blood, which was insufficient; in other words, the conscience of the*

Jew was still heavy with realization that sin had only been covered, not taken away; only the Cross could take away sin [Jn. 1:29]);

"*Which stood* only in meats and drinks, and divers washings, and carnal Ordinances *(refers to the entirety of the Levitical system, which could only present Types and Shadows)*, **imposed *on them* until the time of Reformation.** *(The Cross, to which all of this pointed, would address all of this once and for all.)*

"But Christ being come *(the little word 'but' is the pivot upon which all the arguments swing)* **an High Priest** *(presented by the Apostle to show how marvelously the one Offering of our Lord Jesus Christ transcends all the Types and Shadows of the old)* **of good things to come** *(should have been translated, 'of the good things realized')*, **by a greater and more perfect Tabernacle** *(presents Christ Himself as the more Perfect Tabernacle)*, **not made with hands, that is to say, not of this building** *(Christ is not a flimsy structure like the Tabernacle of old)*;

"Neither by the blood of goats and calves *(proclaims by the fact of the continued need of more Sacrifices that it was not properly effected)*, **but by His Own Blood** *(presents the price paid)* **He entered in once into the Holy Place** *(presents Christ doing what no other Priest had ever done; He offered a Sacrifice that was complete, which means it would never have to be repeated; thereby, the Heavenly Tabernacle was opened to Him; and if opened to Him, it was opened to us as well)*, **having obtained Eternal Redemption *for us.*** *(This proclaims what was accomplished by the giving of Himself on the Cross)*" **(Heb. 9:8-12).**

As we have stated, Jesus did go down into Paradise, which was a part of Hell, where the righteous souls were, but there was no record that He ever went into the burning Pit. This is the place to which Jesus was referring when He said to the dying thief, *"Today shall you be with Me in Paradise"* (Lk. 23:43).

He was speaking of that place in the heart of the Earth where He would go. The other thief would go to the punishment side of Hell where the rich man was.

HE LED CAPTIVITY CAPTIVE

After Jesus died on the Cross, He went down into Paradise to *"lead captivity captive"* (Eph. 4:8). This strange term means that all of the Old Testament Saints were actually captives of Satan, in effect, kept in this place against their will, in fact, awaiting the coming of Christ. And let it be understood, when Jesus went down into this place, He did not go there as a defeated worm, as some claim, but He went as a victorious conqueror, which, in fact, He was. That is what the Scripture means when it says that Christ descended first into Hell, the lower parts of the Earth (Ps. 16:10; Acts 2:27; Eph. 4:8-10). He captured these righteous souls from Satan, and there was nothing the Evil One could do about it, leading them captive to Heaven when He ascended on high. This fulfilled Psalms 68:18.

Prior to this, as stated, all righteous souls went into Hades or Sheol when they died, along with the souls of the wicked who went to another compartment of that place. These two compartments had a great gulf between them (Lk. 16:19-31), in effect, separating the two. Since the Cross, every Believer upon death immediately goes to Heaven to await the Resurrection of the body (II Cor. 5:8; Phil. 1:21-24; Heb. 12:23; Rev. 6:9-11).

When the wicked die, they continue to go into this torment compartment of Hades or Sheol until the end of the Millennium. Then death and Hell will deliver up the wicked souls, who will be reunited with their bodies and resurrected to be sentenced to the Lake of Fire, which will take place at the Great White Throne Judgment (Rev. 20:11-15).

In this context a person could say that Jesus went to Hell, but it in no way means that He went down into the burning flames of the Pit as a sinner. Nor was He molested by Satan, triumphed over by the powers of darkness, and then suddenly justified by

God and born again as the *"Firstborn among many brethren"* (Rom. 8:29). This is an erroneous teaching that does not understand the Scriptural sense of the Atonement and the vicarious Sacrifice paid by Christ at Calvary's Cross as a Sin Offering.

As well, of Jesus during the three days and nights He was in the heart of the Earth, the Scripture says:

> **"By which also He went** *(between the time of His Death and Resurrection)* **and preached** *(announced something)* **unto the spirits in prison** *(does not refer to humans, but rather to fallen Angels; humans in the Bible are never referred to in this particular manner; these were probably the fallen Angels who tried to corrupt the human race by cohabiting with women [II Pet. 2:4; Jude, Vss. 6-7]; these fallen Angels are still locked up in this underworld prison)***;**
>
> **"Which sometime** *(in times past)* **were disobedient** *(this was shortly before the Flood)***, when once the longsuffering of God waited in the days of Noah** *(refers to this eruption of fallen Angels with women taking place at the time of Noah; this was probably a hundred or so years before the Flood)***, while the Ark was a preparing** *(these fallen Angels were committing this particular sin while the Ark was being made ready, however long it took; the Scripture doesn't say!)***, wherein few, that is, eight souls were saved by water.** *(This doesn't refer to being Saved from sin. They were saved from drowning in the Flood by being in the Ark)***"** **(I Pet. 3:19-20).**

What Jesus said to these fallen Angels we aren't told, but the following must be said.

FROM THE CROSS TO THE RESURRECTION

The Word of God relates only two things to us, even as we have enumerated, which Christ did during His three days and nights in the heart of the Earth, between His Death on Calvary

and His Resurrection. They are:

- **He preached to these fallen Angels who were locked up and, in fact, are still locked up at this time in the heart of the Earth. They will, at the Great White Throne Judgment, be placed into the Lake of Fire with their master Satan, where they will remain forever and forever (Rev. 20:10-15).**

The word *"preached"* as Peter used it here, is not the same Greek word used as we normally think of preaching. It actually means that Jesus made an announcement to these Angels, but it doesn't say what that announcement was. Quite possibly, the Cross now being a fact where every sin was atoned and Redemption afforded for all who will believe, He related to them the stern fact that they had failed and failed miserably.

- **He went into the place called Paradise, where He *"led captivity captive,"* meaning that He delivered every righteous soul in that place, taking them with Him to Heaven. The compartment called Paradise is now empty.**

Those two things alone are all that the Scripture says as it regards what Jesus did between the Cross and His Resurrection. The Scripture says absolutely nothing about Jesus going into the burning side of the Pit, where He suffered as a sinner for three days and nights, etc. All of that is a fabrication.

No, Jesus did not die spiritually on the Cross. He did not go to the burning side of Hell. He was not placed under Satan's domain. He was not subject to the Evil One. He was, in fact, the Perfect Sacrifice as our Substitute, given up as a *"Sin Offering."* He died physically, not spiritually.

ARE THOSE WHO SUBSCRIBE TO THE JESUS DIED SPIRITUALLY DOCTRINE, SAVED?

Some are, and some aren't!

If it is to be noticed, those who are in this particular doctrine claim that it's not their business to try to get people Saved, but rather to lead them to a deeper experience with God, which, in effect, will tell them how to get rich, etc. So, precious few

people are Saved under these particular Ministries, whoever they might be.

The reason should be obvious, what they are preaching is error and, in fact, a person cannot be Saved by believing that error. So they don't even try to get people to come to Christ.

The truth is, many of the people in this doctrine, gave their hearts to Christ, and were truly Saved, before believing this particular fabrication. In fact, most people in the Word of Faith teaching have little or no understanding at all of the *"Jesus died spiritually doctrine."* As stated, they have already given their hearts and lives to Christ under other types of ministry. If the cover be pulled off this teaching, most have embraced its concepts, thinking that it is their avenue to riches. To be sure, there are riches involved, but it's only for a few of the preachers and not for the people at all.

Regrettably, the *"Jesus died spiritually doctrine"* repudiates the Cross, referring to it as *"past miseries,"* and *"the worst defeat in human history."* Many, if not most, of their Churches refuse to even sing songs about the Blood, about the Cross, about the great Sacrifice of Christ, concluding and claiming that such are *"defeatist."*

All of that is strange when Paul said, *"I, Brethren, when I came to you, came not with excellency of speech or of wisdom, declaring unto you the Testimony of God.*

***"For I determined not to know anything among you, save Jesus Christ and Him Crucified"* (I Cor. 2:1-2).**

If the Cross of Christ was the primary Message of the Apostle Paul, it had better be our primary Message as well!

CHAPTER EIGHT

Can A Merciful God Condemn A Man To Hell Who Has Never Heard The Gospel, And Justify Himself In Doing So?

QUESTION:

CAN A MERCIFUL GOD CONDEMN A MAN TO HELL WHO HAS NEVER HEARD THE GOSPEL, AND JUSTIFY HIMSELF IN DOING SO?

ANSWER:

Considering that there are nearly seven billion people on Planet Earth at this particular time (2008), and considering that untold millions of these people have never even heard the Name of Jesus even one time, the question of our discussion is signally important.

Before we go into discussion, let's look at the situation not only from the perspective of this present time, but for all time.

ADAM AND EVE

When our first parents disobeyed God, they fell from the level of total God-consciousness, down to the far, far lower level of total self-consciousness. They actually died to the things of God, meaning that He was now no longer their Source of life. Concerning the condition of the unsaved, Paul said:

> **"And you *has He quickened*** *(made alive)*, **who were dead in trespasses and sins** *(total depravity due to the Fall and original sin)*;
>
> **"Wherein in time past you walked according to the course of this world** *(refers to the fact that the unredeemed order their behavior and regulate their lives within this sphere of trespasses and sins)*, **according to the prince of the power of the air** *(pertains to the fact that Satan heads up the system of this world)*, **the spirit that now works in the children of disobedience** *(the spirit of Satan, which fills all unbelievers, thereby working disobedience)*:
>
> **"Among whom** *(the children of disobedience)* **also we**

all had our conversation *(manner of life)* **in times past in the lusts of our flesh** *(evil cravings)*, **fulfilling the desires of the flesh and of the mind** *(the minds of the unredeemed are the laboratory of perverted thoughts, impressions, imaginations, etc.)*; **and were by nature the children of wrath, even as others.** *(God's Wrath is unalterably opposed to sin, and the only solution is the Cross)*" **(Eph. 2:1-3).**

THE TERRIBLE FORCE OF SIN

All the heartache in this world, all the sickness and suffering, all the death and dying, all the war and man's inhumanity to man, has all been caused, is all caused, by sin. Man is hopelessly lost! Not just partially so, not somewhat, but totally and completely lost. This means that due to the Fall, he has no conception of God, at least that which is correct, no understanding of God, and no desire for God, at least within himself. While a desire may definitely be placed in the heart of a sinner because loved ones are praying for him or her, but without that, it is impossible, and due to the fact, that all unbelievers are *"dead in trespasses and sins."* And we must understand, *"dead is dead."*

All of this means that the unsaved person must be Born-Again.

BORN-AGAIN

Jesus addressed one of the religious leaders of Israel by the name of Nicodemus. He was very religious, but in truth, was lost. In other words, he wasn't Saved.

Jesus said to him:

"Verily, verily, I say unto you, Except a man be born *again* *(the term, 'born again,' means that man has already had a natural birth, but now must have a Spiritual Birth, which comes by Faith in Christ, and what He has done for us at the Cross, and is available to all)*, **he cannot see the**

Kingdom of God *(actually means that without the New Birth, one cannot understand or comprehend the 'Kingdom of God')*" **(Jn. 3:3).**

So in brief, that is man's present plight, and has been his plight since the Fall.

THE SOLUTION TO THE PROBLEM

When Adam and Eve were driven from the Garden of Eden, lest they eat of the Fruit of the Tree of Life and live forever, someone has said that the Lord, although having driven them out, went with them, and in a sense, that is most definitely correct.

Incidentally, while man was originally created in fact to live forever, and will one day soon achieve that again, the truth is, in man's sinful state, if he was allowed to live forever, think of an Adolph Hitler, a Joseph Stalin, and untold others of like ilk, living forever. It is unthinkable!

The Lord gave to the first family a means by which, although fallen, they could have forgiveness of sins, and thereby, communion with Him. It was by virtue of the slain lamb, which is epitomized in the Fourth Chapter of Genesis, which would be a type of the coming Redeemer. For the Lord had promised that One would come, Who would lift man out of this fallen state. In fact, He said this to Satan through the serpent:

"And I will put enmity *(animosity)* **between you and the woman** *(presents the Lord now actually speaking to Satan, who had used the serpent; in effect, the Lord is saying to Satan, 'You used the woman to bring down the human race, and I will use the woman as an instrument to bring the Redeemer into the world, Who will save the human race')*, **and between your seed** *(mankind which follows Satan)* **and her Seed** *(the Lord Jesus Christ)*; **it** *(Christ)* **shall bruise your head** *(the victory that Jesus won at the Cross [Col. 2:14-15])*, **and you shall bruise His Heel** *(the* *sufferings of the Cross)*" **(Gen. 3:15).**

But despite the Lord making a way as He did, still, between Adam and Eve to the time of the flood, a period of approximately 1600 years, the Bible only records two people who were Saved. That was Abel, who was murdered by his brother Cain, and Enoch who was translated that he should not see death (Gen. 5:22-24). There certainly may been others Saved, but only two were recorded. This means that all the hundreds of millions of others who lived during that particular time, died eternally lost.

FROM NOAH TO ABRAHAM

In the flood, every person on Planet Earth lost their life and their soul, with the exception of Noah and his family. So, in essence, every human being on the face of the Earth stems from the three sons of Noah, Shem, Ham, and Japheth. So, from Noah to Abraham, a time frame of approximately 400 years, the only people on Earth at that time, who were Saved, of which we have any knowledge, were Noah, and two of his sons, Shem and Japheth. There is some evidence that Ham did not live for the Lord (Gen. 9:22-27).

From the time of Abraham to Moses, once again a time frame of approximately 400 years, the only ones who lived for God were Abraham and his family. Melchizedek must be included as well, but of him we have scant knowledge, except that he most definitely was a Type of Christ (Gen. 4:17-20). (It is possible that Melchizedek was actually Shem, the son of Noah.)

Even when the Law was given to Israel through Moses, Israel was the only nation, the only people on the face of the Earth, who were monotheistic, meaning they worshipped one God, namely Jehovah. All the balance of the nations were polytheistic, meaning they worshipped many gods, namely demon spirits. And yet, even in Israel as a nation, which up to the time of Christ covered a time frame of approximately 1,500 years, if

the truth be known, only a small portion of Israelites were truly saved. That means that most Israelites died lost, and despite the fact that they had the Law and the Prophets.

ALMOST ALL HAVE DIED LOST

So if the truth be known, up until the time of Christ, a time frame of approximately 4,000 years, only a few were actually Saved. By comparison to the size of the population from the time of Christ to the present time, again, one would have to state that only a few have been Saved. In fact, Jesus said:

***"Because strait is the gate, and narrow is the way, which leads unto life, and few there be that find it"* (Mat. 7:14).**

THE MERCY OF GOD

People being eternally lost, and upon death, eternally consigned to the place called *"Hell,"* has nothing to do with the Mercy of God or the lack thereof. Sin is such a debilitating factor, such a destructive force, always with death attached to its power, that God, despite His infinite mercy, and despite the fact that He is not willing that any should perish, still, lacking the Born-Again experience, God simply cannot allow such individuals into Heaven. If He did, Heaven would soon be a Hell!

Are governmental authorities heartless when they quarantine people with contagious diseases? No! In fact, they would be heartless if they didn't do such, and for all the obvious reasons. It is the same with criminals with murderous intent, plus those who would destroy the fabric of society; they must be locked away, and for the benefit of all mankind. What would you think of a Court that gave license and liberty to murderers to run amok, continuing their murderous intent? I think the answer to that is obvious. God cannot allow sin into Heaven. So, He must quarantine all those who have not been Born-Again, irrespective as to whom they might be, or where they might be. The place of that quarantine is Hell itself.

SIN, THE REASON FOR THE CROSS

One of the most oft quoted Scriptures in the Word of God is the following:

> **"For God so loved the world** *(presents the God kind of love)*, **that He gave His Only Begotten Son** *(gave Him up to the Cross, for that's what it took to redeem humanity)*, **that whosoever believes in Him should not perish, but have Everlasting Life.**
>
> **"For God sent not His Son into the world to condemn the world** *(means that the object of Christ's Mission was to save, but the issue to those who reject Him must and can only be condemnation)*; **but that the world through Him might be Saved** *(Jesus Christ is the only Salvation for the world; there is no other! as well, He is Salvation only through the Cross; consequently, the Cross must ever be the Object of our Faith)*.
>
> **"He who believes on Him is not condemned** *(is not condemned to be eternally lost in the Lake of Fire forever and forever [Rev. 20:11-15])*: **but he who believes not is condemned already, because he has not believed in the Name of the Only Begotten Son of God** *(all of this refers to Christ and what He did at the Cross in order to redeem humanity; Salvation is never by works, but rather by Grace through Faith, with the Cross ever the Object of that Faith)*" **(Jn. 3:16-18).**

One can tell how awful that sin is, by the price that had to be paid in order for sin to be properly addressed and put away. That price was God's only Son dying on a cruel Cross, in other words, giving Himself as the Perfect, Eternal Sacrifice.

THE LOVE OF GOD

As it regards the Love of God, we can only properly understand

the depth of that love, at least as far as a human being can grasp such, as to what God did in order to redeem humanity, which was the giving of His only Son. There is no greater love than that. So for unbelievers to accuse God of lacking in love, simply because that Love and Mercy cannot allow sin into Heaven, simply do not know what they are talking about. To properly understand the horror of sin, we must first of all understand the ransom that was paid, which ransom man owed to God but could not pay, but was paid by the Lord Jesus Christ.

So, God cannot be accused as it regards the terrible plight of the human race. He has done and is doing everything that Heaven can do in order to save man.

Before Christ came, even to which we have already alluded, the Lord instituted the Sacrificial System, which would serve as a substitute until the Substance would come, namely the Lord Jesus Christ. But man then, as man now, had no desire for the Grace offered.

There has never been a time in history, that man has wanted to be saved, and couldn't. In fact, there is some evidence, that irrespective as to whom the person might be, or where that person might be, if somehow, there is a desire for God within his heart, even though it be not known as to how that desire came about, the Lord will somehow, make Salvation available to that person.

We read in the Book of Acts of an Ethiopian who had come into possession of a Scroll of the Prophet Isaiah. He read it, but did not understand what he was reading, so the Lord sent Philip from Samaria to Gaza, a distance of several hundreds of miles, all in order that Philip may testify to this Ethiopian, who gave his heart to Christ. In other words, God has gone to extraordinary lengths to save mankind, and even to save individuals, wherever they might be.

EVANGELISM

One might say that God has done, and is doing all that

Heaven can do to bring men to Christ, thereby, to save them from eternal Hell. It is now the business of every redeemed person to help take *"the greatest story ever told"* to the ends of the Earth. In fact, some of the last Words that our Lord gave to us are in the form of *"The Great Commission,"* He said:

> **"And Jesus came and spoke unto them** *(the same meeting on the mountain, and constitutes the Great Commission)*, **saying, All power is given unto Me in Heaven and in Earth** *(this is not given to Him as Son of God; for, as God nothing can be added to Him or taken from Him; it is rather a power, which He has merited by His Incarnation and His Death at Calvary on the Cross [Phil. 2:8-10]; this authority extends not only over men, so that He governs and protects the Church, disposes human events, controls hearts and opinions; but the forces of Heaven also are at His Command; the Holy Spirit is bestowed by Him, and the Angels are in His employ as ministering to the members of His Body. When He said, 'all power,' He meant, 'all power!')*.
>
> **"Go ye therefore** *(applies to any and all who follow Christ, and in all ages)*, **and teach all nations** *(should have been translated, 'and preach to all nations', for the word 'teach' here refers to a proclamation of truth)*, **baptizing them in the Name of the Father, and of the Son, and of the Holy Spirit** *(presents the only formula for Water Baptism given in the Word of God)*:
>
> **"Teaching them** *(means to give instruction)* **to observe all things** *(the whole Gospel for the whole man)* **whatsoever I have commanded you** *(not a suggestion)*: **and, lo, I am with you always** *(it is I, Myself, God, and Man, Who am — not 'will be' — hence, forever present among you, and with you as Companion, Friend, Guide, Saviour, God)*, ***even*** **unto the end of the world** *(should have been translated 'age')*. **Amen** *(it is the guarantee of My Promise)*" **(Mat. 28:18-20).**

So, it is the responsibility of every single Believer to help take the Gospel Message to the entirety of the world.

And please understand the following:

JESUS CHRIST THE ONLY SAVIOUR

There is only one Way of Salvation, not ten, not five, not even two, only one. That Way is *"Jesus Christ and Him Crucified."* Islam is not the way, Buddhism is not the way, Shintoism is not the way, etc., only the Lord Jesus Christ. He said, and concerning this very thing:

> **"Jesus said unto Him, I am the Way, the Truth, and the Life** *(proclaims in no uncertain terms exactly Who and What Jesus is)***: no man comes unto the Father, but by Me** *(He declares positively that this idea of God as Father, this approach to God for every man is through Him — through what He is and what He has done)***" (Jn. 14:6).**

Men make a terrible mistake when they conclude that people can be saved without accepting Jesus Christ. Please understand the following:

It was our Lord Who gave Himself on the Cross, in order that man might be Saved. Mohammad didn't die on that Cross, and neither did anyone else. In fact, it would have done them no good, and neither would it have done us any good, had they died on Crosses. Jesus Christ Alone could fulfill the demands of a thrice-Holy God. He was God manifested in the flesh. To offer a polluted sacrifice, which Mohammad and all others would have been, would have served no purpose at all. A Sacrifice had to be offered, that was perfect in every respect. Only the Son of God could meet those criteria.

The Lord Jesus Christ is the One Who paid the price. No one else did, because no one else could! So, it stands to reason, that He Alone is the Saviour. Man is a sinner, he must have a Saviour, and that Saviour is the Lord Jesus Christ, and there

is no other. I do not know how to make it clearer, simpler, and more understandable.

IS THAT FAIR?

Men chaff at the idea that Christ Alone is the Way. They want to claim that one religion is as good as the other. In fact, man has been doing that from the dawn of time. Despite the fact that the Lord gave instructions as to how that sins could be forgiven, Cain ignored the instructions of God, and formulated his own religion and thereby, his own salvation, which was no salvation at all! He built an altar, and offered up a sacrifice. In other words, he did not deny there was a God, but he did deny God's Way of Redemption. And as stated, man has been doing that ever since. Cain offered up the fruit of his own hands, whatever in the world that was, and demanded that God accept it. In other words, he was denying the fact that he was a sinner in need of a Saviour. Concerning this, Williams said:

"There was no difference between the brothers, Cain and Abel, but an eternal difference between their sacrifices. They were both corrupt branches of a decayed tree, both born outside Eden, both guilty, both sinners, no moral difference, and both sentenced to death. Abel accepts God's Way, Cain rejects it. Abel's Altar speaks of repentance, of faith, and of the Precious Blood of Christ, the Lamb of God without blemish. Cain's altar tells of pride, unbelief, and self-righteousness.

"Abel's Altar is beautiful to God's eye and repulsive to man's. Cain's altar, beautiful to man's eye and repulsive to God's. These 'altars' exist today, around the one, that is, Christ and His atoning work, few are gathered, around the other many. God accepts the slain lamb and rejects the offered fruit; and the offering being rejected, so of necessity is the offerer."

It is our responsibility to take this Message to the entirety of the world. That's the reason that this Ministry (Jimmy Swaggart Ministries), is doing everything within our power to carry out the Great Commission of our Lord. That's the reason we

have the Telecast in every country in the world where it's possible for us to do so. That's the reason that we ask you for your financial help as well as your prayerful support, that this task be carried out. Two things must be done:

- **The Word of God must be taken to the whole world.**
- **We must be certain that it is the true Word of God which is actually being taken to fallen humanity. Nothing else will suffice!**

Neither I nor you can answer for the generations passed and past. But we most definitely must answer for this generation. As a Believer, and a Minister of the Gospel, our Lord does not hold me responsible for generations over which I had no control. But He most definitely does hold me responsible, and you, for this present time. What are we doing to take the grandest story ever told to others? God, as we have clumsily tried to explain, has done all that He can do, now it's up to us to obey the Great Commission.

Never before in history, has it been possible through the means of modern communications, and we speak of Television, to take the Gospel to the nations of the world as now. In fact, even as I dictate these notes, our Telecast by Satellite, is going into most every Muslim country in the Middle East, as well as Israel. Also, every program is subtitled in Arabic. As we've said many times, Satan can build a fence around these nations, but he cannot build a roof. Actually, at the present time (2008), we are airing Television in all or part in over 100 nations.

In order to get this task completed, we are given the Holy Spirit, the Third Person of the Triune Godhead, and I speak of the Baptism with the Holy Spirit, which is always accompanied by speaking with other Tongues (Acts 2:4).

Actually, along with the Great Commission, Jesus commanded His followers (I said commanded) *"that they should not depart from Jerusalem, but wait for the Promise of the Father, which, said He, you have heard of Me. For John truly baptized with water; but you shall be baptized with the Holy Spirit not many days hence"* (Acts 1:4-5).

And then He said:

"But you shall receive power *(Miracle-working Power)*, **after that the Holy Spirit is come upon you** *(specifically states that this 'Power' is inherent in the Holy Spirit, and solely in His Domain)*: **and you shall be witnesses** *(doesn't mean witnessing to souls, but rather to one giving one's all in every capacity for Christ, even to the laying down of one's life)* **unto Me** *(without the Baptism with the Holy Spirit, one cannot really know Jesus as one should)* **both in Jerusalem, and in all Judaea, and in Samaria, and unto the uttermost part of the Earth** *(proclaims the Work of God as being worldwide)***" (Acts 1:8).**

The Lord said through the great Prophet Ezekiel many years ago, *"Have I any pleasure at all that the wicked should die? Says the Lord GOD: and not that he should return from his ways, and live?"* (Ezek. 18:23).

The Lord also said through the Prophet, *"When I say unto the wicked, You shall surely die; and you give him not warning, nor speak to warn the wicked from his wicked way, to save his life; the same wicked man shall die in his iniquity; but his blood will I require at your hand"* (Ezek. 3:18). This Passage tells us several things. They are:

- **It tells us that ignorance of the Gospel does not save one.**
- **It tells the preacher that the Truth must be presented, irrespective as to how disliked the Truth might be.**
- **It tells us if the preacher does not preach the Truth, or if we fail to take the Gospel to those who do not know, that *"their blood will be required at our hands."* They will still be lost, but we will be responsible.**

If ignorance of the Gospel insures Salvation, then the best thing to do in order to get men Saved, is to stop all preaching, burn all Bibles, close all churches, etc. But we know that's not the way.

In fact, every iota of decency in this world, all prosperity, all

freedom, wherever it may reign, is all because of the Gospel of Jesus Christ. It is the only light in this darkened world. That light being removed, there is nothing left but darkness, and a darkness that steals, kills, and destroys.

I realize that the powers that be little recognize that which I've just stated; however, that in no way abrogates this great Truth. Jesus Christ is the Light of the world (Jn. 8:12).

The answer to the question as it regards all being lost who have never heard the Name of Jesus, meaning they never had the opportunity to accept or reject, is found in the words of Abraham some 4,000 years ago.

As it regarded the destruction of Sodom and Gomorrah, the great Patriarch said to the Lord, *"Shall not the Judge of all the Earth do right?"* (Gen. 18:25).

To be sure, the Judge of all the Earth will most definitely do right.

Due to the reasons given, yes, no person can be allowed into Heaven, unless they have been Born-Again. And yet at the same time, I personally believe according to the Word of God, that every baby, every child below the age of accountability, and that age varies with different children, if they die before reaching that age, whatever it might be, they are instantly taken to Heaven. A child below the age of accountability, cannot reason, and thereby, cannot make a rational judgment. So I believe they are protected, and if dying in that state, Saved. Jesus said, and concerning the little children:

***"Suffer the little children to come unto Me, and forbid them not: for of such is the Kingdom of God"* (Mk. 10:14).**

To answer the question, yes, an all-merciful God, and because of the reasons given, can condemn a soul to eternal Hell, who is not Born-Again, and justify Himself in doing so!

CHAPTER NINE

Is The Doctrine Of Unconditional Eternal Security Scriptural?

QUESTION:

IS THE DOCTRINE OF UNCONDITIONAL ETERNAL SECURITY SCRIPTURAL?

ANSWER:

Basically there are two schools of thought on the matter of security for the Believer. One is Calvinism and the other is Armenianism. Both are based on Scripture, but their conclusions diverge dramatically.

Calvinism emphasizes the Sovereignty of God and His Divine Prerogative. Armenianism stresses man's free will and responsibility.

The doctrine of unconditional eternal security accepts the Calvinistic perspective and states that once a person has been Saved and accepts the atoning Blood of Jesus Christ, he can never be lost afterward no matter what he might do.

The Armenian view is that man has a free will and it is the free will of man that determines his condition. According to his free will, he determined to accept Christ when the Holy Spirit moved upon his heart. As well, free will coupled with the Grace of God maintains his position in Christ; however, if he so desires, God forbid, he can, through his free will, elect to cease believing what got him in, which is Faith in Christ and what Christ did at the Cross. If that happens he will then revert from a Saved condition to a lost condition.

BOTH CONDITIONS ANALYZED

In order to come to a full understanding of both these positions, the Calvinist position and the Armenian position, I feel that they should be analyzed together.

Without question God is Sovereign and this Sovereignty allows Him full latitude in any area whatsoever. At the same time, though, God is always consistent. This means that God,

although He has the Power to do anything, will never abrogate His Nature or His Righteousness. We can, therefore, determine His predictable Reaction by reviewing Scripture. Any doctrine demanding capricious or arbitrary action by God, contrary to other areas in the Word, can be assumed to be errant.

In order to properly evaluate this issue, we will investigate four questions:

- Can a Saved person cease to believe and then be lost?
- Is our Salvation dependent on works or Faith?
- What happens when a Believer sins?
- What are the fruits of the doctrine of unconditional eternal security?

CAN A BELIEVER CEASE TO BELIEVE AND THEN BE LOST?

Some time ago I heard two sermons which asked the same question. One asked, *"Can a Christian be lost?"* And the other asked, *"Can a Born-Again Believer be lost?"*

The motive behind both these sermons was promotion of the doctrine of unconditional eternal security. And what was the conclusion of both the Preachers? That a Born-Again Believer, a Christian, cannot be lost.

Actually, no Born-Again Believer can be lost. Of that the Word of God is clear and plain.

Unfortunately, these Preachers didn't go the one further step necessary to complete their investigation of this matter. They should have also asked the question, *"Can a Born-Again Christian cease to believe in Christ and, thereby, what He did for us at the Cross?"*

Yes, a Believer, if he so desires, can cease to believe in Christ and what Christ has done for us at the Cross. That done, and if they continue in that vein, they will be eternally lost. As stated, it is free will that gets one in. The Scripture says:

"And the Spirit and the Bride say, Come. *(This*

> *presents the cry of the Holy Spirit to a hurting, lost, and dying world. What the Holy Spirit says should also be said by all Believers.)* **And let him who hears say, Come.** *(It means if one can 'hear,' then one can 'come.')* **And let him who is athirst come** *(speaks of Spiritual Thirst, the cry for God in the soul of man)*. **And whosoever will, let him take the Water of Life freely** *(opens the door to every single individual in the world; Jesus died for all and, therefore, all can be Saved, if they will only come)*" **(Rev. 22:17).**

As free will gets one in, free will can get one out and keep one out, if that is what the person so desires.

Some claim that if a person is truly Saved, then they won't want out.

That most definitely is the case with me and millions of others; however, there are some unfortunately, who for whatever reason, elect to turn their back on Christ and what He did at the Cross. Never forget, the loss of Faith, is the loss of the soul.

BIBLICAL EXAMPLES

The Word of God records any number of personalities who were at one time in the Grace of God, but who subsequently fell from Grace. After their fall from Grace, these individuals were lost.

LUCIFER

Lucifer was once without sin and walked perfectly within the Grace of God. Read Ezekiel 28:12-19, where the fall from Grace of Lucifer is so poignantly described, and his ultimate end so graphically revealed.

ANGELS

Then, there are the uncounted millions of Angels created by

God. Of these, one-third rebelled and chose to follow Lucifer in his insurrection against God. Every one of these became destined, at that moment, to join Lucifer ultimately in the fiery Pit (Mat. 25:41).

ADAM AND EVE

Our First Parents were created in God's Grace and Favor (Gen. 1:26-31). And, what happened? They fell from Grace and lost the Eternal Residence they would have enjoyed if only they had obeyed God and walked in His Statutes. Adam was a son of God (Lk. 3:38) but he lost his sonship, through transgression. No specific mention is made anywhere within the Word of God of Adam or Eve's subsequent salvation from sin.

NADAB AND ABIHU

These two men, Nadab and Abihu, were sons of Aaron — God's anointed, who served as the first High Priests of the Children of Israel after the captivity. Yet, as recounted in Leviticus 10:1-2, they disobeyed God. And, what was their instantaneous end? They were destroyed by fire from God.

KORAH, DATHAN, AND ABIRAM

These three, Korah, Dathan, and Abiram rebelled against God. Korah was a Levite, actually a Priest, an incense bearer before God in the worship services of the Israelites. And, what happened to him and his fellow rebels? They were cast into the Pit and, consequently, eternally lost, because of their decision to turn away from God.

SAUL, THE FIRST KING OF ISRAEL

The other day I read the answer of a Preacher who was asked whether Saul, Israel's first king, was Saved when he died.

And what was the Preacher's answer? *"Yes,"* he said, *"Saul was Saved and went to Heaven."*

Of course, this Preacher was a devotee of the doctrine of unconditional eternal security. If this doctrine were valid, of course, his answer would be correct. But, what does the Bible say about Saul's fate?

***"So Saul died for his transgression which he committed against the LORD, even against the Word of the LORD, which he kept not, and also for asking counsel of one who had a familiar spirit, to enquire of it; and enquired not of the LORD: therefore He slew him, and turned the kingdom unto David the son of Jesse"* (I Chron. 10:13-14).**

If that sounds like the account of a faithful Child of God being taken home to be with the Lord, I must be reading a version of the Bible differently from that used by the Preacher quoted above. It seems obvious to me from these Passages that Saul was not Saved when he died, nor did he go to Heaven.

MANY TURNED AWAY FROM GRACE

Turning to the New Testament we find, in St. John 6:66, that many of the faithful — the very Disciples who worked personally with our Lord — turned away from His Grace and walked with Him no more. In Luke 8:13, the Words of our Saviour Himself tell us that many, in times of temptation fall away after receiving the Word.

ANANIAS AND SAPPHIRA

Just the other day a radio Preacher stated that Ananias and Sapphira were Saved, and even though they lost fellowship with God, they still went to Heaven upon their deaths. This Preacher was, as well, a proponent of the doctrine of unconditional eternal security.

To accept the concept that Ananias and Sapphira died Saved, just doesn't conform to God's Principles as laid out in the balance

of His Word. It is stated unequivocally in Acts 5:3-4, and 9, that they lied to God and the Holy Spirit. And, what is the fate of liars according to God's Word? In Revelation 21:8, we are told that liars are to be cast into the Lake of Fire. What happens to those cast into the Lake of Fire?

Revelation 20:10 says they *"shall be tormented day and night forever and ever."* According to God's Word, the fate of Ananias and Sapphira is quite different from that described by the radio Preacher.

HYMENAEUS AND ALEXANDER

In I Timothy 1:19-20, Paul refers in passing to Hymenaeus and Alexander. He states that they, though once being in the Faith, have made their faith shipwreck by putting it away.

We are admonished in many places throughout the Bible to avoid the special wrath God has reserved for those who turn away after coming to know the Light. In the Old Testament (Ex. 32:33), the Lord said, *". . . Whosoever has sinned against Me, him will I blot out of My Book."*

In Deuteronomy 30:17-20, He said, *". . . But if your heart turn away . . . you shall surely perish. . . ."*

In Ezekiel 3:20-21, we are told, *"When a righteous man turns from his righteousness and commits iniquity . . . he shall die in his sin. . . ."*

Jesus spoke (Mat. 5:13) of the salt which has lost its savor. What is it good for? Only to be cast out.

In John 8:31, our Lord said, *"If you continue in My Word, you are My Disciples. . . ."*

In Galatians 5:4, Paul accused some in the Churches of Galatia of having *"fallen from Grace."*

In I Timothy 4:1, he said, *"expressly . . . some shall depart from the Faith, giving heed to seducing spirits, and doctrines of devils."*

Peter said, *"Give diligence to make your calling and election sure, for if you do these things, you shall never fall"* (II Pet. 1:10).

He also said (II Pet. 2:20-22), *"If, after they have escaped the pollutions of the world through the knowledge of the Lord and Saviour Jesus Christ, they are again entangled therein, and overcome, the latter end is worse . . . than the beginning."*

Those who do not overcome will have their names blotted out of the Book of Life (Rev. 3:5; Ex. 32:32-33; Ps. 69:28).

THE DEFECTING OF JEWISH BELIEVERS

Paul said:

> **"For *it is* impossible for those who were once enlightened** *(refers to those who have accepted the Light of the Gospel, which means accepting Christ and His great Sacrifice)*, **and have tasted of the Heavenly Gift** *(pertains to Christ and what He did at the Cross)*, **and were made partakers of the Holy Spirit** *(which takes place when a person comes to Christ)*,
>
> **"And have tasted the good Word of God** *(is not language that is used of an impenitent sinner, as some claim; the unsaved have no relish whatsoever for the Truth of God, and see no beauty in it)*, **and the powers of the world to come** *(refers to the Work of the Holy Spirit within hearts and lives, which the unsaved cannot have or know)*,
>
> **"If they shall fall away** *(should have been translated, 'and having fallen away')*, **to renew them again unto Repentance** *('again' states they had once repented, but have now turned their backs on Christ)*; **seeing they crucify to themselves the Son of God afresh** *(means they no longer believe what Christ did at the Cross, actually concluding Him to be an imposter; the only way any person can truly repent is to place his Faith in Christ and the Cross; if that is denied, there is no Repentance)*, **and put *Him* to an open shame** *(means to hold Christ up to public ridicule; Paul wrote this Epistle because some Christian Jews were going back into Judaism, or seriously contemplating doing so)*" **(Heb. 6:4-6).**

The following is what was taking place with some of these Christian Jews.

While all who came to Christ during the time of the Early Church had to suffer persecution in some way, still, the Jews who came to Christ were submitted, at least in most cases, to even a greater persecution and opposition.

In many of these cases, their family actually held a funeral for them. Thereafter, they were treated as if they were dead. If they were met on the street, their closest loved one would not even acknowledge their presence. If a member of the family died, they were not allowed to come to the funeral. As stated, having accepted Christ, they were treated by their family as one dead, that is, if their family rejected Christ.

Many of the Jews could not handle such persecution and, thereby, gave up serving the Lord and, as well, going back into Judaism. To do so, they had to reject Christ and what He did at the Cross, and do so publicly. It is to these people, or those contemplating doing such, to whom Paul is writing.

He, in effect, tells them that if they do this thing, and remain in that state, despite the fact that they have been Saved, they will now be eternally lost. As we have stated, it's Faith that gets one in and Faith that keeps one in. But if a person so desires, they can renounce their Faith in Christ, which is what these Jews were doing.

AN ERRONEOUS CONCLUSION

There was a particular Greek Scholar who is now with the Lord, after whom I have studied quite extensively. I personally believe that he loved the Lord very much, but yet, he was a devotee to the doctrine of unconditional eternal security.

Concerning the Passage in Hebrews, Chapter 6, which we have just quoted, he stated, and I paraphrase:

The Greek Text makes it very clear in these Passages that these Jews had truly once been Saved, but upon going back into Judaism, thereby renouncing Christ, they had reverted to

a lost condition.

Knowing this was irrefutable in the Greek Text, I wondered how he was going to justify his statement, and maintain his doctrine of unconditional eternal security. Here's what he said, and again I paraphrase:

"Admitting these Jews had truly been saved, and admitting that they had turned their backs on Christ, and reverted to a lost condition, still, this could only happen to Jews, and could only happen to Jews who lived at that particular time."

As I've stated, I believe this dear Brother loved the Lord very much; however, claiming that such could only happen to Jews, and Jews who lived at that particular time, is ridiculous to say the least!

If it was possible for those Jews to lose their Salvation, which the Bible plainly says they did, then it's possible for anyone.

ARE WE SAVED AND KEPT BY WORKS OR BY FAITH?

What we are really asking here is, *"Do we have to worry about losing our Salvation?"*

The Scripture says:

> **"For by Grace** *(the Goodness of God)* **are you Saved through Faith** *(Faith in Christ, with the Cross ever as its Object)***; and that not of yourselves** *(none of this is of us, but all is of Him)***: *it is* the Gift of God** *(anytime the word 'Gift' is used, God is speaking of His Son and His Substitutionary Work on the Cross, which makes all of this possible)***:**
>
> **"Not of works** *(man cannot merit Salvation, irrespective what he does)***, lest any man should boast** *(boast in his own ability and strength; we are allowed to boast only in the Cross [Gal. 6:14])***" (Eph. 2:8-9).**

We are further told, *"The Just shall live by Faith."*

> **"Now the Just shall live by Faith** *(Faith in Christ*

> *and the Cross [Hab. 2:4]):* **but if *any man* draw back** *(proclaims the fact that such can be done, and refers to Believers transferring their Faith from Christ and the Cross to other things),* **My soul shall have no pleasure in him.** *(As should be obvious, God is grieved over the conduct of any person who would do such)*" **(Heb. 10:38).**

All of this means that Salvation is given to the Believer, not by works, or by acts of righteousness, but as a Gift through the act of Faith. It is, of course, maintained in exactly the same way.

Our status as Believers is not a matter of works, but always of *"Faith."* Even though a sinner does good works, he does not become acceptable to God on the basis of those works. We can only become acceptable to God through Grace, on the basis of Faith; however, the Object of Faith which is so very, very important, must always be the Cross of Christ (Rom. 6:1-14; 8:1-2, 11; I Cor. 1:17-18, 23; 2:2; Gal. 6:14; Col. 2:14-15).

With our acceptance, through Faith, of the fact that Jesus Christ died for our sins, and with the acceptance of His Sacrifice as atonement for our sins, we receive forgiveness by God's Grace.

The sinner accepts Jesus' Sacrifice by Faith, and by Faith he throws himself on the Mercy of God, knowing that God will accept His Son's Sacrifice as payment in full for those sins.

The Believer now sees himself, through Faith, clothed with the Righteousness of Christ. This is a *"standing"* imputed to the Believer through no intrinsic merit — it is strictly a Gift from God.

The Believer's *"state,"* however, must not be confused with his *"standing."* We stand clothed in the Righteousness of Jesus Christ, whatever our *"state."* This standing with God is a result of Grace, i.e., *"the Goodness of God,"* through Faith — God's Grace and the Believer's Faith. Beyond this, of course, Righteousness in the Believer's life is a matter of Spiritual Growth, a progressive Sanctification by obedience to — and cooperation with — God's Holy Spirit (II Pet. 1:5-7; Rom. 6:12). Once

again, this is done by the Believer placing his Faith in Christ and the Cross, maintaining his Faith in Christ and the Cross, which then gives the Holy Spirit latitude to work within our lives, thereby bringing about the desired result of Righteousness and Holiness. This is God's Prescribed Order of Victory. He has no other order (Rom. 6:1-4; 8:1-2, 11).

PERFECT CHRISTIANS?

Is the Christian, then, perfect?

Of course not. He will make mistakes from time to time. Sad to say, at times he will even sin. He need not, however, doubt his Salvation, as long as he has Faith in Christ Jesus as the Author of his Salvation. As long as the Believer has Faith in Christ and what Christ has done for us at the Cross, the Lord will never repudiate His Word, which guarantees the Salvation of the Believer. On that basis, the Believer need never doubt his Salvation.

IF THE BELIEVER SINS, DOES HE LOSE HIS SALVATION?

It seems clear, both through experience and through Scripture, unfortunately, that Christians do sin. When the Christian does sin, his recourse always is forgiveness through Christ. The Scripture says:

THE INTERCESSION OF CHRIST

> **"Wherefore He** *(the Lord Jesus Christ)* **is able also to save them to the uttermost** *(proclaims the fact that Christ Alone has made the only true Atonement for sin; He did this at the Cross)* **who come unto God by Him** *(proclaims the only manner in which man can come to God)*, **seeing He ever lives to make intercession for them.** *(His very Presence by the Right Hand of the Father guarantees such, with*

nothing else having to be done [Heb. 1:3])" **(Heb. 7:25).**

The fact that Christ is constantly making intercession for all Believers, tells us that all Believers constantly need intercession.

We live in an ungodly world. Jesus told His Disciples, and you and me as well, that they needed their feet washed continually. He was not speaking literally, but rather symbolically. He said:

THE WASHING OF THE FEET

"He rose from supper *(He rose from the table when the preparation had been completed)*, **and laid aside His Garments** *(physically, His outer Robe; Spiritually, He laid aside the expression of His Deity, while never losing the possession of His Deity)*; **and took a towel** *(refers to the action of the lowliest slave or servant in a household; it represents the servant spirit possessed by Christ)*, **and girded Himself** *(wrapped Himself in the towel; spiritually speaking, it refers to His Human Body provided for Him by the Father [Heb. 10:5] in order to serve as a Sacrifice on the Cross for sin)*.

"After that He poured water into a basin *(spiritually, it referred to the Holy Spirit, which would pour from Him like a River [Jn. 7:38-39])*, **and began to wash the Disciples' feet** *(presenting the servant principle which we are to follow, but even more particularly the cleansing guaranteed by the Holy Spirit concerning our daily walk, which comes about according to our Faith in Christ and what He did for us at the Cross)*, **and to wipe *them* with the towel wherewith He was girded** *(refers to the Incarnation, which made possible His Death on Calvary that atoned for all sin and made cleansing possible for the human race)*.

"Then cometh He to Simon Peter *(seems to indicate it was Peter to whom He first approached)*: **and Peter said unto him, Lord, do you wash my feet?** *('The flesh'* *cannot understand Spiritual Realities; it is too backward or too forward, too courageous or too cowardly; it is incapable of ever being right, and it is impossible to improve, consequently, it must 'die.')*

"Jesus answered and said unto him, What I do you know not now; but you shall know hereafter *(when Peter was filled with the Spirit, which he was on the Day of Pentecost)***.**

"Peter said unto Him, You shall never wash my feet *(the Greek Text actually says, 'Not while eternity lasts'; Calvin said, 'With God, obedience is better than worship')***. Jesus answered him, If I wash you not, you have no part with Me** *(the statement as rendered by Christ speaks to the constant cleansing needed regarding our everyday walk before the Lord, which the washing of the feet [our walk], at least in part, represented)***.**

"Simon Peter said unto Him, Lord, not my feet only, but also *my* hands and *my* head *(Chrysostom said, 'In his deprecation he was vehement, and his yielding more vehement, but both came from his love')***.**

"Jesus said to him, he who is washed needs not save to wash *His* feet *(as stated, pertains to our daily walk before God, which means that the Believer doesn't have to get Saved over and over again; the 'head' refers to our Salvation, meaning that we do not have to be repeatedly Saved, while the 'hands' refer to our 'doing,' signifying that this doesn't need to be washed because Christ has already done what needs to be done; all of this is in the Spiritual Sense)***, but is clean every whit** *(refers to Salvation, and pertains to the Precious Blood of Jesus that cleanses from all sin; the infinite Sacrifice needs no repetition)***: and you are clean, but not all** *(refers to all the Disciples being Saved with one exception, which was Judas)***" (Jn. 13:4-10).**

It was the *"feet"* only that Jesus mentioned, because such represents our constant walk before God. Inasmuch as we are

living in a polluted world, this means that we need the intercession of Christ 24 hours a day, 7 days a week, etc.

No, if a Believer sins, he doesn't lose his Salvation.

THE CHRISTIAN AND SIN

No true Christian wants to sin. In fact, sin is abhorrent to such an individual; consequently, such a Christian will struggle against sin with all of his strength and power, because he hates sin.

Unfortunately, most of the Churches presently are filled with people who have never been Born-Again. As a result, sin is a constant part of their lives, with no intention of giving it up, unless something has become very debilitating to them. But, most of the time, in such cases, they are unable to overcome the problem, and remain bound by some type of vice.

ROMANS, CHAPTER SEVEN

But the truth is every Christian must, to a degree, go through the Seventh Chapter of Romans. There is no exception to this.

When the believing sinner comes to Christ, shortly, in some way, he or she will fail the Lord. Such will come as a shock, but it will happen. The Believer then sets about to not make the same mistake again. Invariably, he tries to do such by means of the flesh, which guarantees failure.

Then, the sin nature begins to be resurrected, not because of the sin, whatever it may have been, but because the Believer's Faith is in something other than Christ and the Cross. To be sure, whatever it is in which the Believer has placed his Faith is, no doubt, very religious, and perhaps even correct in its own right, but not in the way it's presently being used.

One can hear these schemes over Christian Television constantly. Believers are told that if they will take the Lord's Supper every day, or some such time frame, this will guarantee them prosperity and victory over sin, etc. While the Lord's

Supper is a viable, Scriptural Ordinance, still, there's nothing in the Bible to substantiate such a claim.

Other preachers claim that if the Believer is having a problem, he should select two or three Scriptures, memorize them, and quote them over and over, which will bring God on the scene. Now, while it's perfectly proper for Believers to memorize Scriptures and, in fact, all should do such, still, there's nothing in the Bible that will guarantee victory by such methods.

With faith wrongly placed, which means that such a Believer is now living in a state of spiritual adultery, this greatly hinders the Holy Spirit from helping the Believer to be what he ought to be. In fact, such a Believer is living in a state of sin, and no matter how hard he struggles to be otherwise. That's what Paul was talking about when he said:

> **"For the good that I would I do not** *(if I depend on self, and not the Cross)*: **but the evil which I would not** *(don't want to do)*, **that I do** *(which is exactly what every Believer will do no matter how hard he tries to do otherwise, if he tries to live this life outside of the Cross [Gal. 2:20-21])*.
>
> **"Now if I do that I would not** *(which is exactly what will happen if the Believer tries to live this life outside of God's Prescribed Order)*, **it is no more I that do it, but sin** *(the sin nature)* **that dwells in me** *(this emphatically states that the Believer has a sin nature; in the original Greek Text, if it contains the definite article before the word 'sin' which originally did read 'the sin,' it is not speaking of acts of sin, but rather the sin nature or the evil nature; the idea is not getting rid of the sin nature, which actually cannot be done, but rather controlling it, which the Apostle has told us how to do in Rom., Chpts. 6 and 8; when the Trump sounds, we shall be changed and there will be no more sin nature [Rom. 8:23])*" **(Rom. 7:19-20).**

As stated, while it's imperative that every Believer go through the Seventh Chapter of Romans, still, it's not the Will of

God that the Believer remain there all of his life; unfortunately, that is the case with most modern Christians.

Not understanding God's Prescribed Order of Victory, it is *"Oh wretched man that I am . . ."* (Rom. 7:24).

GOD'S PRESCRIBED ORDER OF VICTORY

If it is possible to reduce the meaning of the New Covenant, which is the meaning of the Cross, down to the lowest, possible, common denominator, maybe the following will help:

FOCUS: The Lord Jesus Christ (Jn. 14:6).

OBJECT OF FAITH: The Cross of Christ (Rom. 6:1-14).

POWER SOURCE: The Holy Spirit (Rom. 8:1-2, 11).

RESULTS: Victory (Rom. 6:14).

Let's use the same formula now, but with a different direction.

FOCUS: Works

OBJECT OF FAITH: Performance

POWER SOURCE: self

RESULTS: Defeat!

Unfortunately, most of the Church world is functioning in the latter diagram instead of the former.

SIN AND SEPARATION FROM CHRIST

For the person who is truly a Believer, which means that such a person abhors sin, the fact of sin and failure will not separate such a person from the Lord. It will cause tremendous difficulties and problems, but it will never separate the Believer from the Lord Jesus Christ. If it did, there would not be any Believers left. The only thing that will separate one from Christ is for one to cease believing. As we have repeatedly stated, it's Faith in Christ and what He did for us at the Cross that got us in, and keeps us in; however, if the person ceases to believe in Christ and what He did at the Cross, one will then revert to an unsaved state. In fact, and as just stated, this is the one sin, and actually the only sin, that will separate a person from Christ (Heb. 6:4-6).

THE CROSS OF CHRIST

God's Answer for sin, and His only Answer for sin, is the Cross of Christ (Rom. 6:1-14; I Cor. 1:17-18; 2:2; Col. 2:14-15).

This means that the Cross was the only answer for the believing sinner coming to Christ, and the only answer for the Saint remaining in Christ. There is no other solution, because there need be no other solution.

Most Believers have at least a modicum of understanding as it regards the Cross of Christ respecting their Salvation. In fact, one of the greatest phrases ever uttered is, *"Jesus died for me!"* However, when it comes to the Cross of Christ as it refers to Sanctification, in other words, how we live for God on a daily basis; most Believers have no understanding whatsoever.

As we have stated, the Believer must understand the following:

• Jesus Christ is the source of all things that we receive from God (Col. 2:9).

• The Cross of Christ is the Means by which these things are received, which refers to everything from Salvation to Sanctification (Rom. 6:3-5; I Cor. 1:17-18; 2:2; Gal. 6:14).

• The Holy Spirit superintends all that is done (Rom. 8:1-2, 11).

• In other words, the Believer must understand that whatever needs to be done in our lives, we cannot do it ourselves. It is the Holy Spirit Alone Who can carry out that which is needed. He does so strictly on the basis of the Finished Work of Christ. This means that our Faith must be exclusively in Christ and what Christ did for us at the Cross. That being done, and continuing to be done, the Holy Spirit can then function within our hearts and lives developing us as He should. While the Bible does not teach sinless perfection, it most definitely does teach that sin is not to have dominion over us (Rom. 6:14).

ETERNAL SECURITY

Believers can have eternal security if they claim it on God's Terms, not on the terms of man. Thankfully, the Terms of our

Lord are not hard at all. In fact, Jesus said, *"My Yoke is easy, and My Burden is light"* (Mat. 11:30). Faith alone is required, but it must be Faith in the correct object, and that correct Object is *"Jesus Christ and Him Crucified"* (I Cor. 1:23).

"I can see far down the mountain,
"Where I've wandered many years,
"Often hindered on my journey,
"By the ghosts of doubts and fears.
"Broken vows and disappointments,
"Thickly strewn along the way,
"But the Spirit has led unerring,
"To the land I hold today."

CHAPTER TEN

What Is The Sin Nature?

QUESTION:

WHAT IS THE SIN NATURE?

ANSWER:

The sin nature is that which happened to Adam and Eve as a result of the Fall, and has come down to every human being from then until now. In other words, the very nature of Adam and Eve was that of sin, and is likewise of all who have followed thereafter.

Anyone and everyone who is not Born-Again, is ruled totally and completely by the sin nature. This means that everything they do, irrespective as to what it is, lends itself to sin. When the person comes to Christ, the sin nature is made dormant, meaning totally ineffective; however, if the Believer doesn't function according to God's Prescribed Order of Victory, which is the Cross of Christ, the Believer will find himself being ruled again in some manner by the sin nature.

THE SIXTH CHAPTER OF ROMANS

In the great Sixth Chapter of Romans, the Apostle Paul gives us God's Prescribed Order of Victory. He explains what that victory is, and he also explains the presence and potential of the sin nature.

Some sixteen times in this one Chapter the Apostle deals with the sin nature. One time, he uses the word *"sin"* in the capacity of acts of sin (Vs. 15).

In the original Greek which is the language in which the Apostle wrote this Epistle, some sixteen times he placed before the word *"sin"* what is referred to as the definite article, making it read *"the sin."* In the Fourteenth Verse where he said *"For sin shall not have dominion over you,"* he did not use the definite article, but he did use the word *"sin"* as a noun instead of a verb, which makes it mean the same thing, i.e., *"the sin nature."*

So starting with the Second Verse, he actually wrote, *"How shall we, who are dead to the sin, live any longer therein?"*

Why did the King James translators not place it exactly as the Apostle gave it to us?

I cannot answer that question. Perhaps, it reads clumsy in English, and they thereby left it out. Unfortunately, when most people read the Sixth Chapter or Romans, they think that Paul is speaking of acts of sin, which causes them to miss the entire point of what the Apostle is saying. As stated, he is dealing with the *"sin nature,"* or the *"evil nature."* The Book of Romans can be divided according to the following:

- **Romans 1: Paul addresses the Gentile world, and concludes it to be abysmally lost.**
- **Romans 1-2: Paul addresses the Jewish world, and puts it in the same category, which to say the least, did not endear him to the Jews.**
- **Romans 4-5: The Holy Spirit through the Apostle gives us the answer to this dilemma, which is Justification by Faith. Paul is at pains to proclaim the fact that works are out. It is all by Faith.**
- **Romans 6: Inasmuch as the Apostle has told the world how to be justified in Chapters 4 and 5, the Holy Spirit now tells Believers how to live for God. The first two Verses of the Chapter tell us the problem is *"sin."* Verses 3 through 5 tell us that the solution is *"the Cross of Christ,"* and only the Cross of Christ. As the Cross of Christ is the solution for the sinner, it is also the solution for the Saint. As Verses 3 through 5 tell us the answer is the Cross, the balance of the Chapter tells us that if we do not place our Faith exclusively in Christ and the Cross that the sin nature will rule within our lives.**
- **Chapter 7: This Chapter tells us what happens to the Believer when he is ruled by the sin nature. Unfortunately, every Believer has to go through Chapter 7 to one degree or the other. Most Believers, however, not understanding the Cross as it refers to Sanctification, remain in the Seventh Chapter all their lives. It's not a very pleasant place to be.**

• **Chapter 8: Someone has said that Chapter 6 gives us the *"mechanics"* of the Holy Spirit, which tells us how He works. Chapter 8 gives us the *"dynamics"* of the Holy Spirit, which tells us what He can do after we understand how He does it. This is the Chapter of Victory, where the Believer is meant to live, after he understands God's Prescribed Order given to us in the Sixth Chapter, which is the Cross of Christ.**

• **Chapters 9-11: Many people mistake these Chapters as pertaining to Prophecy. While they do contain some Prophecy, still that is not the objective of the Holy Spirit. The Holy Spirit through the Apostle is telling us that as Israel lost her way, because she rejected the Righteousness of Christ, and was, therefore, cut off, that the Church will be cut off as well, if we ignore God's Prescribed Order.**

• **Chapters 12-16: The Holy Spirit in these Chapters proclaims the practicality of everyday life and living for the Believer, after the Believer understands God's Prescribed Order, which again we state, is the Cross of Christ.**

THE SIXTH CHAPTER OF ROMANS IS THE PIVOT CHAPTER OF THE BIBLE

Virtually the entirety of the Bible is given over to telling Believers how to live for God. While, of course, information is given as to how the sinner is to be Saved and graphically so, virtually the entirety of the Sacred Text from Genesis 1:1 through Revelation 22:21 is given over to the *"why"* and *"how"* of living for God. Before Chapter 6, the summation of the entirety of the Word of God strains toward this one Chapter. Now that the Cross is historic, everything following in the Word of God strains back to that great Chapter. Unfortunately, most Believers little understand this all-important Chapter, or else have an improper view of what the Holy Spirit is saying through the Apostle. One might say the entirety of the Chapter is made up of telling the Believer how to have victory over the sin nature, which is through the Cross of Christ and the Cross of Christ alone.

GOD'S PRESCRIBED ORDER OF VICTORY

The following is copied directly from THE EXPOSITOR'S STUDY BIBLE. The first two Verses tell us that the problem is sin. Yes, even though we are now Believers and have been Born-Again, still, the problem is sin. In Verses 3 through 5 we are told, as previously stated, that the solution to the problem of sin, and the only solution, in fact, is the Cross of Christ. In these three Verses, we are told how the answer is in the Cross. In the Sixth Verse we are told if the Cross of Christ is the Object of our Faith, and continues to be the Object of our Faith, then the sin nature will be made ineffective. We quote:

> **"What shall we say then?** *(This is meant to direct attention to Rom. 5:20.)* **Shall we continue in sin, that Grace may abound?** *(Just because Grace is greater than sin doesn't mean that the Believer has a license to sin.)*
>
> **"God forbid** *(presents Paul's answer to the question, 'Away with the thought, let not such a thing occur')*. **How shall we, who are dead to sin** *(dead to the sin nature)*, **live any longer therein?** *(This portrays what the Believer is now in Christ.)*
>
> **"Know you not, that so many of us as were baptized into Jesus Christ** *(plainly says that this Baptism is into Christ and not water [I Cor. 1:17; 12:13; Gal. 3:27; Eph. 4:5; Col. 2:11-13])* **were baptized into His Death?** *(When Christ died on the Cross, in the Mind of God, we died with Him; in other words, He became our Substitute, and our identification with Him in His Death gives us all the benefits for which He died; the idea is that He did it all for us!)*
>
> **"Therefore we are buried with Him by baptism into death** *(not only did we die with Him, but we were buried with Him as well, which means that all the sin and transgression of the past were buried; when they put Him in the Tomb, they put all of our sins into that Tomb as well)*: **that like as Christ was raised up from the dead by the Glory**

of the Father, even so we also should walk in Newness of Life *(we died with Him, we were buried with Him, and His Resurrection was our Resurrection to a 'Newness of Life')*.

"For if we have been planted together *(with Christ)* **in the likeness of His Death** *(Paul proclaims the Cross as the instrument through which all Blessings come; consequently, the Cross must ever be the Object of our Faith, which gives the Holy Spirit latitude to work within our lives)*, **we shall be also *in the likeness* of *His* Resurrection** *(we can have the 'likeness of His Resurrection,' i.e., 'live this Resurrection Life,' only as long as we understand the 'likeness of His Death,' which refers to the Cross as the means by which all of this is done)*:

"Knowing this, that our old man is Crucified with *Him* *(all that we were before conversion)*, **that the body of sin might be destroyed** *(the power of sin broken)*, **that henceforth we should not serve sin** *(the guilt of sin is removed at conversion, because the sin nature no longer rules within our hearts and lives)*" **(Rom. 6:1-6).**

In a nutshell, that is God's Prescribed Order. It is the Cross of Christ, and by that, we are not speaking of a wooden beam. We are speaking of the benefits of the Cross, what Jesus did there, and did for all for us, which will never have to be repeated, amended, added to, or taken from. That's the reason that the Holy Spirit through Paul could refer to this Covenant as *"The Everlasting Covenant"* (Heb. 13:20).

HOW CAN THE SIN NATURE BE REVIVED IN THE BELIEVER, IF IT IS MADE INEFFECTIVE BY THE CROSS?

As the Sixth Verse tells us, the moment we were Saved, i.e., *"born again,"* the sin nature was unplugged so to speak. It was made totally ineffective. Whereas it had ruled us totally and completely before conversion, it is now made dormant. So, that

being the case, how is it the greatest problem for the Believer?

The problem is, the sin nature has revived, and how does that happen?

To which we have already alluded in this answer, when the believing sinner comes to Christ, he is made a new creation, with old things passing away, and all things becoming new (II Cor. 5:17). But very shortly after we were Saved, we failed in some way. In other words, we sinned! What it was, or what type of sin we committed, is relatively insignificant at the moment. The fact is we sinned.

When this happened, it shocked us. Being a new creation in Christ we now hate sin. So, in order that this thing not be repeated, whatever it might be, we set out to stop the reoccurrence. I think I can say without fear of contradiction, that every single time the new Believer sets about to stop the reoccurrence of the failure, we invariably rely on the flesh. In other words, we do not place our Faith in Christ and the Cross, and that mostly out of ignorance, but rather we try to devise ways and means which originate out of our own minds, or the mind of someone else, as to how to walk in victory. That's where the problem arises.

It's not the sin that we commit that causes a revival of the sin nature. It is rather the incorrect object of our Faith, which means that now we are committing spiritual adultery (Rom. 7:1-4), which means we greatly limit the Holy Spirit as to what He can do within our lives.

THE HOLY SPIRIT

The Believer must understand the following:

Whatever we need to be in Christ, our growing in Grace and the Knowledge of the Lord, the Fruit of the Spirit, etc., all must be done exclusively by the Holy Spirit. All of these grand things that we want to be, and we know we need to be, within our own ability and strength, within our own talents and education and motivation, we cannot bring to pass, and no matter how hard we try. This is a Work that only the Holy Spirit can do. But now we have a major problem.

We have placed our faith in something other than the Cross of Christ, and please remember the Cross of Christ is the only Object of Faith allowed by the Spirit.

The story of the Bible is the Story of Jesus Christ and Him Crucified. So, if we place our Faith in anything except the Cross of Christ, we are going outside of the Word of God. In other words, to a great degree we are doing the same thing that Cain did in the Fourth Chapter of Genesis, when he offered up the labor of his own hands, instead of the lamb which typified Christ. God did not accept it, as God could not accept it. And neither can He accept our faith being in something other than Christ and Him Crucified.

Now don't misunderstand, Christ is no longer on a Cross — that Work is finished completely. He is now at the Right Hand of the Father and, in fact, we, spiritually speaking, are seated with Him, or we are supposed to be (Eph. 2:6). We are speaking of the benefits of the Cross, for which Jesus died, and all the great things that were accomplished in the giving of Himself as the supreme Sacrifice, which was accepted by God in totality. As we have repeatedly stated, it was all for us. The moment we think we can obtain something from the Lord, or be what we ought to be outside of the Sacrificial, Atoning Work of Christ on the Cross, that's when we fail, and that's what causes the revival of the sin nature.

As stated, it was not our failure that caused its revival, but us placing our Faith in something other than Christ and the Cross. When that happens, by us placing our Faith in something other than the Cross, failure is guaranteed. It doesn't matter how hard we try, it doesn't matter how zealous we are, and it doesn't matter how consecrated we are. The failure will not only continue, but it will get worse and worse as time goes on, with the sin nature ruling our lives in some way. Yes, we are still Saved, even Spirit-filled, but no matter what, we simply cannot live for God victoriously, unless we understand the Victory of the Cross.

THE APOSTLE PAUL

The Believer should understand, that the Apostle Paul was Saved on the road to Damascus, having seen Christ and spoken with Him, even blinded by a Light from Heaven, and then filled with the Holy Spirit some three days later, as Ananias prayed for him, and then began to preach the Gospel of Jesus Christ, and irrespective of all of these great and wonderful things happening to him, he still couldn't live a victorious, overcoming, Christian life, victorious one might say, over the world, the flesh, and the Devil. Now, if Paul couldn't do it, how in the world do you think you can?

In Paul's defense, there was no one else at that time who knew or understood God's Prescribed Order as well. In fact, it was to the Apostle Paul that this great truth was given, which is the meaning of the New Covenant that was and is the meaning of the Cross (Gal. 1:1-12).

How long that Paul lived in this state of spiritual failure, as described for us in Romans, Chapter 7, we aren't told. But more than likely, it was several years. Listen to the Apostle. He said:

> **"For I was alive without the Law once** *(Paul is referring to himself personally and his conversion to Christ; the Law, he states, had nothing to do with that conversion; neither did it have anything to do with his life in Christ)***: but when the Commandment came** *(having just been Saved, and not understanding the Cross of Christ, he tried to live for God by keeping the Commandments through his own strength and power; in his defense, no one else at that time understood the Cross; in fact, the meaning of the Cross, which is actually the meaning of the New Covenant, would be given to Paul)***, sin revived** *(the sin nature will always, without exception, revive under such circumstances, which results in failure)***, and I died** *(he was not meaning that he physically died, as would be obvious, but that he died to the Commandment; in other words, he failed to obey no matter*

how hard he tried; let all Believers understand that if the Apostle Paul couldn't live for God in this manner, neither can you!)" **(Rom. 7:9).**

The entirety of the Seventh Chapter of Romans is a glimpse into Paul's life before this great truth was given to him. When the truth of the Cross was given to him Personally by Christ, and then Paul gave it to us in his fourteen Epistles, most definitely when he wrote these words he full well understood God's Prescribed Order, and was living victorious. We must take a lesson from him.

SINLESS PERFECTION?

The Bible doesn't teach sinless perfection. And anyone who thinks they are sinlessly perfect, should think about the Intercessory Work of Christ (Heb. 7:25). Christ intercedes for us (for Believers) in the matter of sin, twenty-four hours a day, seven days a week, in fact, never ceasing, simply because we need it. Whenever Believers, ignorantly or otherwise, are placing their faith in something other than the Cross of Christ, they are living in a state of sin, for this is rebellion against God and His Way. In fact, such individuals, who presently include almost the entirety of the modern Church, are living in a state of spiritual adultery (Rom. 7:1-4). Yes, they are Saved, and thank God they are. I remember the day that I lived in the same state. I did it in ignorance, but nevertheless, it was a state of rebellion against God and I suffered greatly for it, as all suffer greatly who live in such a state.

While the Bible doesn't teach sinless perfection, it does teach that *"sin is not to have dominion over us"* (Rom. 6:14), and that speaks of dominion by the sin nature.

DOMINION

The word *"dominion"* in the Greek is *"kurieno,"* and means

"to rule, to be lord of, to exercise lordship over." **This doesn't mean that the sin nature exercises lordship in every capacity, but in some way it does in some capacity, making this Christian experience far less than it is meant to be.**

So, if we do not subscribe to God's Prescribed Order, then the sin nature will have dominion over us. The tragedy is, the modern Church, understanding virtually nothing about the Cross of Christ as it refers to Sanctification, is, in fact, being dominated in some way by the sin nature. That refers to untold millions of Believers.

LAW OR GRACE

Romans 6:14 says:

"For sin shall not have dominion over you: for you are not under the Law, but under Grace."

The *"Law"* that Paul mentions here, can refer to the Law of Moses, or it can refer to religious laws that we devise presently, or someone else for that matter. In fact, the modern Church is full of religious laws. While these laws may be correct and good in their own way, they will not set the captive free, and will not give power to the Believer to live the life he should live. Paul also said this:

> **"I am Crucified with Christ** *(as the Foundation of all Victory; Paul, here, takes us back to Rom. 6:3-5)*: **nevertheless I live** *(have new life)*; **yet not I** *(not by my own strength and ability)*, **but Christ lives in me** *(by virtue of me dying with Him on the Cross, and being raised with Him in Newness of Life)*: **and the life which I now live in the flesh** *(my daily walk before God)* **I live by the Faith of the Son of God** *(the Cross is ever the Object of my Faith)*, **Who loved me, and gave Himself for me** *(which is the only way that I could be Saved)*.
>
> **"I do not frustrate the Grace of God** *(if we make anything other than the Cross of Christ the Object of our*

> *Faith, we frustrate the Grace of God, which means we stop its action, and the Holy Spirit will no longer help us)*: **for if Righteousness *come* by the Law** *(any type of Law)*, **then Christ is dead in vain.** *(If I can successfully live for the Lord by any means other than Faith in Christ and the Cross, then the Death of Christ was a waste)*" **(Gal. 2:20-21).**

In the Twenty-first Verse just quoted, we are clearly and plainly told that we can achieve nothing by trying to formulate and obey religious laws. How much clearer does it need to be!

SANCTIFICATION

Showing us the conflict between the sin nature and our regenerated spirit, the great Apostle also said:

> **"Let not sin** *(the sin nature)* **therefore reign** *(rule)* **in your mortal body** *(showing that the sin nature can once again rule in the heart and life of the Believer, if the Believer doesn't constantly look to Christ and the Cross; the 'mortal body' is neutral, which means it can be used for Righteousness or unrighteousness)*, **that you should obey it in the lusts thereof** *(ungodly lusts are carried out through the mortal body, if Faith is not maintained in the Cross [I Cor. 1:17-18])*.
>
> **"Neither yield you your members** *(of your mortal body)* ***as* instruments of unrighteousness unto sin** *(the sin nature)*: **but yield yourselves unto God** *(we are to yield ourselves to Christ and the Cross; that alone guarantees victory over the sin nature)*, **as those who are alive from the dead** *(we have been raised with Christ in 'Newness of Life')*, **and your members *as* instruments of Righteousness unto God** *(this can be done only by virtue of the Cross and our Faith in that Finished Work, and Faith which continues in that Finished Work from day-to-day [Lk. 9:23-24])*" **(Rom. 6:12-13).**

Sadly, this Truth, the Truth of Victory over the sin nature,

which is one of the most important, found in the Word of God, is little known by most modern Believers. As a result, they are consigned to live a life far less than intended.

If you will place your Faith exclusively in Christ and the Cross, and do so constantly, while Satan will definitely not quit knocking on your door, still, victory will be yours, and in totality, and permanently *"and you shall know the Truth, and the Truth shall make you free"* (Jn. 8:32).

CHAPTER ELEVEN

What Does It Mean To "Fall From Grace"?

QUESTION:

WHAT DOES IT MEAN TO "FALL FROM GRACE"?

ANSWER:

***"Christ is become of no effect unto you, whosoever of you are justified by the Law; you are fallen from Grace"* (Gal. 5:4).**

A PERSONAL ILLUSTRATION

Sometime back I happened to view a program over Television consisting of several Preachers, who strangely enough were discussing another Preacher who had had some difficulties, but who was not present. They surmised the sin that he committed, meant that he had fallen from Grace. They all concurred! Some of these Preachers were household names, but with some of them I was not acquainted. But yet, the striking thing about this is, every single one of those Preachers sitting on that dais that day addressing the subject, were themselves at that very time *"fallen from Grace."*

How did I know that?

Was I intimately acquainted with all of these men?

As stated, I only knew a couple of them, and with the others I was not acquainted at all. So how can I be so sure of my statement?

The very thing that brings one into the Grace of God and keeps one in the Grace of God, of that, none of these Preachers were aware. If they did have understanding of that of which I speak, they most definitely would have addressed the subject very readily. They didn't, because they simply did not know God's Prescribed Order of Life and Living.

WHAT IS THE GRACE OF GOD?

I suppose that Grace is addressed in the lexicon of Christian

terminology as much and maybe more than anything else. But yet, most Believers simply do not have a correct understanding as to what Grace is, hence, the reason for the fallen condition for the Preachers in question.

The Grace of God is simply, the *"Goodness of God"* extended to undeserving Believers. It's not something that one can earn, not something that one can merit, not something that is readily available, except on God's terms. And that is critical!

Everything that Believers receive from the Lord comes in the form of a gift. God has nothing for sale! Neither can anything be earned in any way or manner. It is all under the heading of a gift, and is readily available if we meet God's Conditions. And I might quickly add, those conditions are very simple, and can be met by anyone at any time.

THE CROSS OF CHRIST

Some time back I was handed a book of approximately a hundred pages in length on the Grace of God. I read it, hurriedly I might add, and found that the Brother, even though he said some good things about Grace, made no mention at all of the Cross of Christ. Please understand the following:

Jesus Christ is the Source of all things that we receive from God, and the Cross is the Means by which these things are received, all superintended by the Holy Spirit (Rom. 8:2). In other words, it is the Cross of Christ that makes the Grace of God possible to all who meet God's Conditions.

THE CONDITION FOR RECEIVING THE GRACE OF GOD

If you'll notice the word *"condition"* is in the singular, meaning there is really only one condition. That one condition is Faith; however, for it to be Faith that God will recognize, it must without fail be exclusively in the Cross of Christ. And that is why I said those Preachers mentioned at the beginning

of this article were all *"fallen from Grace."* I realize that's quite a statement, but I know it to be true. In fact, all of these men claimed great Faith; however, it was a nebulous faith that the Lord will not recognize, which is par for the course, regrettably, for most Christians. The Lord only recognizes Faith that is exclusively in Christ and what He did for us at the Cross. We keep going back to the statement that Jesus Christ is the Source, while the Cross is the Means that we receive all things, with the Holy Spirit being the Superintendent. Listen to Paul, and I quote from THE EXPOSITOR'S STUDY BIBLE:

"For Christ sent me not to baptize *(presents to us a Cardinal Truth)*, **but to preach the Gospel** *(the manner in which one may be saved from sin)*: **not with wisdom of words** *(intellectualism is not the Gospel)*, **lest the Cross of Christ should be made of none effect.** *(This tells us in no uncertain terms that the Cross of Christ must always be the emphasis of the Message.)*

"For the preaching *(Word)* **of the Cross is to them who perish foolishness** *(Spiritual things cannot be discerned by unredeemed people, but that doesn't matter; the Cross must be preached just the same, even as we shall see)*; **but unto us who are Saved it is the Power of God.** *(The Cross is the Power of God simply because it was there that the total sin debt was paid, giving the Holy Spirit, in Whom the Power resides, latitude to work mightily within our lives)*" **(I Cor. 1:17-18).**

The great Apostle then said:

"I, Brethren, when I came to you, came not with excellency of speech or of wisdom *(means that he depended not on oratorical abilities, nor did he delve into philosophy, which was all the rage of that particular day)*, **declaring unto you the Testimony of God** *(which is Christ and Him Crucified)*.

"For I determined not to know any thing among you *(with purpose and design, Paul did not resort to the knowledge or philosophy of the world regarding the preaching of the Gospel)*, **save Jesus Christ, and Him Crucified** *(that and that alone is the Message which will save the sinner, set the captive free, and give the Believer perpetual victory)*" **(I Cor. 2:1-2).**

And finally:

"But God forbid that I should glory *(boast)*, **save in the Cross of our Lord Jesus Christ** *(what the opponents of Paul sought to escape at the price of insincerity is the Apostle's only basis of exultation)*, **by Whom the world is Crucified unto me, and I unto the world.** *(The only way we can overcome the world, and I mean the only way, is by placing our Faith exclusively in the Cross of Christ and keeping it there)*" **(Gal. 6:14).**

FRUSTRATING THE GRACE OF GOD

Paul also said:

"I am Crucified with Christ *(as the Foundation of all Victory; Paul, here, takes us back to Rom. 6:3-5)*: **nevertheless I live** *(have new life)*; **yet not I** *(not by my own strength and ability)*, **but Christ lives in me** *(by virtue of me dying with Him on the Cross, and being raised with Him in Newness of Life)*: **and the life which I now live in the flesh** *(my daily walk before God)* **I live by the Faith of the Son of God** *(the Cross is ever the Object of my Faith)*, **Who loved me, and gave Himself for me** *(which is the only way that I could be Saved)*.

"I do not frustrate the Grace of God *(if we make anything other than the Cross of Christ the Object of our Faith, we frustrate the Grace of God, which means we stop*

> *its action, and the Holy Spirit will no longer help us)*: **for if Righteousness *come* by the Law** *(any type of Law)*, **then Christ is dead in vain.** *(If I can successfully live for the Lord by any means other than Faith in Christ and the Cross, then the Death of Christ was a waste)*" **(Gal. 2:20-21).**

When the Believer places his Faith in anything other than Christ and Him Crucified, such serves to frustrate the Grace of God.

The word *"frustrate"* in the Greek is *"atheteo,"* and means *"to set aside, to neutralize or violate, to bring to naught, to reject."*

In the last several decades, the modern church has all but abandoned the Cross. While the Cross is still the emblem of Christianity so to speak and rightly so, still, the Salvation experience respecting the Cross is about the limit of the understanding of most. As it regards Sanctification, in other words, how we live for God, most people don't have a clue as to how the Cross plays into this. Listen to our Lord:

TAKING UP THE CROSS DAILY

Jesus said:

> **"And He said to *them* all, If any *man* will come after Me** *(the criteria for Discipleship)*, **let him deny himself** *(not asceticism as many think, but rather that one denies one's own willpower, self-will, strength, and ability, depending totally on Christ)*, **and take up his cross** *(the benefits of the Cross, looking exclusively to what Jesus did there to meet our every need)* **daily** *(this is so important, our looking to the Cross; that we must renew our Faith in what Christ has done for us, even on a daily basis, for Satan will ever try to move us away from the Cross as the Object of our Faith, which always spells disaster)*, **and follow Me** *(Christ can be followed only by the Believer looking to the Cross, understanding what it accomplished, and by that means*

alone [Rom. 6:3-5, 11, 14; 8:1-2, 11; I Cor. 1:17-18, 21, 23; 2:2; Gal. 6:14; Eph. 2:13-18; Col. 2:14-15]).

"For whosoever will save his life shall lose it *(try to live one's life outside of Christ and the Cross)***: but whosoever will lose his life for My sake, the same shall save it** *(when we place our Faith entirely in Christ and the Cross, looking exclusively to Him, we have just found 'more abundant life' [Jn. 10:10])***" (Lk. 9:23-24).**

Jesus as well said:

"And whosoever does not bear his Cross *(this doesn't speak of suffering as most think, but rather ever making the Cross of Christ the Object of our Faith; we are Saved and we are victorious not by suffering, although that sometimes will happen, or any other similar things, but rather by our Faith, but always with the Cross of Christ as the Object of that Faith)***, and come after Me** *(one can follow Christ only by Faith in what He has done for us at the Cross; He recognizes nothing else)***, cannot be My Disciple** *(the statement is emphatic! if it's not Faith in the Cross of Christ, then it's faith that God will not recognize, which means that such people are refused [I Cor. 1:17-18, 21, 23; 2:2; Rom. 6:3-14; 8:1-2, 11, 13; Gal. 6:14; Eph. 2:13-18; Col. 2:14-15])***" (Lk. 14:27).**

Almost all of the Bible is given over to telling us how to live for God. It was to the Apostle Paul that the meaning of the New Covenant was given by our Lord, and Paul gave it to us in his fourteen Epistles. As well, virtually the entirety of the content of these Epistles is, as we've just said, given over to telling us how to live a victorious, overcoming, Christian life. Understanding that, we should know and realize how important this is. In the center of all this is the Lord Jesus Christ (Jn. 1:1-2). The only way to Christ is through the Cross. One might say it in the following manner:

• The only way to God is through Jesus Christ (Jn. 14:6).

• The only way to Jesus Christ is through the Cross (Rom. 6:3-5).

• The only way to the Cross is an abnegation of self (Lk. 9:23).

TO SUM UP . . .

• When one falls from Grace, this stops most of the action of the Holy Spirit on our behalf (Rom. 8:2).

• One falls from Grace by placing one's faith in something other than the Cross of Christ. And no matter how beneficial the *"something"* might be in its own right, this is Faith that God will not recognize (Gal. 5:1-4).

• The Holy Spirit works entirely within the framework of the Finished Work of Christ. What Jesus did there, gives Him the legal right to carry forth His Mission, without which He is greatly hindered (I Cor. 1:18).

CHAPTER TWELVE
Is Tithing In The New Covenant?

QUESTION:

IS TITHING IN THE NEW COVENANT?

ANSWER:

The Truth is, tithing was and is in every Covenant.

THE SACRIFICE OF ABEL

"And Abel, he also brought of the firstlings of his flock and of the fat thereof. And the LORD had respect unto Abel and to his offering" **(Gen. 4:4).**

The word *"firstlings,"* refers to the firstborn of the flock that was offered in sacrifice, which, no doubt, the Lord instructed Abel to do.

Established with the First Family, and constituted when Israel became a Nation, God established the principle that every firstborn male belonged to the Lord (Ex. 13:2-15). As well, the firstborn male clean animals were sacrificed to the Lord also; the firstborn son of the family was redeemed. The picture is a beautiful one. As it regards man, God exercised the right of ownership, but He did not do it by killing, but instead, by giving life. All of this was a Type of God's Firstborn, so to speak, the Lord Jesus Christ, Who, in fact, He would give in sacrifice. So, Abel was instructed to use a firstborn of his flock as a sacrifice, which would picture the Lord Jesus Christ and, as well, was a picture of tithing.

God must come first in all things in our lives, and that refers to our financial resources as well.

Jesus said:

> **"Therefore take no thought** *(don't worry)***, saying, What shall we eat? or, What shall we drink? or, Wherewithal shall we be clothed?** *(The Greek Text actually means that even one anxious thought is forbidden. Such shows a*

distrust of the Lord.)

"(For after all these things do the Gentiles seek:) *(Gentiles had no part in God's Covenant with Israel; consequently, they had no part in God's Economy, and, basically, had to fend for themselves)* **for your Heavenly Father knows that you have need of all these things** *(the phrase is meant to express the contrast between those who do not know the Lord and those who do; if we live for Him, ever seeking His Will, we have the guarantee of His Word, which He will provide for us; is God's Word good enough? I think it is!)*.

"But seek you first the Kingdom of God, and His Righteousness *(this gives the 'condition' for God's Blessings; His interests are to be 'first')*; **and all these things shall be added unto you** *(this is the 'guarantee' of God's Provision)*.

"Take therefore no thought for the morrow *(don't worry about the future)*: **for the morrow shall take thought for the things of itself** *(this is meant to refer back to Verse 27)*. **Sufficient unto the day *is* the evil thereof** *(this means that we should handle daily difficulties in Faith, and have Faith for the future that the present difficulties will not grow into larger ones; we have God's assurance that they won't, that is, if we will sufficiently believe Him)*" **(Mat. 6:31:34).**

So, the Law of the *"firstling"* or firstborn applies to our finances as well, which, of course, includes tithing, *"seek ye first the Kingdom of God. . . ."*

TITHING

The first mention of Tithing in the Bible is found with Abraham. This is extremely important Scripturally for the simple reason that it was to Abraham that the Lord gave the great meaning of *"Justification by Faith."* In other words, the

Abrahamic Covenant, which is Justification by Faith, comes down to us presently, which in a sense makes us children of Abraham. We will look at tithing first and I quote from THE EXPOSITOR'S STUDY BIBLE:

> **"And the king of Sodom went out to meet him** *(Abraham)* **after his return from the slaughter of Chedorlaomer, and of the kings who were with him, at the Valley of Shaveh, which is the king's dale.** *(As we shall see here, there is no time so dangerous to the Christian as the morrow after a great Spiritual Victory.)*
>
> **"And Melchizedek** *(this man appears on the scene, who is a King and a Priest and, above all, who is a Type of Christ [Ps. 110:4; Heb. 5:5-6]; some Scholars believe that Melchizedek could actually have been Shem, the son of Noah; Shem was alive at this time, and actually lived for about 60 years more; in fact, some think he died when Abraham was about 150 years of age; his name means, 'King of Righteousness' and 'King of Peace' [Heb. 7:2])* **king of Salem** *(Jerusalem)* **brought forth bread and wine** *(the 'bread and wine' symbolize the broken Body and shed Blood of our Lord, which was necessary for the Salvation of mankind [Mat. 26:29; Mk., Chpt. 14; Lk. 22:15; Rom. 8:21])*: **and he was the Priest of the Most High God.** *(Melchizedek, as a Priest, symbolized the coming Christ, Who is our Great High Priest [Heb. 7:15-17]. David prophesied, about a thousand years after Abraham, 'The Lord has sworn, and will not repent, You [Christ] are a Priest forever after the order of Melchizedek' [Ps. 110:4]. Abraham is here introduced to God by a different name than he had previously known, 'El Elyon,' meaning 'Most High God.')*
>
> **"And he** *(Melchizedek)* **blessed him** *(Abraham)*, **and said, Blessed be Abram of the Most High God, Possessor of heaven and Earth:** *(Melchizedek blessing Abraham means that the standing of Melchizedek was greater than*

that of Abraham. The reason? Melchizedek was a Type of Christ [Heb. 7:4, 7].)

"And blessed be the Most High God, Who has delivered your enemies into your hand. *(We find here that Melchizedek did not come forth when Abraham was in pursuit of Chedorlaomer, but when the king of Sodom was in pursuit of Abraham. This makes a great moral difference. Mackintosh says: 'A deeper character of communion was needed to meet the deeper character of conflict.')* **And he gave him tithes of all.** *(This is the first time that 'tithes' are mentioned in Scripture. It refers to a tenth part. Abraham paid tithe to Melchizedek, who was a Type of Christ; consequently, Abraham's children, who make up the Church presently, are to continue to pay tithe to those carrying out the Work of God)***" (Gen. 14:17-20).**

CHILDREN OF ABRAHAM

As we have stated, the Abrahamic Covenant, which is Justification by Faith, presents God's Means and Method of Regeneration. We are justified in the sight of God, Whose Sight alone matters, strictly by Faith, which refers to the believing sinner having Faith in Christ and what Christ did for us at the Cross. As should be understandable, that was and is God's Means and Method of Redemption, which meaning was given to Abraham, and which remains His Standard of Righteousness presently, and ever shall remain His Standard. It and it alone is the means of Salvation.

Concerning this, Paul said:

"Even as Abraham believed God *(proclaims the fact that the Patriarch was justified by Faith, not works)*, **and it was accounted to him for Righteousness.** *(The Righteousness of God is imputed to a person only on the basis of Faith in Christ, and what Christ has done at the Cross [Jn. 8:56].)*

> **"Know you therefore that they which are of Faith** *(presents Faith, and Faith alone, as the foundation; but the Object of Faith must ever be the Cross)*, **the same are the children of Abraham** *(the legitimate sons of Abraham)*.
>
> **"And the Scripture, foreseeing that God would justify the heathen through Faith** *(proclaims the Word of God as the Foundation of all Things)*, **Preached before the Gospel unto Abraham,** ***saying*****, In you shall the nations be blessed** *(Gen. 12:1-3)*.
>
> **"So then they** *(whomsoever they might be)* **which be of Faith** *(in Christ and the Cross)* **are blessed with Faithful Abraham.** *(He received Justification by Faith, and so do we!)*" **(Gal. 3:6-9).**

Inasmuch as we presently are Children of Abraham, and because of the Doctrine of Justification by Faith, as Abraham paid tithe to Melchizedek who was a Type of Christ, likewise, we presently as Believers must pay tithe to those who are carrying out the Work of Christ.

Where did Abraham learn about tithing?

It's quite possible that the Lord revealed such to him; however, there is also the possibility, that the principal of tithing was handed down to the First Family, and practiced by Abel and, as well, was practiced by the few people who lived for God from the time of Abel to the time of Abraham, a time span of nearly 2,000 years.

JACOB

We hear of tithing again as it regards Jacob, the grandson of Abraham. I quote again from THE EXPOSITOR'S STUDY BIBLE:

> **"And Jacob awaked out of his sleep, and he said, Surely the LORD is in this place; and I knew it not** *(for the first time, the Lord reveals Himself to Jacob; this is the*

*night that Jacob was 'born from above'; all of this tells us that all hopes of the flesh must die before the Spirit can properly be revealed to us)***.**

"And he was afraid, and said, How dreadful is this place! this is none other but the House of God, and this is the Gate of Heaven *(could be translated, 'How all-inspiring is this place!'; the 'Gate of Heaven' is Jesus Christ)***.**

"And Jacob rose up early in the morning, and took the stone that he had put for his pillows, and set it up for a pillar, and poured oil upon the top of it *(the 'stone' is a Type of Christ, with the 'oil' serving as a symbol of the Holy Spirit; no doubt, he was inspired by the Lord to do this)***.**

"And he called the name of that place Beth-el: but the name of that city was called Luz at the first *('Beth-el' means 'House of God'; 'Luz' means 'separation'; the Lord can turn 'Luz' into the 'House of God,' only as the Believer is separated from the world)***.**

"And Jacob vowed a vow *(the first recorded vow in the Bible)***, saying, If God be with me** *(should read, 'Since God be with me')***, and will keep me in this way that I go, and will give me bread to eat, and raiment to put on,**

"So that I come again to my father's house in peace *(free from Esau's avenging threats)***; then shall the LORD be my God:**

"And this stone *(representing Christ)***, which I have set for a pillar, shall be God's House** *(all of this sets the stage for the Holy Spirit making the Believer His Sanctuary; it was all made possible by the Cross [Jn. 14:16-20])***: and of all that You shall give me I will surely give the tenth unto you.** *(This obviously means that Jacob gave a tenth of his vast herds of sheep and cattle to the Lord as a Sacrifice. If that, in fact, was the case, we now find Jacob offering up Sacrifices to a degree as no one else. If the tithe which we propose to give to the Lord doesn't advance the grand Message of 'Jesus Christ and Him Crucified' [I Cor. 1:23; 2:2], then we actually aren't really* *paying tithe. The first occasion of tithing mentioned in the Bible was when Abraham paid tithes to Melchizedek, who was a Type of Christ as our Great High Priest. Jesus would become this by dying on the Cross as a Sacrifice [14:18-20]. So both occasions of paying tithes speak to the Cross)*" **(Gen. 28:16-22).**

TITHING IN THE LAW

Actually, under the Law, Israel was required to give to the Lord not merely a tenth, but rather twenty-three and a third percent of their income. It was as follows:

- ***"You shall truly tithe all the increase of your seed, that the field brings forth year by year"* (Deut. 14:22).**
- ***"And the Levite that is within your gates; you shall not forsake him; for he has no part nor inheritance with you"* (Deut. 14:27).**

The first tithe was for the Levites, which included the Priests, as it regarded their service to the Tabernacle. In fact, this was their only means of support (Lev., Chpt. 27; Num., Chpt. 18). This ten percent was to be paid on a constant basis.

- ***"And if the way be too long for you, so that you are not able to carry it; or if the place be too far from you, which the LORD your God shall choose to set His Name there, when the LORD Your God has blessed you:***

***"Then shall you turn it into money, and bind up the money in your hand, and shall go unto the place where the LORD your God shall choose"* (Deut. 14:24-25).**

The Lord as well, ordered that Israel deduct ten percent of their income and for it to be laid aside as it regarded their expenses concerning the Feast's, which they were required to attend each year. There were three national Feasts, which took place in April, June, and October. In fact, a representative male of every household was required to attend. Many times, the entire family went. This was so important that the Lord demanded that Israel lay aside ten percent of their income in

order to pay these expenses in traveling to and fro to these Feasts, so they would have no excuse.

- ***"At the end of three years you shall bring forth all the tithe of your increase the same year, and shall lay it up within your gates:***

***"And the Levite, (because he has no part nor inheritance with you,) and the stranger, and the fatherless, and the widow, which are within your gates, shall come, and shall eat and be satisfied; that the LORD your God may bless you in all the work of your hand which you do"* (Deut. 14:28-29).**

This was the third tithe that was required, but was to actually only be given every third year. In other words, instead of ten percent a year as the other two tithes this one was only three and a third percent a year, totaling ten percent at the end of three years. It was to be given to the poor and needy, and was actually a part of God's Welfare Plan.

So, twenty-three and a third percent was required by the Lord under the Law for His People Israel — ten percent to provide for the Priesthood, ten percent to cover the person's expenses in attending the Feasts, then three and a third each year for the poor.

UNDER THE NEW COVENANT

Tithing under the New Covenant, as we have stated, comes to us by the means of Abraham, because we are children of Abraham.

If Abraham's children paid tithe, and such is proven by the experience of Jacob, we as the children of Abraham are to do likewise.

Many Believers have it in their mind that tithing originated with the Law. And inasmuch as the Law of Moses has been fulfilled in Christ, then tithing is no more incumbent upon modern Believers.

In the first place, and as we have proven, tithing did not begin with the Law, but probably at the very beginning of time, and was spelled out clearly under Abraham.

Under the Law, the care for the Priests, and the upkeep of the Temple were done so by Tithe. Unfortunately, at times, Israel was not too faithful.

Presently, and I speak of the New Covenant, the Priesthood is no more, that being replaced by the Ministry (Eph. 4:11). Our task now, as well, is not the Temple, for there is no Temple as such under the New Covenant, but rather, the taking of the Gospel to the world. Jesus said:

> **"Go you therefore** *(applies to any and all who follow Christ, and in all ages)*, **and teach all nations** *(should have been translated, 'and preach to all nations,' for the word 'teach' here refers to a proclamation of truth)*, **baptizing them in the Name of the Father, and of the Son, and of the Holy Spirit** *(presents the only formula for Water Baptism given in the Word of God)*:
>
> **"Teaching them** *(means to give instruction)* **to observe all things** *(the whole Gospel for the whole man)* **whatsoever I have commanded you** *(not a suggestion)*: **and, lo, I am with you always** *(it is I, Myself, God, and Man, Who am — not 'will be' — hence, forever present among you, and with you as Companion, Friend, Guide, Saviour, God)*, ***even*** **unto the end of the world** *(should have been translated 'age')*. **Amen** *(it is the guarantee of My Promise)*" **(Mat. 28:19-20).**

And as someone has well said, the Gospel of Jesus Christ and Him Crucified can only go as far as the dollar takes it.

WHERE TO TITHE

Unfortunately, most of the giving presently goes to that which is really not the Gospel of Jesus Christ, but something else altogether. So we must not only be faithful to give to the Work of God, but, as well, give to where the true Work of God is actually being carried out, which refers to the Message of

the Cross. The Holy Spirit through Paul emphatically states this. The Church at Philippi had sent Paul a generous offering while he was in prison in Rome, the offering, incidentally, which he, no doubt, desperately needed. So, in the letter he wrote to the Church at Philippi, thanking them for their offering, he said the following:

> **"Not because I desire a gift** *(presents the Apostle defending himself against the slanderous assertion that he is using the Gospel as a means to make money)*: **but I desire fruit that may abound to your account.** *(God keeps a record of everything, even our gifts, whether giving or receiving.)*
>
> **"But I have all, and abound: I am full** *(proclaims the fact that the Philippian gift must have been generous)*, **having received of Epaphroditus the things *which were sent* from you** *(Epaphroditus had brought the gift from Philippi to Rome)*, **an odour of a sweet smell** *(presents the Old Testament odors of the Levitical Sacrifices, all typifying Christ)*, **a Sacrifice acceptable, well-pleasing to God.** *(For those who gave to Paul, enabling him to take the Message of the Cross to others, their gift, and such gifts presently, are looked at by God as a part of the Sacrificial Atoning Work of Christ on the Cross. Nothing could be higher than that!)*
>
> **"But my God shall supply all your need** *(presents the Apostle assuring the Philippians, and all other Believers as well, that they have not impoverished themselves in giving so liberally to the cause of Christ)* **according to His Riches in Glory** *(the measure of supply will be determined by the wealth of God in Glory)* **by Christ Jesus** *(made possible by the Cross)*" **(Phil. 4:17-19).**

The true Gospel of Jesus Christ is, *"Jesus Christ and Him Crucified"* (I Cor. 1:23). This is the Gospel that must be supported. Anything else is of little consequence.

THE BLESSINGS OF TITHING

The old adage *"you can't outgive God,"* to be sure, is one hundred percent true.

The worst thing that a Christian can do, when finances are tight, and he's wondering how in the world he's going to pay all the bills, is to say in his heart, *"I cannot afford to give anything to the Lord this month,"* etc. That is a big, big mistake.

When the Holy Spirit was to give a dissertation on *"giving,"* as it regards the Work of God to the Early Church, through Paul he used as an example the poorest Churches of all, those in Macedonia. The following is what Paul said:

> **"Moreover, Brethren, we do you to witness of the Grace of God bestowed on the Churches of Macedonia** *(northern Greece)***;**
>
> **"How that in a great trial of affliction** *(Macedonia was greatly impoverished due to political and military problems)* **the abundance of their joy and their deep poverty abounded unto the riches of their liberality.** *(Despite their deep poverty, they gave liberally to the Work of God.)*
>
> **"For to *their* power, I bear record** *(Paul knew their financial circumstances)***, yes, and beyond *their* power *they were* willing of themselves** *(they gave beyond what it seemed they could give)***;**
>
> **"Praying us with much entreaty that we would receive the gift** *(knowing their impoverished circumstances, Paul didn't want to take the gift, but they insisted)***, and *take upon us* the fellowship of the Ministering to the Saints.** *(Paul was receiving an Offering from all the Churches for the poor Saints at Jerusalem.)*
>
> **"And *this they did*** *(gave far beyond what seemed to be their ability)***, not as we hoped** *(meaning much greater than he had hoped)***, but first gave their own selves to the Lord** *(this means it was the Will of the Lord for them to do*

> *what they did)*, **and unto us by the Will of God.** *(They had great confidence in Paul and his Ministry. As we see here, the Holy Spirit used Macedonia as an example)*" **(II Cor. 8:1-5).**

The Holy Spirit used these impoverished Churches as an example, and for reason. It addresses itself perfectly to the Christian who thinks he cannot afford to give to God. My advice is whatever else we have to take off the list, above all, put the Lord first. This is the only way to get out of debt, to get one's feet on solid financial footing, put God first. Tithing should be a minimum, with offerings given on top of that as we are able to do so, or else the Lord speaks to us about a certain amount.

Paul then wrote:

> **"But this** ***I say,*** **He which sows sparingly shall reap also sparingly** *(if we give little to the Lord, He will bless little)*; **and he which sows bountifully shall reap also bountifully.** *(If we give bountifully, He will bless bountifully. This is a Promise of the Lord)*" **(II Cor. 9:6).**

I cannot help but believe that the Lord blessed the Macedonians abundantly.

But there is something else about this that we must understand.

It's not necessarily the amount that one gives, but it's how much we have left. There are some people who could only give $25 in today's money, but to God it is a bountiful amount, and simply because they don't have much. And there are others who give $1,000 and it's an insult to the Lord because He has blessed them abundantly so, and yet they aren't reciprocating.

Jesus called attention to a poor widow by saying the following:

> **"And He looked up** *(our Lord was in the covered colonnade of that part of the Temple which was open to*

the Jewish women; here was the treasury with its thirteen boxes on the wall, where the people could give offerings), **and saw the rich men casting their gifts into the treasury** *(implying that they were making a show of their gifts, desiring to impress the people by the amount, etc.)*.

"And He saw also a certain poor widow casting in thither two mites *(was probably worth something less than a U.S. dollar in 2003 purchasing power)*.

"And He said, Of a truth I say unto you *(presents a new concept of giving)*, **that this poor widow has cast in more than they all** *(the term 'poor widow' means that she worked very hard for what little she received)*:

"For all these have of their abundance cast in unto the offerings of God *(means that they had much left, constituting very little given, at least in the Eyes of God)*: **but she of her penury** *(poverty)* **has cast in all the living that she had** *(spoke of her gift, as small as it was, being larger than all others combined because she gave all; God judges our giving by many factors; motive plays very heavily into the account)*" **(Lk. 21:1-4).**

PAUL AND TITHE

Even though the statement we will now give, as it regards Paul, is not directly about tithing but rather the superiority of the New Covenant over the Old, still, the point is made regarding tithing continuing under the New Covenant.

I believe that Paul wrote Hebrews. He said:

"But he *(Melchisedec)* **whose descent is not counted from them** *(from Israel)* **received Tithes of Abraham, and blessed him who had the Promises.** *(This proclaims the fact that Melchisedec blessed Abraham, despite the fact that it was Abraham to whom the great Promises of God had been given. The only way one could be greater than Abraham is that he would be a Type of Christ, which*

Melchisedec was.)

"And without all contradiction *(means that what he is saying cannot be contradicted)* **the less** *(Abraham)* **is blessed of the better** *(Melchisedec, who was a Type of Christ; this has Paul saying that Christ is better than any other system, and is the only One Who can properly Bless)*.

"And here men who die receive Tithes *(refers to the Levitical Priesthood, which, in fact, was still being carried on at the time Paul wrote these words)*; **but there he *receives them*** *(refers back to the Passage in Genesis where Melchisedec is recorded as having received Tithes)*, **of whom it is witnessed that he lives.** *(This refers to the Eternal Priesthood of Christ, of which Melchisedec was the Type.)*

"And as I may so say, Levi also, who receives Tithes *(because Tithes were paid to Levi, i.e., 'the Priestly Order,' in no way means this was the superior Order)*, **paid Tithes in Abraham.** *(This struck a telling blow in Paul's argument regarding the superiority of the Priestly Order of Melchisedec. If Abraham paid Tithes to Melchisedec [which he was instructed by the Lord to do], and Abraham is the father of the Jewish people [meaning Levi was in his loins], then Levi also paid Tithes to Melchisedec. This placed the whole of the Jewish system as second to that of Christ.)*

"For he *(Levi)* **was yet in the loins of his father** *(Abraham)*, **when Melchisedec met him.** *(This makes the New Covenant better than the Old, which is the argument of the Book of Hebrews)*" **(Heb. 7:6-10).**

CHAPTER THIRTEEN

What Does The Term "Church Government" Mean?

QUESTION:

WHAT DOES THE TERM "CHURCH GOVERNMENT" MEAN?

ANSWER:

The word *"government"* regarding civil functions means, *"the continuous exercise of authority over and the performance of functions for a political unit."*

It also means, *"the organization, machinery, or agency through which a political unit exercises authority and performs functions and which is usually classified according to the distribution of power within it."*

Of course, this relates to civil government, but the word *"government"* would basically mean the same in Church administration. God ordained Civil Government (Rom. 13:1-7), and He also ordains Church Government (I Cor. 12:28); however, that is where the similarity ends. Civil government is guided and directed by man, while Church Government is guided and directed by God — at least that's the way it should be. Too often Civil Government is guided by demon spirits and, too often Church Government is guided by men — with Jesus Christ treated as a passive Head instead of an active Head, if, in fact, given any place at all.

Many books have been written on Church Government, and I'm certain that some contain valuable information; however, the Holy Spirit did not give an ironclad formula in the Bible regarding Church Government, even though in a sense, the entirety of the Bible could be said to be the *"Government of God."*

Men love government, but they are not too interested in that given in the Bible. That's the reason that in most Church circles Jesus is looked at as basically a passive Head.

Men love to rule; they love to wield authority. They really enjoy telling other men what to do. Jesus referred to this when He said to His Disciples:

"You know that they which are accounted to rule over the Gentiles exercise lordship over them; and their great ones exercise authority upon them." (Mk. 10:42).

Then He said:

"But so shall it not be among you: but whosoever will be great among you, shall be your minister (servant)*"* (Mk. 10:43).

So the Passage just quoted would place most Church Government in the position of being unscriptural and, in fact, the very opposite of what the Word of God demands.

The basic problem with most Church Government is that it has borrowed the ways of the world, brought them into the Church and tried to make them work. God will have no part of it.

As we attempt to define this very important subject, we will, of necessity, be brief. At the same time, we will assume that the reader desires to know what the Word of God says, and not what man says. Some of the statements we will make will be shocking, but they will, we believe, be Biblical.

JESUS IS THE HEAD OF THE CHURCH

"And He is the Head of the Body, the Church . . ." (Col. 1:18).

The great problem with this, as stated, is that the majority of the Church treats Christ as a passive Head instead an active Head; however, Christ is the Head of the Church, which means the Pope is not, a General Superintendent is not, a General Overseer is not, or any other mortal.

The Catholic Church claims that the Pope is the Vicar of Christ on Earth, which means he is the substitute or agent for Christ. That would mean Christ is the Heavenly Head with the Pope being the earthly head. This, of course, is spurious and totally unscriptural. There is no human earthly head. Christ is both the heavenly and earthly Head.

The Protestant world of Denominationalism, however, is little different from Roman Catholic Popery. In many circles, it more or less teaches the same thing. Its error is little different,

if any at all, from Catholic error.

As Head of the Church, Christ, through the agency of the Holy Spirit, calls men and women to preach the Gospel. He also anoints them (Mat., Chpt. 10). Men cannot call men to preach; neither should they tell men where to preach nor what to preach. Ideally, the God-called Preacher is to be led by the Holy Spirit in all those decisions.

THE FIVEFOLD CALLING

"And He gave some, Apostles; and some, Prophets; and some, Evangelists; and some, Pastors and Teachers;

***"For the perfecting of the Saints, for the work of the Ministry, for the edifying of the Body of Christ"* (Eph. 4:11-12).**

Religious leaders are fond of talking about *"spiritual authority."* It should be noted, however, that all *"spiritual authority"* as given in the Word of God has to do with authority over Satan and demon spirits, and never over fellow human beings.

***"And when He had called unto Him His Twelve Disciples, He gave them power against unclean spirits, to cast them out, and to heal all manner of sickness and all manner of disease"* (Mat. 10:1).**

> **"And these signs shall follow them who believe** *(not these 'sins' shall follow them who believe)***; In My Name shall they cast out devils** *(demons — Jesus defeated Satan, fallen Angels, and all demon spirits at the Cross [Col. 2:14-15])***; they shall speak with new Tongues** *(Baptism with the Holy Spirit with the evidence of speaking with other Tongues [Acts 2:4])***;**
>
> **"They shall take up serpents** *(put away demon spirits [Lk. 10:19] has nothing to do with reptiles)***; and if they drink any deadly thing, it shall not hurt them** *(speaks of protection; in no way does it speak of purposely drinking poison, etc., in order to prove one's faith; the word, 'if,' speaks of accidental ingestion)***; they shall lay hands on**

the sick, and they shall recover *(means to do so 'in the Name of Jesus' [Acts 5:12; 13:3; 14:3; 19:11; 28:8; I Tim. 4:14; II Tim. 1:6; Heb. 6:2; James 5:14])*" **(Mk. 16:17-18).**

"Behold, I give unto you power to tread on serpents and scorpions, and over all the power of the enemy: and nothing shall by any means hurt you *(this is the domain of Spiritual Authority; it is only over spirit beings, and not at all over humans)*" **(Lk. 10:19).**

Let us say it again, and because it is so important.

Every single Spirit-filled Believer on Earth, be they Preacher or otherwise, has spiritual authority, whether it is being used or not. This authority is to be used over the powers of darkness and never over other human beings. Ignore so-called religious leaders who demand obedience, because they have some supposed spiritual authority, and because they were elected on the fifteenth ballot to some religious office. Their demands aren't Biblical and their position isn't Biblical as well.

In true Biblical Church Government or true Biblical authority, there is no such thing as a *"Superintendent, General Superintendent, Overseer, General Overseer, Bishop, Moderator, President,"* etc., or any other such title. It is not necessarily wrong to have, hold, or form these offices as long as it is remembered that they are man-made and, thereby, carry no spiritual authority. They are a part of man-made Church Government but not a part of Biblical Church Government.

THE NEW TESTAMENT

The New Testament is the criteria for all Doctrine, correction and instruction in Righteousness (II Tim. 3:16). The New Testament describes the Early Church with Jesus Christ as its Builder. Through the Holy Spirit, He laid down its Doctrine and Government.

Many so-called religious leaders have insinuated that the Early Church is incomplete as it relates to Government and,

therefore, needs something added. This, in effect, says that the Lord did not know what He was doing in the building of His Church, and through man He is still writing the Bible. That is foolishness at best and heresy at worst. Early Church Doctrine and Government were inspired by the Holy Spirit and He mandated it as He desired it to be. Man has no right to take from them or add to them in any manner; consequently, New Testament Church Government does not include any type of spiritual authority for man-made offices or positions.

THE OFFICE OF THE BISHOP

***"This is a true saying, If a man desire the Office of Bishop, he desires a good work"* (I Tim. 3:1).**

Men have attempted to take the title *"Bishop"* and make it apply to a higher office in the Church. This is prominent in both the Catholic Church and the Protestant Church; however, one will look in vain for such an office in the New Testament Church.

The title *"Bishop,"* as it related to a higher office began to be bestowed on individuals as the Church went into spiritual declension. Down through history that title has been used for that purpose quite frequently. But once again, this is a man-made office, and it has no spiritual equivalency in the New Testament Church.

Actually, the words or titles *"Bishop," "Elder," "Pastor," "Shepherd," "Overseer,"* and *"Presbyter,"* as used in the Word of God, all have reference to the same calling — *"Pastor."* In other words, they all mean a man or woman who is Called by God to preach the Gospel and to pastor a local Church.

Paul and Peter used these titles interchangeably, meaning that they all pertain to the office of *"Pastor"* (I Pet. 2:25; I Tim. 5:17; Titus 1:5-7; Acts 20:28).

Consequently, Churches that form boards of *"Elders"* have basically done so unscripturally unless those individuals are Preachers of the Gospel in a local Church. Appointing a group of businessmen (or women) or professionals in various

walks of life and calling them *"Elders"* has no Scriptural basis. Likewise, as we have stated, giving an individual the title of *"Bishop,"* denoting some type of man-made higher office, is unscriptural as well. A Bishop is the same as an Elder, and they're both the same as the Pastor of a local Church — as stated, the words are interchangeable. It is not wrong to use these titles, providing one understands that they all denote the Pastor of a local Church and nothing else.

DENOMINATIONS

"Unto the Angel of the Church of Ephesus write . . ." (Rev. 2:1).

The New Testament records no such thing as a Denomination. It simply did not exist; consequently, it must always be understood that any and all Denominations are man-originated and not God-originated. No, it's not wrong to have, form, participate in, or belong to a Denomination as long as one understands that it is a man-originated organization, carrying no spiritual authority, and is merely a tool to accomplish the Work of God.

The segmenting of the Body of Christ is not Scriptural; however, it did not begin with the Baptist Church, the Methodist Church, and so forth. It started in the Early Church, and it began as a work of Satan. Paul said:

"Now this I say, that every one of you says, I am of Paul; and I of Apollos; and I of Cephas; and I of Christ.

"Is Christ divided? . . ." (I Cor. 1:12-13).

So, Satan attempted through *"contentions"* to segment the Body of Christ even at that early date. He was not successful, but at a later time he would become very successful. Segmentation of the Body of Christ is a curse that we have to live with, but it was never the intention of the Holy Spirit that Christ be divided.

As we have stated, a Denomination consisting of a group of people of like faith, ideally, should be a tool, just as a computer or a printing press is a tool, to help carry out the Work of

God on Earth. There is nothing unscriptural about that. But, sadly, most Denominations go into Denominationalism, which is very much akin to racism.

Racism basically says, *"If you are not my color or in my group, then you are somewhat less than I am."*

Denominationalism basically is of the same spirit. It says, *"If you do not belong to my Denomination then you are less of a Christian than I am — if you are a Christian at all."*

Denominationalism and racism are both unscriptural and ungodly. It is sad, but most Denominations fall into this category.

HIERARCHIES

When a religious Denomination ceases to be a tool to carry out the Work of God and spiritually declines into Denominationalism, almost invariably a hierarchy is formed.

The word *"hierarchy"* means *"a ruling body of clergy organized into orders or ranks each subordinate to the one above it."* There is not even the hint of a hierarchy in the New Testament, yet the Church world presently is full of hierarchies. A hierarchy, applying *"spiritual authority"* to its man-made offices, then proceeds to give guidance and direction which filters down through the hierarchical layers to be disseminated among the *"ordinary"* Preachers and laity.

The hierarchy, claiming legitimate spiritual authority, then asserts either by outright declaration or by implication, that its word is to be treated the same as God's Word. The underlings, whomever they might be, are ordered to obey or else.

The Catholic Church, as an example, is one great hierarchy with the Pope at the head. His word, functioning as law, filters down through the Cardinals and Bishops to the Priests and is then disseminated to the parishioners. It is totally unscriptural.

I should be quick to add, however, that many of the Protestant Denominations, albeit with different names for the hierarchy, are basically following the same pattern. The

hierarchy frowns on an individual outside of the loop receiving direction from the Lord regarding even his own ministry.

The *"ideal"* Protestant hierarchy functions best when each Preacher is placed, positioned, and even in some cases told what to preach — all by the hierarchy. Individuals who seek God and hear from the Lord concerning their types and places of Ministry are frowned upon and, ultimately, even pushed aside. In effect, the hierarchy takes the place of the Holy Spirit.

There are a few Godly Preachers in this system, and there are many Godly people, but the system itself is unscriptural and, at times, evil.

THE LOCAL CHURCH

In the New Testament, there is no higher authority than the local Church; however, the course and direction of the local Church were set by the Holy Spirit through Apostles. We will address the Office of the Apostle in a moment.

When Jesus addressed the seven Churches of Asia in Revelation, Chapters 2 and 3, He addressed each local Church individually. He addressed His Message, by and large, to the Pastor. He did not address a district headquarters or a Denominational headquarters. It would have been very easy for Him to have addressed the *"Mother Church in Jerusalem,"* but He did not.

Why?

The answer is simple. The Church in Jerusalem was not looked at by the Lord as any more important than any other Church. That is very hard for man to accept. Men who rule over other men love to have *"headquarters,"* and they love to be the head. But there is no hint in the New Testament that the Lord ever recognized any particular Church as *"headquarters."* Each Church was addressed distinctly and separately, being held accountable for its own actions. True, some Churches were, no doubt, much larger than others, with some being much more productive than others. But in God's Eyes, each Church was its own corporate body; answerable directly to its Head Who was

the Lord Jesus Christ. It did not answer to any hierarchy, state headquarters, district headquarters, or national headquarters.

It seems from II Corinthians, Chapters 8 and 9 that a loose fellowship of Churches was all that the Holy Spirit countenanced. Even the Apostle Paul (who planted most of these Churches) when given instructions by the Holy Spirit, usually *"beseeched"* the individuals to heed these instructions instead of demanding that they do so (I Cor. 1:10).

APOSTLES

Paul said:

"And He gave some, Apostles; and some, Prophets; and some, Evangelists; and some, Pastors and Teachers;

"For the perfecting of the Saints, for the Work of the Ministry, for the edifying of the Body of Christ:

***"Till we all come in the unity of the Faith, and of the knowledge of the Son of God, unto a perfect man, unto the measure of the stature of the fullness of Christ"* (Eph. 4:11-13).**

The Office of the Apostle is a New Covenant or New Testament entity. There were no designated Apostles in the Old Testament.

To explain the role of the Apostle, however, we will need to go back first of all to the Old Testament.

The Nation of Israel, which was the only monotheistic people in the world, meaning they worshipped one God, Jehovah, were guided by the God-called Prophet. Regrettably, for every true Prophet of God, there seemed to be several false prophets which sought ever to lead the people astray, and which generally succeeded.

The Office of the Prophet was first occupied by Samuel, even though there definitely were Prophets before him. But Samuel was the first one to fill this Office, and simply because it was then that Israel had finally become a Nation, of sorts.

It was the Prophet, at least those who were God-called, who served as Preachers of Righteousness, who stood as a warning

to the Nation when it was going astray, which was often, and who set the Spiritual Tone for all the people. While the king was definitely important as should be obvious, still, the Lord guided the Nation, at least tried to, through the Office of the Prophet.

For instance, it was Nathan the Prophet who was sent by the Lord to David when the king determined to build the Temple, telling him the true purpose as it regarded the Mind of God (II Sam. 7:1-17). It was Nathan, as well, who was sent by the Lord to David when the king had sinned greatly as it regarded Bathsheba and the murder of her husband. The first Message was a delight to deliver, the second message the very opposite (II Sam. 12:1-15).

Jesus told Israel shortly before they crucified Him, *"O Jerusalem, Jerusalem, you who killed the Prophets, and stoned them who are sent unto you, how often would I have gathered your children together, even as a hen gathers her chickens under her wings, but you would not!*

***"Behold, your house is left unto you desolate"* (Mat. 23:37-38).**

While the Office of the Prophet is maintained in the New Covenant, as it regards the course and direction of the Church, that is set by Christ through the Holy Spirit by the means of Apostles.

An Apostle is known by the critical Message he has, which is to be delivered to the Church. While others may preach the same Message, whatever that might be, the one who is truly an Apostle, will deliver the Word given to him by the Lord with much greater authority. This is the manner in which the Church is guided. Unfortunately, man attempts to change that direction, thereby instituting his own means and ways, which God can never bless.

As stated, an Apostle is known by the Message that God has given him, which is desperately needed by the Church, and to be sure, such a one cannot be appointed by man, elected by popular ballot, etc. Actually, most who refer to themselves as Apostles are self-appointed, or rather appointed by other men, who the Lord doesn't recognize. Most of the time, those who are truly Apostles, and with the Message to prove such,

are little recognized, if at all, by religious hierarchy. In fact, true Apostles are always a threat to religious hierarchy, simply because they cannot be controlled.

But even though most true Apostles are little accepted or even recognized as such, still, the Message which the Lord has given them, which the Church desperately needs, somehow finds its way, and by the Power of the Holy Spirit, into the Body of Christ.

One of the reasons that the Apostle Paul had to constantly reaffirm his Apostleship was because he was little accepted. That's the reason that he said:

"Paul, an Apostle, (not of men, neither by man, but by Jesus Christ, and God the Father, Who raised Him from the dead)" **(Gal. 1:1).**

While the original Twelve accepted him readily, there were many others in the Early Church who did not, somewhat looking at him as an interloper; nevertheless, it was to Paul that the meaning of the New Covenant was given, which is the meaning of the Cross, which, in a sense, made Paul the Moses of the New Testament.

If I remember correctly, there were twenty-four men who were designated by the Holy Spirit as Apostles in the Early Church.

Neither James nor Jude, the brothers of our Lord, referred to themselves as Apostles, although Paul did refer to James as such. He said:

"But other of the Apostles saw I none, save James the Lord's Brother" **(Gal. 1:19). Actually, both James and Jude were Apostles, inasmuch as their Books were included in the Canon of Scripture. More than likely, James and Jude did not refer to themselves as Apostles, because they did not believe in Christ during His earthly Ministry (Jn. 7:5). Nevertheless, they were Apostles.**

DEACONS

"Wherefore, brethren, look you out among you seven men of honest report, full of the Holy Spirit and wisdom, whom we may

appoint over this business" (Acts 6:3).

Actually, the word *"deacons"* is not found in the Passage just quoted; nevertheless, most Bible Scholars feel it is referring to Deacons.

The present practice in most Churches of *"deacon boards"* running the Churches and hiring and firing the Pastors is unscriptural.

This is in no way meant to demean the Godly Office of the Deacon, but it is meant to point out the unscriptural position that is, by and large, adhered to in today's Church climate.

Nowhere in the New Testament Church, which must be our example, are Deacons given authority over the Pastor of the Church.

The Deacons were chosen by the Apostles. They were not voted on by the Body of the Church. While it is true that the Apostles did not personally select each one (that was left to others), still, they were the ones who gave the instructions for it to be done, and they presided over their selection (Acts 6:6). These Deacons performed two tasks:

1. They *"served tables"* (Acts 6:2). This meant they attended to the tables where collections were received and distributions to the people were made — in other words, they took care of at least some part of the business of the Church.

2. It also seems that at least some of them were Preachers (Acts 6:8).

The qualities that Deacons should have, are very similar to the qualities the Pastors should have (I Tim. 3:1-13).

It appears that the Holy Spirit originated this Office to be filled by Deacons so that Pastors would not be loaded down with the necessary business of the Church (which can be a hindrance to personal consecration). They freed the Apostles to say:

". . . We will give ourselves continually to prayer, and to the Ministry of the Word" (Acts 6:4).

The modern-day Church has strayed to a large extent from the New Testament pattern of Church Government. It must be understood that to the degree the Church deviates from the

Word, to that degree it will suffer spiritual declension. The Holy Spirit intends for us to follow the Word. As previously stated, it must not be added to, taken from, or, above all, ignored. If we do so, we purchase for ourselves ultimate spiritual destruction. If we adhere to the Word to the best of our ability, then we will reap the Blessing that always comes from doing such.

THE SYSTEM

We must also understand that to adhere to the Word of God will, most of the time, mean bucking the system so to speak, fighting the tide, and, thereby, being ostracized. Many attempt to console themselves with the idea that even though they are a part of the system, they are not controlled by it; however, to support an evil system (if, in fact, it is evil) is to do violence to the Word of God and to aid and abet the Work of Satan to some degree.

When Paul said, *"Wherefore come out from among them, and be you separate, says the Lord . . ."* (II Cor. 6:17), he was speaking not only of the world, but of the apostate Church as well. Today, the greatest hindrance to the Work of God is not the world; it is still the apostate Church (II Tim. 3:1-9). At least one of the areas where Satan causes the greatest hindrance in the Church is in what we call *"Church Government."* In these last days, his activity in this area will not diminish, but will increase.

God's Church is a glorious Church, but most of what is referred to as *"Church"* is not God's Church, but rather, man's church. I have no desire to be a part of man's church. I do desire with all my heart to be a part of God's Church. And by His Grace and the precious shed Blood of Jesus Christ being applied to my heart and life, thank God, I am.

"And I say also unto you, That you are Peter *(the Lord changed his name from Simon to Peter, which means* *'a fragment of a rock')*, **and upon this rock** *(immovable mass; Jesus is the Living Rock on which the Redeemed as living stones are built; for other foundation can no man lay [I Cor. 3:11])* **I will build My Church** *(the Church belongs to Christ, and He is the Head [Col. 1:18])*; **and the gates of Hell shall not prevail against it** *(the power of death caused by sin, shall not prevail against it, which victory was won at the Cross [Vss. 21, 24])*.

"And I will give unto you *('you' refers to all Believers)* **the keys of the Kingdom of Heaven** *(refers to symbols of authority, the privilege of preaching or proclaiming the Gospel, which is the privilege of every Believer)*: **and whatsoever you shall bind on Earth shall be bound in Heaven** *(Christ has given the authority and power to every Believer to bind Satan and his minions of darkness, and to do so by using the Name of Jesus [Mk. 16:17-18; Lk. 10:19])*: **and whatsoever you shall loose on Earth shall be loosed in Heaven** *(looses the Power of God according to the usage of the Name of Jesus; this is the authority of the Believer)*" **(Mat. 16:18-19).**

CHAPTER FOURTEEN

Is The Keeping Of The Sabbath Incumbent Upon Christians?

QUESTION:

IS THE KEEPING OF THE SABBATH INCUMBENT UPON CHRISTIANS?

ANSWER:

No!

First of all, the Christian should understand that Sunday is not the Sabbath. Saturday is the Sabbath.

Second, the old Jewish Sabbath was a day of rest and not necessarily of worship as it regarded the Lord. The people were supposed to rest on this day, and even the animals were supposed to rest on this particular day. The Fourth Commandment stated:

"Six days you shall labor, and do all your work:

"But the seventh Day is the Sabbath of the LORD your God: in it you shall not do any work, you, nor your son, nor your daughter, your manservant, nor your maidservant, nor your cattle, nor your stranger that is within your gates:

***"For in six days the LORD made Heaven and Earth, the sea, and all that in them is, and rested the seventh day: wherefore the LORD blessed the Sabbath Day, and hallowed it"* (Ex. 20:8-11).**

The Sabbath and, in fact, every single thing that pertained to the Law, and in every capacity, spoke of Christ in some manner, whether in His Intercessory Work, His Atoning Work, or His Meditorial Work. In fact, the Jewish Sabbath was one of the greatest types of all, in that it symbolized the *"rest"* that would be incumbent in Christ. That's what Jesus was talking about when He said:

> **"Come unto Me** *(is meant by Jesus to reveal Himself as the Giver of Salvation)*, **all *you* who labor and are heavy laden** *(trying to earn Salvation by works)*, **and I will give you rest** *(this 'rest' can only be found by placing one's Faith in Christ and what He has done for us at the*

Cross [Gal. 5:1-6]).

"Take My Yoke upon you *(the 'yoke' of the 'Cross' [Lk. 9:23])*, **and learn of Me** *(learn of His Sacrifice [Rom. 6:3-5])*; **for I am meek and lowly in heart** *(the only thing that our Lord Personally said of Himself)*: **and you shall find rest unto your souls** *(the soul can find rest only in the Cross)*.

"For My Yoke *is* easy, and My Burden is light *(what He requires of us is very little, just to have Faith in Him, and His Sacrificial Atoning work)*" **(Mat. 11:28-30).**

In the Law of Moses, everything was *"doing," "doing," "doing!"*

In Christ, it is *"believing," "believing," "believing,"* and because Christ has already done all the work so to speak.

That is what the Sabbath was supposed to represent, the *"rest"* that would come in Christ.

ACCEPTING CHRIST

When one accepts Christ now, in effect, one is keeping the Fourth Commandment, because everything now is in Christ. In fact, Christ fulfilled every particle of the Law, every nuance of the Law. Nothing was left unfulfilled. This means that the Law, or no part of the Law is now incumbent upon Believers, and that includes Sabbath-keeping.

Concerning what Jesus did as it regards the Law, Paul said:

"For Christ *is* the end of the Law for Righteousness *(Christ fulfilled the totality of the Law)* **to everyone who believes** *(Faith in Christ guarantees the Righteousness which the Law had, but could not give)*" **(Rom. 10:4).**

All of this means, even as we have already stated, that Christ fulfilled the Law in every respect, in effect, doing it for us because we could not do it for ourselves and, therefore, the Law

is no more, i.e., not binding upon Believers. The truth is, when we accepted Christ, we were transferred from the position of Lawbreaker to the position of Law-keeper. Christ being our Substitute, our identification with Him grants us the victory which he purchased for us with His Own Blood.

THE CROSS

In His Life and Living, Christ kept the Law perfectly and in every respect. And it must be understood, He did all of this for us. But there still remained the broken law, meaning that all were guilty, none excluded, for all had broken the Law of God. Regarding the Law per se, the life and living of our Lord answered that, and when it came to the broken Law, the Cross answered that. Paul also said:

> **"Blotting out the handwriting of Ordinances that was against us** *(pertains to the Law of Moses, which was God's Standard of Righteousness that man could not reach)*, **which was contrary to us** *(Law is against us, simply because we are unable to keep its precepts, no matter how hard we try)*, **and took it out of the way** *(refers to the penalty of the Law being removed)*, **nailing it to His Cross** *(the Law with its decrees was abolished in Christ's Death, as if Crucified with Him)*;
>
> **"*And* having spoiled principalities and powers** *(Satan and all of his henchmen were defeated at the Cross by Christ Atoning for all sin; sin was the legal right Satan had to hold man in captivity; with all sin atoned, he has no more legal right to hold anyone in bondage)*, **He** *(Christ)* **made a show of them openly** *(what Jesus did at the Cross was in the face of the whole universe)*, **triumphing over them in it.** *(The triumph is complete and it was all done for us, meaning we can walk in power and perpetual victory due to the Cross.)*
>
> **"Let no man therefore judge you in meat, or in**

drink, or in respect of an holyday, or of the new moon, or of the Sabbath *Days* *(the moment we add any rule or regulation to the Finished Work of Christ, we have just abrogated the Grace of God)***:**

"Which are a shadow of things to come *(the Law, with all of its observances, was only meant to point to the One Who was to come, Namely Christ)***; but the Body** *(Church)* ***is* of Christ** *(refers to 'substance and reality,' as opposed to shadow)***" (Col. 2:14-17).**

THE SABBATH AS A TYPE

In the Law of Moses, there was a most stringent penalty for breaking the Sabbath — death. The Scripture says:

"Six days shall work be done, but on the seventh day there shall be to you an holy day, a Sabbath of Rest to the LORD: whosoever does work therein shall be put to death.

***"You shall kindle no fire throughout your habitations upon the Sabbath Day"* (Ex. 35:1-3).**

Concerning this, what distinguishes God's People is participation in God's Rest. Christ is God's Rest (Heb., Chpt. 4). The honor, or dishonor, done to the Sabbath was the test under Law. The honor, or dishonor, done to Christ is the test under Grace. Death was the penalty of dishonoring the old Jewish Sabbath; a similar penalty attaches to dishonoring Christ, which is spiritual death.

This severe penalty was attached to the Jewish Sabbath simply because of Who and What (Christ) it represented (Redemption).

SUNDAY

There isn't a Passage in the New Testament that records a distinctive gathering of Christians on the Jewish Seventh-day Sabbath. On the contrary, the records show that Christians gathered on Sunday, the first day of the week, referred to as

"the Lord's Day" **(Rev. 1:10).**

"The first day of the week *(Sunday)* **comes Mary Magdalene early, when it was yet dark, unto the Sepulchre" (Jn. 20:1).**

"Then the same day at evening, being the first day of the week *(proclaims the first gathering on a Sunday)*, **when the doors were shut where the Disciples were assembled for fear of the Jews, came Jesus and stood in the midst, and said unto them, Peace be unto you" (Jn. 20:19).**

"And, after eight days again His Disciples were within, and Thomas with them *(presents Jesus meeting with them again on Sunday, the First Day of the week, the Day of His Resurrection)*: **then came Jesus, the doors being shut, and stood in the midst, and said, Peace be unto you" (Jn. 20:26).**

"And upon the first day of the week *(Sunday)*, **when the Disciples came together to break bread** *(Sunday had become the main day of worship)*, **Paul preached unto them, ready to depart on the morrow; and continued his speech until midnight" (Acts 20:7).**

"Now concerning the collection for the Saints, as I have given orders to the Churches of Galatia, even so do you.

"Upon the first day of the week *(Sunday, which replaced the Jewish Sabbath of Saturday)* **let every one of you** *(no exceptions)* **lay by him in store, as God has prospered him** *(give to the Work of the Lord on this day)*, **that there be no gatherings when I come" (I Cor. 16:1-2).**

RIGID OBSERVANCE OF DAYS IS REBUKED BY PAUL

The Apostle said:

"But now, after that you have known God *(refers to Saving Grace, knowing God through the acceptance of*

Jesus Christ, which is the only way He can be known), **or rather are known of God** *(refers to the Lord knowing us in a saving way)*, **how turn you again to the weak and beggarly elements** *(when the substance is reached and sonship established, going back to the 'rudiments,' i.e., symbols and sacraments, is not progress, but ignorance)*, **whereunto you desire again to be in bondage?** *(Bondage to the sin nature! It refers to leaving the Cross, and making other things the object of Faith.)*

"You observe days, and months, and times, and years. *(The Judaizers were attempting to get the Galatians to go into Law-keeping in conjunction with Christ, which cannot work.)*

"I am afraid of you *(afraid for your spiritual welfare)*, **lest I have bestowed upon you labour in vain.** *(If one leaves Faith in Christ and the Cross and embraces other things, which means to look to those other things for life and victory, the Holy Spirit will have bestowed upon such a person labor in vain)*" **(Gal. 4:9-11).**

The Sabbath is not named among the necessary requirements of the Gospel, which was handed down by James, at the first General Counsel so to speak, conducted in Jerusalem. Paul was present as well! James said:

"For it seemed good to the Holy Spirit, and to us *(proclaims without a doubt that the Holy Spirit led and guided these proceedings)*, **to lay upon you no greater burden than these necessary things** *(when men leave the Word of God, they get into a lot of 'unnecessary things')*;

"That you abstain from meats offered to idols, and from blood, and from things strangled, and from fornication: from which if you keep yourselves, you shall do well. Fare ye well" (Acts 15:28-29).

If it is to be noticed, and let us repeat what we have said,

the Sabbath is not mentioned here as a requirement regarding Christians.

REAL AND ETERNAL REST IS IN CHRIST, NOT IN A DAY

Paul said:

"There remains *(what the Law couldn't do, Christ would do)* **therefore a Rest to the People of God.** *(This is found only in Christ and through what He did at the Cross, to which everything in the Old Testament pointed.)*

"For he who is entered into His *(God's)* **Rest** *(due to what Christ did at the Cross, anyone can enter into this 'Rest')*, **he also has ceased from his own works** *(we enter in by Faith, which refers to Faith in Christ and what He did at the Cross)*, **as God *did* from His.** *(God rested on the seventh day when Creation was finished. And we can Rest in Christ because the Plan of Redemption is finished, of which God's Rest was a type)*" **(Heb. 4:9-10).**

OBSERVING THE LAW TO KEEP THE SABBATH WOULD OBLIGATE A PERSON TO KEEP THE WHOLE LAW OF MOSES

"Behold *('mark my words!')*, **I Paul say unto you** *(presents the Apostle's authority regarding the Message he brings)*, **that if you be circumcised, Christ shall profit you nothing.** *(If the Believer goes back into Law, and Law of any kind, what Christ did at the Cross on our behalf will profit us nothing. One cannot have it two ways.)*

"For I testify again to every man who is circumcised *(some of the Galatian Gentiles were being pressured by false teachers to embrace the Law of Moses, which meant they would have to forsake Christ and the Cross, for it's not possible to wed the two; as well, it's not possible* *to wed any Law to Grace)*, **that he is a debtor to do the whole Law** *(which, of course, is impossible; and besides, the Law contained no Salvation)*" **(Gal. 5:2-3).**

Had there been any explicit commands to worship on a certain day, or to keep a certain day, even the first day, it would have brought about the same bondage as the Law of Moses. The higher ideals and principles of Christianity would have then been regulated to days and seasons, which God promised to abolish (Isa. 1:13; Hos. 2:11) and which He did abolish (II Cor. 3:6-15; Gal. 3:19-25; Eph. 2:14-15; Heb. 6:20).

CHAPTER FIFTEEN

What Is The Difference Between The Great White Throne Judgment And The Judgment Seat Of Christ?

QUESTION:

WHAT IS THE DIFFERENCE BETWEEN THE GREAT WHITE THRONE JUDGMENT AND THE JUDGMENT SEAT OF CHRIST?

ANSWER:

There is a world of difference between the two. At the Great White Throne Judgment only the unsaved will be there. At the Judgment Seat of Christ, only Believers will be at this particular Judgment.

We'll look at the Great White Throne Judgment first.

THE GREAT WHITE THRONE JUDGMENT

I quote from THE EXPOSITOR'S STUDY BIBLE:

"And I saw a Great White Throne *(proclaims the final Judgment of the unredeemed, which will take place at the end of the Kingdom Age)*, **and Him Who sat on it** *(proclaims none other than God; however, we must understand that it is the Person of the Godhead, the Lord Jesus Christ [Mat. 25:31]; He is the Saviour today; He will be the Judge tomorrow)*, **from Whose Face the Earth and the Heaven fled away; and there was found no place for them.** *(This means a New Heaven and New Earth are in the offing.)*

"And I saw the dead, small and great, stand before God *(pertains to the second Resurrection, the Resurrection of Damnation [I Cor., Chpt. 15; I Thess. 4:13-18; Jn. 5:29])*; **and the Books were opened: and another Book was opened, which is *the Book* of Life: and the dead were Judged out of those things which were written in the Books, according to their works** *(proclaims the manner of Judgment)*.

"And the sea gave up the dead which were in it; and death and Hell delivered up the dead which were in them *(points to the fact that every unredeemed person who has ever lived will face the Great White Throne Judgment; none will be exempted)*: **and they were Judged every man according to their works** *(records the fact that this Judgment is not arbitrary, but is based on absolute Justice)*.

"And death and Hell were cast into the Lake of Fire *(combined, includes the wicked of all ages)*. **This is the second death** *(Eternal separation from God and the Lake of Fire)*.

"And whosoever was not found written in the Book of Life *(refers to the record of all the Redeemed)* **was cast into the Lake of Fire.** *(This includes every single individual who isn't Redeemed, beginning with Adam and Eve. That is, if they didn't come back to God)*" **(Rev. 20:11-15).**

Even though, I think, the notes given in THE EXPOSITOR'S STUDY BIBLE explain this Judgment, perhaps it would be more helpful to flesh it out somewhat.

WHO WILL BE AT THE GREAT WHITE THRONE JUDGMENT?

Every unsaved person who has ever lived will be at this Judgment, beginning with Adam and Eve, if, in fact, they did not come back to the Lord.

At the time of this Judgment, will be what is referred to as the Resurrection of Damnation. Concerning this, Jesus said:

"Verily, verily, I say unto you *(always signals a statement of the highest authority, and proclaims Jesus as that Authority)*, **The hour is coming, and now is, when the dead shall hear the Voice of the Son of God: and they who hear shall live** *(has a double meaning: 1. It refers to people being Saved, thereby, coming from spiritual death* *to Spiritual Life; and, 2. It refers to the coming Resurrection of Life, when all Saints will be Resurrected)*.

"For as the Father has Life in Himself *(refers to God as the Eternal Fountain of Life, the Source Ultimate)*; **so has He given to the Son to have Life in Himself** *(Jesus saying that He is not merely a participator in this 'Life,' but, in fact, is, as well, the Source of Life and, in Truth, the Ultimate Source exactly as the Father; consequently, He again claims Deity)*;

"And has given Him Authority to execute judgment also *(this speaks of 'The Judgment Seat of Christ,' which will be for all Believers and, as well, the 'Great White Throne Judgment,' which will be for all the unsaved)*, **because He is the Son of Man** *(refers to Him paying the price on Calvary's Cross, and by the merit of such, He will also be the 'Judge')*.

"Marvel not at this *(these statements, as given by Christ, left the religious leaders of Israel speechless)*: **for the hour is coming, in the which all who are in the graves shall hear His Voice** *(speaks of the Resurrection of Life and the Resurrection of Damnation; again, these statements proclaim Christ as the Lord of both life and death)*,

"And shall come forth *(portrays both Resurrections as we shall see, and according to His 'Voice')*; **they who have done good, unto the Resurrection of Life** *(pertains to the First Resurrection, or as commonly referred, 'The Rapture' [I Thess. 4:13-18])*; **and they who have done evil, unto the Resurrection of Damnation** *(this last Resurrection will take place approximately a thousand years after the First Resurrection of Life [Dan. 12:2; Rev., Chpt. 20])*" **(Jn. 5:25-29).**

At this Resurrection of Damnation, every unsaved person who has every lived will be given an indestructible body for their soul and spirit.

This will be quite different from the *"Glorified Body"* which

will be given to all Saints at the First Resurrection of Life, inasmuch as the Holy Spirit is the life force of that body, whereas the body that will be given to the unredeemed is merely indestructible.

So, at this time, every single unsaved person who has ever lived, as stated, will be at this Judgment, none excluded.

WHEN WILL IT BE CONDUCTED?

The Apostle John gave us the answer to this. He said:

"And when the thousand years are expired *(should have been translated, 'finished')*, **Satan shall be loosed out of his prison** *(is not meant to infer a mere arbitrary act on the part of God; He has a very valid reason for doing this)*,

"And shall go out to deceive the nations which are in the four quarters of the Earth, Gog and Magog *(the main reason the Lord allows Satan this latitude is, it seems, to rid the Earth of all who oppose Christ; George Williams says: 'The Creation Sabbath witnessed the first seduction, and the Millennial Sabbath will witness the last'; the 'Gog and Magog' spoken of by John is a Hebrew term expressive of multitude and magnitude; here it embraces all nations, 'the four quarters of the Earth')*, **to gather them together to battle: the number of whom *is* as the sand of the sea** *(proclaims the fact that virtually all of the population at that particular time, which did not accept Christ during the Kingdom Age, will throw in their lot with Satan)*.

"And they went up on the breadth of the earth, and compassed the camp of the Saints about, and the beloved city *(pictures Satan coming against Jerusalem with his army, which will be the last attack against that city)*: **and fire came down from God out of Heaven, and devoured them.** *(Stipulates that the Lord will make short work of this insurrection. In fact, very little information is* *given regarding this event, as is obvious.)*

"And the Devil who deceived them was cast into the Lake of Fire and brimstone *(marks the end of Satan regarding his influence in the world, and, in fact, in any part of the Creation of God)*, **where the Beast and the False Prophet *are*** *(proclaims the fact that these two were placed in 'the Lake of Fire and Brimstone' some one thousand years earlier [Rev. 19:20])*, **and shall be tormented day and night forever and ever.** *(This signifies the Eternity of this place. It is a matter of interest to note that Satan's first act is recorded in Gen., Chpt. 3 [the third Chapter from the beginning], whereas his last act on a worldwide scale is mentioned in Rev., Chpt. 20 [the third Chapter from the end])*" **(Rev. 20:7-10).**

WHERE WILL THIS JUDGMENT BE CONDUCTED?

Even though the Scripture is not clear as it regards this question, there is some indication, I think, that it will be conducted on Earth.

In the first place, this Judgment, as stated, will be conducted immediately after the Devil makes his last effort against the Lord and the city of Jerusalem. Immediately after that, John gave us the account of the Great White Throne Judgment (Rev. 20:11-15).

Sadly and regrettably, almost all human beings who have ever lived died eternally lost. Jesus personally said concerning this:

"Enter you in at the strait gate *(this is the Door, Who is Jesus [Jn. 10:1])*: **for wide *is* the gate, and broad *is* the way, that leads to destruction, and many there be which go in thereat** *(proclaims the fact of many and varied religions of the world, which are false, and lead to eternal hellfire)*:

"Because strait *is* the gate, and narrow *is* the way, which leads unto life, and few there be that find it *(every* *contrite heart earnestly desires to be among the 'few'; the requirements are greater than most are willing to accept)"* **(Mat. 7:13-14).**

Control of this Earth has been the contest from the beginning until now. There is evidence that Satan, then known as Lucifer the mighty Archangel of God, at one time ruled the Earth, which was before Adam and Eve. He ruled it under the Lord in Righteousness and Holiness; however, at a point in time the record seems to indicate that he took his eyes off Christ, and placed them on himself. The Scripture says concerning this:

***"You were perfect in your ways from the day that you wee created, till iniquity was found in you"* (Ezek. 28:15).**

The Scripture also says: *"How are you fallen from Heaven O Lucifer, son of the morning! how are you cut down to the ground, which did weaken the nations!"* (Isa. 14:12).

The rebellion of Lucifer against God probably caused the catastrophe which occurred between the First and Second Verses of Genesis, Chapter 1.

At the temptation of Christ, the Scripture also says:

"Again *(the third temptation)*, **the Devil took Him up into an exceeding high mountain** *(not definitely known, but probably Nebo)*, **and showed Him all the kingdoms of the world, and the glory of them** *(showed them to Him, not in a physical sense, but rather in a spiritual sense)*;

"And said unto Him, All these things will I give You, if You will fall down and worship me *(the temptation was that Christ abrogate the Cross, through which He would regain all things)*.

"Then said Jesus unto him, Get thee hence, Satan *(presents Christ for the first time Personally addressing Satan)*: **for it is written, you shall worship the Lord your God, and Him only shall you serve** *(Satan desires that mankind worship and serve him; we are to worship* *and serve the Lord Alone)*.

"Then the Devil left Him *('departed from Him for a season,' meaning that there would be other temptations [Lk. 4:13])*, **and, behold, Angels came and ministered unto Him** *(in what manner they ministered, we aren't told)*" **(Mat. 4:8-9).**

And then considering that the Lord, after the Kingdom Age, and after the Heavens and the Earth have been renovated by fire (II Pet. 3:10-13), the Lord will transfer, as stated, His Headquarters from Heaven to Earth (Rev. 21:1-5).

Considering all of this, it stands to reason that Earth will be the scene of this great Judgment.

CONSIDERING THAT ALL WHO APPEAR AT THIS JUDGMENT ARE LOST, WHY IS THE JUDGMENT NECESSARY?

It is necessary because of the eternal Justice of God.

The Scripture says:

"And I saw the dead, small and great, stand before God; and the Books were opened: and another Book was opened, which is the Book of Life: and the dead were Judged out of those things which were written in the Books, according to their works" **(Rev. 20:12).**

Two sets of Books are kept in Heaven. They are:

1. The Books containing the actions of every individual who has ever lived.

2. The Book of Life which contains the names of all the redeemed.

It is a sobering thought to understand that every single thing we do, when it's done, where it is done, how it is done, and what is done, all and without exception, are written down in the Book. And yet, for everyone who accepts Christ, all of the failures, sins, and transgressions are erased. The Blood of Jesus Christ has cleansed from all sin (I Jn. 1:7). And that

word *"cleansed"* refers to a cleansing of our heart and life and, as well, cleansed from the Book. But if Christ is not accepted, then in black and white, one might say, the account of all wrongdoing is forever registered.

In other words, no unredeemed person will have any excuse, because everything they've ever done is registered, and that they will not be able to deny. They will then have no excuse.

As it regards *"The Book of Life"* every person whose name is in that Book, is there because of Jesus Christ and what He did for us at the Cross, and our acceptance of Him as Saviour and Lord (Jn. 3:16).

In other words, the Lord at this Judgment will show them, as well, the *"Book of Life,"* and that their name is not written there.

We must remember every one of these people will be consigned to the Lake of Fire, which will be forever and forever. Considering the terrible conclusion of the matter, the idea is, God will go to all lengths to show these people the Justice of His Judgment.

WHO WILL BE THE JUDGE?

As we quoted some time back, the Lord Jesus Christ will be the Judge. The Scripture says:

***"For the Father judges no man, but has committed all judgment unto the Son"* (Jn. 5:22).**

This is only right inasmuch as Jesus is also the Saviour and, in fact, the only Saviour, by which was made possible by the Cross.

There is animosity in this world against the God of the Bible; however, the greater animosity of all is against the Lord Jesus Christ.

Why?

He said of Himself, *"I am the Way, the Truth, and the Life: no man comes unto the Father but by Me"* (Jn. 14:6).

Men bridle at that statement that Jesus is the only Way,

and if He is rejected, eternal Hell is the result. That is blunt, but it happens to be true. So, if He is the only Saviour, then it is right that He be the only Judge. Therefore, men can accept Him today as their Saviour, or else they will face Him tomorrow as their Judge, but face Him they will! Pure and simple, Jesus, although incarnated into human form, still, is God. John the Beloved said of Him:

> **"In the beginning** *(does not infer that Christ as God had a beginning, because as God He had no beginning, but rather refers to the time of Creation [Gen. 1:1])* **was the Word** *(the Holy Spirit through John describes Jesus as 'the Eternal Logos')*, **and the Word was with God** *('was in relationship with God,' and expresses the idea of the Trinity)*, **and the Word was God** *(meaning that He did not cease to be God during the Incarnation; He 'was' and 'is' God from eternity past to eternity future)*.
>
> **"The same was in the beginning with God** *(this very Person was in eternity with God; there's only one God, but manifested in three Persons — God the Father, God the Son, God the Holy Spirit)*.
>
> **"All things were made by Him** *(all things came into being through Him; it refers to every item of Creation one by one, rather than all things regarded in totality)*; **and without Him was not any thing made that was made** *(nothing, not even one single thing, was made independently of His cooperation and volition)*.
>
> **"In Him was Life** *(presents Jesus, the Eternal Logos, as the first cause)*; **and the Life was the Light of men** *(He Alone is the Life Source of Light; if one doesn't know Christ, one is in darkness)*" **(Jn. 1:1-4).**

In this age of psychology, which incidentally claims that man is not at fault, but rather that he is only a victim, the idea of a Judgment is denied. Humanistic psychology denies the culpability of man. But the Bible says different. It says:

> **"As it is written** *(Ps. 14:1-3)*, **There is none righteous, no, not one** *(addresses the complaint of the Jews and clinches the argument with the Scriptures, which the Jews could not deny)*:
>
> **"There is none who understands** *(proclaims total depravity)*, **there is none who seek after God** *(man left on his own will not seek God and, in fact, cannot seek God; he is spiritually dead)*.
>
> **"They are all gone out of the Way** *(speaks of the lost condition of all men; the 'Way' is God's Way)*, **they are together become unprofitable** *(refers to the terrible loss in every capacity of wayward man)*; **there is none who does good, no, not one** *(the Greek Text says, 'useless!')*" **(Rom. 3:10-12).**

Man is culpable, and he will have to answer to God for his rejection of the Lord Jesus Christ. This means that humanistic psychology is a lie.

HOW CAN THESE MANY PEOPLE BE JUDGED?

The question pertains to the mechanics of the situation.

Considering that there have been between ten billion and twenty billion people, all who have ever lived, even from the beginning, and who died lost, the numbers are staggering.

As to the how that all of this will be done, it is impossible for us to now say; however, one thing is certain, it will be very simple for God to do such considering that He is Omnipotent, Omniscient, and Omnipresent.

Concerning His Knowledge, the Scripture says:

> **"He tells the number of the stars; he calls them all by their names.** *(If we take this literally, and we certainly should, this means that God calls all the stars by name.*
>
> "*In the 1950's, astronomers claimed that there were about 40 sextillion stars in the vast universe, which are*

suns to other Planets. They have presently increased that number, but have left it open-ended. [Forty sextillion is the number 40 followed by twenty-one zeros.] At any rate, God knows the exact number, for He made them [Isa. 45:18].

"It is said that there are approximately 500,000 words in Webster's Unabridged Dictionary. If all the names of all the stars were put in books of this size, it would take 80 quadrillion books to list the name of every star. [Eighty quadrillion is the number 80 followed by 15 zeros.])

"Great is our LORD, and of great Power; His understanding is infinite. *(Considering Verse 4, the phrase, 'Great is our LORD,' has to be summed up as a gross understatement)***" (Ps. 147:4-5).**

How He will do it, we cannot say, but that He will do it, is for certain.

WHAT WILL BE THE JUDGMENT HANDED DOWN?

The Scripture says concerning this all-important question:

***"And whosoever was not found written in the Book of Life was cast into the Lake of Fire"* (Rev. 20:15).**

This includes every single individual who isn't redeemed, beginning with Adam and Eve, that is, if they didn't come back to God, and there is no record that they did.

Where is the Lake of Fire?

Every evidence is it is in the heart of the Earth. The Scripture says:

***"For as Jonah was three days and three nights in the whale's belly; so shall the Son of Man be three days and three nights in the heart of the Earth"* (Mat. 12:40).**

Inasmuch as Jesus was talking about His Death on the Cross of Calvary, and where He would go after death, we have to conclude that this is the location of Hell. Jesus gives us a description of this place in Luke 16:19-31.

The Scripture also says, *"And death and Hell were cast into*

the Lake of Fire. This is the second death" **(Rev. 20:14).**

There is some indication here that Hell is different than the Lake of Fire. At any rate, whether different or not, it is eternal, and the awfulness of such defies all description. That's the reason we should labor to get everyone into the Kingdom of God that is possible for us to do so.

THE JUDGMENT SEAT OF CHRIST

Whereas, as the Great White Throne Judgment, only unbelievers will be present, at the Judgment Seat of Christ, only Believers will be present.

The Scripture says:

> **"But why do you judge your brother?** *(Is any Believer qualified to judge another Believer? 'Your Brother' is another reason for not judging. It is inconsistent with the recognition of the Brotherhood of Believers.)* **or why do you set at nought your brother?** *(There is only one reason for refusing fellowship, and that reason is unconfessed, unrepentant, habitual sin in a person's life [I Cor., Chpt. 5].)* **for we shall all stand before the Judgment Seat of Christ** *(we will be judged there, not for our sins, those having been handled at the Cross, but as it regards our stewardship and our motives, etc.; gain or loss of reward will be the result)***.**
>
> **"For it is written** *(Isa. 45:23)***, As I live, says the Lord** *(God cannot die)***, every knee shall bow to Me, and every tongue shall confess to God** *(to make a confession of God's Honor, and as well, to praise Him)***.**
>
> **"So then every one of us shall give account of himself to God** *(each is responsible, meaning that the blame cannot be shifted elsewhere)***" (Rom. 14:10-12).**

Paul also said:

> **"Wherefore we labour** *(are ambitious)***, that, whether**

present *(with Christ)* **or absent** *(still in this world)*, **we may be accepted of Him** *(approved by Him, which we will be if our Faith is in Christ and the Cross)*.

"For we must all appear before the Judgment Seat of Christ *(this will take place in Heaven, and will probably transpire immediately before the Second Coming)*; **that every one may receive the things *done* in *his* body, according to that he has done, whether *it be* good or bad.** *(This concerns our life lived for the Lord. Sins will not be judged here, but rather our motivation and faithfulness, for sin was judged at Calvary)*" **(II Cor. 5:9-10).**

WHO WILL BE AT THE JUDGMENT SEAT OF CHRIST?

As we've already stated, only Believers will be there. But this includes every Believer who has ever lived, with the first one, of which we are aware, being Abel. Every Bible Great will be there, plus untold millions of others of which we have no knowledge. What a story all will have to tell and how interesting all of it will be. As well, there will be plenty of time in the eternal future to hear the story of each and every one, as the song says, *"How we made it through."* What a joy it will be to hear Paul talk about his Ministry, his work for Christ, and to talk to Peter, and John, plus the great Prophets of the Old Testament, such as Isaiah, Jeremiah, Ezekiel, Daniel, etc.

WHERE WILL THIS JUDGMENT BE CONDUCTED?

Undoubtedly, it will be conducted in Heaven. Everyone who is included in the First Resurrection of Life will also be at this Judgment. This time frame will include the seven years of the Great Tribulation. This means that all who accept Christ during those final years will be included in the Resurrection of Life, meaning that they too will be given Glorified Bodies.

Concerning that seven year period, John wrote and said:

"And in those days shall men seek death, and shall not find it; and shall desire to die, and death shall flee from them. *(For pain to be so bad that people want to die is bad indeed! Evidently pain-killing drugs will not work. It will be interesting how medical doctors diagnose all of this, to say the least.)*

"And the shapes of the locusts *were* like unto horses prepared unto battle; and on their heads *were* as it were crowns like gold, and their faces *were* as the faces of men. *(These are demon spirits, but will be invisible. If they could be seen, this is what they would look like. We aren't told their origin in the Bible. We know they were not originally created in this manner, but evidently became this way in the revolution instigated by Lucifer against God [Isa. 14:12-20; Ezek. 28:11-19].)*

"And they had hair as the hair of women, and their teeth were as *the teeth* of lions. *(They were, no doubt, originally created by God to perform a particular function of praise and worship, even as the 'living creatures,' but they have suffered this fate due to rebellion against God.)*

"And they had breastplates, as it were breastplates of iron; and the sound of their wings *was* as the sound of chariots of many horses running to battle. *(We are given a glimpse here into the spirit world. This is the reason such foolish efforts as humanistic psychology are helpless against such foes. The only answer is Christ and the Cross.)*

"And they had tails like unto scorpions, and there were stings in their tails: and their power *was* to hurt men five months. *(This Judgment is limited to five months, which tells us Satan can only do what God allows him to do.)*

"And they had a king over them, *which is* the Angel of the bottomless pit *(gives us further insight into the spirit world of darkness)*, **whose name in the Hebrew tongue *is* Abaddon, but in the Greek tongue has *his* name Apollyon.** *(This is a powerful fallen Angel, who* *evidently threw in his lot with Lucifer in the great rebellion against God. Only four Angels are named in Scripture, 'Gabriel, Michael, Lucifer, and Apollyon,' the first two being Righteous.)*

"One woe is past *(refers to the fifth Trumpet Judgment)*; ***and,*** **behold, there come two woes more hereafter.** *(The word 'behold' calls attention to the fact that the two remaining 'woes' will be exceedingly horrific)*" **(Rev. 9:6-12).**

Actually, the First Resurrection of Life will incorporate several Raptures, which will take place at the end. They are:

- **The General Rapture explained in I Thess. 4:13-18. This Rapture will take place shortly before the advent of the Great Tribulation.**
- **The Rapture of the man child, which speaks of Jews, actually 144,000 Jews, which will be raptured at about the midpoint of the Great Tribulation (Rev. 12:5).**
- **The Rapture of the Tribulation Saints. This pertains to those who died as martyrs for their testimony of Jesus Christ during the entirety of the Great Tribulation (Rev. 7:9-17). This corresponds with Rev. 6:11.**
- **The Rapture of the two witnesses (Rev. 11:3-12).**

All of these groups, as stated, will be included in the First Resurrection of Life, and at the end of the Great Tribulation Period, and will all be in Heaven. So it stands to reason that Heaven is the place where this Judgment Seat will be held.

WHEN WILL THE JUDGMENT SEAT OF CHRIST BE CONDUCTED?

For all Believers to be included, which we most definitely will, it will have to be conducted immediately before the Second Coming. In fact, this Coming will take place during the Battle of Armageddon (Rev. 19:15-21).

The Apostle John described the Second Coming in this fashion:

"And I saw Heaven opened *(records the final Prophetic hour regarding the Second Coming, without a doubt the greatest moment in human history)*, **and behold a white horse** *(in effect, proclaims a war horse [Zech. 14:3])*; **and He Who sat upon him *was* called Faithful and True** *(faithful to His Promises and True to His Judgments; He contrasts with the false Messiah of Rev. 6:2, who was neither faithful nor true)*, **and in Righteousness He does Judge and make war** *(refers to the manner of His Second Coming)*.

"His eyes *were* as a flame of fire *(represents Judgment)*, **and on His Head *were* many crowns** *(represents the fact that He will not be Lord of just one realm; He will be Lord of all realms)*; **and He had a Name written, that no man knew, but He Himself** *(not meaning that it is unknown, but rather it is definitely unknowable; it will remain unreachable to man, meaning that its depths can never be fully plumbed)*.

"And He *was* clothed with a vesture dipped in Blood *(speaks of the Cross where He shed His Life's Blood, which gives Him the right to Judge the world)*: **and His Name is called The Word of God.** *(His revealed Name is the Word of God, for He revealed God in His Grace and Power to make Him known, so the Believer can say, 'I know Him')*

"And the armies *which were* in Heaven followed Him upon white horses *(these 'armies' are the Saints of God, in fact, all the Saints who have ever lived, meaning we will be with Him at the Second Coming)*, **clothed in fine linen, white and clean.** *(Harks back to Verse 8. It is the Righteousness of the Saints, all made possible by the Cross)*" **(Rev. 19:11-14).**

In fact, the JUDGMENT SEAT OF CHRIST could very well take place immediately before the MARRIAGE SUPPER OF THE LAMB. And this will be immediately prior to the Second Coming.

Concerning the Marriage Supper of the Lamb, John also wrote:

"And after these things *(pertains to specifically Chapter 18, but also the entire Book of Revelation in a broader sense,)* **I heard a great voice of much people in Heaven** *(proclaims 'praise,' which is the exact opposite of what is happening on Earth)*, **saying, Alleluia; Salvation, and Glory, and Honour, and Power, unto the Lord our God** *(the song here, and it is a song, does not begin with ascribing 'Salvation' to God, as the English version suggests; it rather affirms the fact; 'The Salvation is God's; it is the echo of the ancient utterance — "Salvation belongs unto God"')*:

"For true and righteous *are* His Judgments *(neither man nor spirit beings, in all honesty, can fault God for what He has done regarding the system of this world)*: **for He has Judged the great whore** *(pertains to every false way of Salvation, irrespective of what it might be; no matter how beautiful it might look outwardly, the Lord refers to it as the 'great whore')*, **which did corrupt the Earth with her fornication** *(this refers to all the religions of the world, and for all time; however, it also refers to the fact that if the Preacher is not preaching 'Jesus Christ and Him Crucified' as the answer to man's dilemma, then in some manner he is preaching and projecting a type of 'spiritual fornication' [Rom. 7:1-4])*, **and has avenged the blood of His servants at her hand.** *(Almost all of the persecution against the true Saints of God in this world, and for all time, has come from apostate religion. It started with Cain [Gen., Chpt. 4].)*

"And again they said, Alleluia. *(This 'praise of the Lord' is because of the destruction of the literal city of Babylon. The 'Alleluia' in Verse 1 was proclaimed concerning the destruction of Mystery Babylon.)* **And her smoke rose up for ever and ever** *(proclaims the fact that her Judgment is Eternal)*.

"And the four and twenty Elders and the four Beasts

(Living Ones) **fell down and worshipped God Who sat on the Throne** *(the 24 Elders represent all the Redeemed of all the ages; they are, in fact, 24 men; the 'four Living Ones' represent the Creation of God, and how that Creation can now serve its full purpose as originally intended)*, **saying, Amen; Alleluia.** *(This 'Alleluia' signals the end of all evil, and the beginning of all Righteousness.)*

"And a voice came out of the Throne *(is silent regarding the identity)*, **saying, Praise our God, all you His Servants, and you who fear Him, both small and great.** *(Every true Believer will praise the Lord, and should do so continually.)*

"And I heard as it were the voice of a great multitude *(this 'great multitude' consists of every single Believer who has ever lived, all the way from Abel to the last one Saved in the Great Tribulation)*, **and as the voice of many waters, and as the voice of mighty thunderings** *(this is praise that expresses itself, and not merely the thoughts of a silent heart)*, **saying, Alleluia: for the Lord God Omnipotent Reigns.** *(This 'Alleluia' pertains to the Lord reigning as King, and doing so forever. Satan does not reign. The Lord God Omnipotent Reigns, and He is 'All-powerful.')*

"Let us be glad and rejoice *(all the Redeemed are about to be joined in Holy Matrimony to the Lamb Who has Saved them)*, **and give honour to Him** *(God has made it possible for mankind to be Redeemed, and did so through the Sacrifice of His Son, the Lord Jesus Christ)*: **for the marriage of the Lamb is come, and His Wife has made herself ready.** *(This presents a scene that will take place in Heaven immediately before the Second Coming. The 'Wife' is the Redeemed of all ages.)*

"And to her was granted that she should be arrayed in fine linen, clean and white: for the fine linen is the Righteousness of Saints. *(The 'fine linen' is symbolic of 'Righteousness,' which was afforded by what Christ did at the Cross.)*

"And he said unto me, Write, Blessed *are* they which are called unto the Marriage Supper of the Lamb. *(The man speaking to John says this. The word 'Lamb' is used, signifying that all of this is made possible because of what Jesus did at the Cross.)* **And he said unto me, These are the true sayings of God.** *(This refers again to the fact that all of this is made possible by what Jesus did regarding His Finished Work)*" **(Rev. 19:1-9).**

As we have stated, THE JUDGMENT SEAT OF CHRIST could very well take place immediately before the MARRIAGE SUPPER OF THE LAMB, with that event taking place immediately before the Second Coming.

WHO WILL BE THE JUDGE?

Inasmuch as it is THE JUDGMENT SEAT OF CHRIST it stands to reason that Christ will be the Judge. As we've already quoted concerning THE GREAT WHITE THRONE JUDGMENT, all Judgment has been committed to the Son (Jn. 5:22).

Concerning Christ the Apostle Paul wrote:

"In Whom we have Redemption through His Blood *(proclaims the price that was paid for our Salvation)*, ***even*** **the forgiveness of sins** *(at the Cross, the Lord broke the power of sin, and took away its guilt [Rom. 6:6])*:

"Who is the Image of the invisible God *(the Son is the exact reproduction of the Father; a derived Image)*, **the Firstborn of every creature** *(actually means Jesus is the Creator of all things)*:

"For by Him were all things created *(presents the Justification of the title given Christ in the preceding Verse)*, **that are in Heaven, and that are in earth, visible and invisible** *(things seen and not seen)*, **whether *they be* thrones, or dominions, or principalities, or powers** *(refers to both Holy and fallen Angels)*: **all things were created by**

Him, and for Him *(Christ is the Creator of all [Jn. 1:3])*:

"And He is before all things *(preexistence)*, **and by Him all things consist.** *(All things come to pass within this sphere of His Personality, and are dependent upon it.)*

"And He is the Head of the Body, the Church *(the Creator of the world is also Head of the Church)*: **Who is the Beginning** *(refers to Christ as the Origin or Beginning of the Church)*, **the firstborn from the dead** *(does not refer to Jesus being Born-Again as some teach, but rather that He was the first to be raised from the dead as it regards the Resurrection, never to die again)*; **that in all *things* He might have the preeminence.** *(He is the First and Foremost as it relates to the Church.)*

"For it pleased *the Father* that in Him should all fulness dwell *(this 'fullness' denotes the sum total of the Divine Powers and Attributes)*" **(Col. 1:14-19).**

In essence, one might say, the Lord Jesus Christ has Saved us, and He has the right to judge us!

WHAT TYPE OF JUDGMENT WILL IT BE?

This Judgment has absolutely nothing to do with sin or sins. This was handled at Calvary when we came to Christ and was Born-Again. Plainly and clearly the Scripture says:

"But if we walk in the Light, as He is in the Light, we have fellowship one with another *(if we claim fellowship with Him, we will at the same time walk in the Light, which is the sphere of His Walk)*, **and the Blood of Jesus Christ His Son cleanses us from all sin.** *(Our Faith being in the Cross, the shed Blood of Jesus Christ, constantly cleanses us from all sin)*" **(I Jn. 1:7).**

No Believer will ever have to answer for a single sin committed, that being forever handled by Christ. To suggest the

opposite, is to claim that Calvary did not pay it all, which thinking is an abomination.

That's why Paul said:

> **"But God forbid that I should glory** *(boast)*, **save in the Cross of our Lord Jesus Christ** *(what the opponents of Paul sought to escape at the price of insincerity is the Apostle's only basis of exultation)*, **by Whom the world is Crucified unto me, and I unto the world.** *(The only way we can overcome the world, and I mean the only way, is by placing our Faith exclusively in the Cross of Christ and keeping it there)*" **(Gal. 6:14).**

So, understanding that all sin and sins have been handled at the Cross of Christ, then what will this Judgment consist of?

It will consist of the stewardship of the individual, regarding what Christ has given us, and it will, as well, incorporate motives. What did we do with what Christ gave us? What were our motives as it regards the reason for the doing?

Paul said:

> **"Now he who plants and he who waters are one** *(literally means in the Greek, 'one thing')*: **and every man shall receive his own reward according to his own labour.** *(Paul did not say, 'according to his own success,' but rather 'labor.' God hasn't called us to be successful, but He has called us to be Faithful.)*
>
> **"For we are labourers together with God** *(pertains to Labor in the harvest)*: **you are God's husbandry** *(God's field, God's tilled land)*, ***you are*** **God's building** *(Vineyard)*.
>
> **"According to the Grace of God which is given unto me, as a wise masterbuilder** *(in essence, Paul, under Christ, founded the Church)*, **I have laid the foundation** *(Jesus Christ and Him Crucified)*, **and another builds thereon** *(speaks of all Preachers who followed thereafter, even unto this very moment, and have built upon this Foundation)*.

But let every man take heed how he builds thereupon. *(All must preach the same Doctrine Paul preached, in essence, 'Jesus Christ and Him Crucified.')*

"For other foundation can no man lay than that is laid *(anything other than the Cross is another foundation and, therefore, unacceptable to the Lord)*, **which is Jesus Christ** *(Who He is, God manifest in the flesh, and What He did, Redemption through the Cross)*.

"Now if any man build upon this foundation gold, silver, precious stones *(presents Paul using symbols; the first three are materials which will stand the test of fire, symbolic of the Word of God which is the Standard)*, **wood, hay, stubble** *(will not stand the test of fire)*;

"Every man's work shall be made manifest *(at the Judgment Seat of Christ)*: **for the day shall declare it** *(the time of the Judgment Seat of Christ)*, **because it shall be revealed by fire** *(the fire of God's Word)*; **and the fire shall try every man's work of what sort it is.** *('Fire' in the Greek is 'puri,' and speaks of the ability of Christ, Who will be the Judge and Who sees through everything we do [Rev. 2:18]. He Alone knows our very motives!)*

"If any man's work abide which he has built thereupon *(assuming it to be true)*, **he shall receive a reward** *(pertains to that which will be eternal, although we aren't told what it will be)*.

"If any man's work shall be burned, he shall suffer loss *(refers to the loss of reward, but not Salvation)*: **but he himself shall be Saved; yet so as by fire.** *(Actually, this means the person is Saved 'despite the fire.' While the fire of the Word of God will definitely burn up improper works, it will not touch our Salvation, that being in Christ and the Cross)*" **(I Cor. 3:8-15).**

REWARD

As the Apostle has stated, and plainly so, Believers can gain

reward or lose reward at the Judgment Seat of Christ, which will stand for all eternity. We should not forget that!

It seems the reward will be based, more than anything, on our faithfulness to the Cross of Christ. That is symbolized as *"gold, silver, and precious stones."* Everything else is symbolized by *"wood, hay, and stubble."* Faithfulness to the Cross and what it represents, will be the test. I think we can say that without fear of contradiction. That's what the great Apostle said in this very letter:

> **"For I determined not to know any thing among you** *(with purpose and design, Paul did not resort to the knowledge or philosophy of the world regarding the preaching of the Gospel)*, **save Jesus Christ, and Him Crucified** *(that and that alone is the Message, which will save the sinner, set the captive free, and give the Believer perpetual victory)*" **(I Cor. 2:2).**

The Price that Jesus paid, which was the giving of Himself in Sacrifice, is that and that alone which stands between mankind and eternal Hell. We must never forget that. That's why the great Apostle said:

> **"But we preach Christ Crucified** *(this is the Foundation of the Word of God and, thereby, of Salvation)*, **unto the Jews a stumblingblock** *(the Cross was the stumblingblock)*, **and unto the Greeks foolishness** *(both found it difficult to accept as God a dead Man hanging on a Cross, for such Christ was to them)*;
>
> **"But unto them who are called** *(refers to those who accept the Call, for the entirety of mankind is invited [Jn. 3:16; Rev. 22:17])*, **both Jews and Greeks** *(actually stands for both 'Jews and Gentiles')*, **Christ the Power of God** *(what He did at the Cross Atoned for all sin, thereby, making it possible for the Holy Spirit to exhibit His Power within our lives)*, **and the Wisdom of God.** *(This Wisdom*

devised a Plan of Salvation which pardoned guilty men and at the same time vindicated and glorified the Justice of God, which stands out as the wisest and most remarkable Plan of all time)" **(I Cor. 1:23-24).**

Again, let us state, that faithfulness to the Message of the Cross will be the criteria by which we are judged. We must never forget that! That will be the criteria for the sentence concerning every Believer as it regards THE JUDGMENT SEAT OF CHRIST.

WHAT WILL THE REWARD BE?

We aren't told exactly as to what it will be; however, this we do know, whatever the Lord does, it is far beyond what we may even ask or think.

We are possibly given a hint in Paul's first Letter to the Corinthians. He said:

> **"*There are* also celestial bodies** *(heavenly bodies, such as the Sun, Moon, etc.)*, **and bodies terrestrial** *(earthly bodies, which refer to human beings, animals, trees, etc.)*: **but the glory of the celestial *is* one, and the *glory* of the terrestrial *is* another** *(the glory differs)*.
>
> **"*There is* one glory of the Sun, and another glory of the Moon, and another glory of the Stars: for *one* Star differs from *another* Star in glory.** *(Paul has a point here, which we will see in the next Verse.)*
>
> **"So also *is* the Resurrection of the dead.** *(Some Saints, due to greater faithfulness, will have greater glory than others, which is the point of the previous Verse.)* **It is sown in corruption** *(refers to the grave)*; **it is raised in incorruption** *(refers to the Glorified Form and the type of Body God will provide)*:
>
> **"It is sown in dishonour** *(refers to the awful indignity of 'dust to dust')*; **it is raised in glory** *(the same body, but*

glorified): **it is sown in weakness** *(death)*; **it is raised in power** *(life)*:

"It is sown a natural body *(was energized by 'blood,' before death)*; **it is raised a Spiritual Body** *(energized by the Holy Spirit, not blood, and will be of immortal substance)*. **There is a natural body** *(which we now have)*, **and there is a Spiritual Body.** *(The Glorified Body of our Lord is the example, and our Glorified Body will be like His [I Jn. 3:2])*" **(I Cor. 15:40-44).**

The Reward could very well be greater glory for some, and for all the obvious reasons, than for others. As to exactly what that will consist of, we do not now know. But again I state, to be sure, whatever the reward is, and whatever the glory is, it will be beyond that of which we could ask or even think. Paul again said:

"But as it is written *(Isa. 64:4)*, **Eye has not seen, nor ear heard, neither have entered into the heart of man** *(the purpose is to show that we cannot come to a knowledge of God through these normal ways of learning)*, **the things which God has prepared for them who love Him.**

"But God has revealed *them* unto us by His Spirit *(tells us the manner of impartation of Spiritual Knowledge, which is Revelation)*: **for the Spirit searches all things, yes, the deep things of God.** *(The Holy Spirit is the only One amply qualified to reveal God because He is God, and He is the member of the Godhead Who deals directly with man)*" **(I Cor. 2:9-10).**

"Now unto Him Who is able *(presents God as the Source of all Power)* **to do exceeding abundantly above all that we ask or think** *(so far beyond our comprehension that the Holy Spirit could give us this explanation only in these terms)*, **according to the power that works in us" (Eph. 3:20).**

CHAPTER SIXTEEN

Do All Suicides Die Lost?

QUESTION:

DO ALL SUICIDES DIE LOST?

ANSWER:

Every minute in the United States and Canada, someone attempts suicide. Mental anguish, suffering, pain, and consternation are only a few of the many reasons for this startling statistic. Not only is suicide personal, but it also affects entire families, causing untold grief and sorrow.

SUICIDES MENTIONED IN THE WORD OF GOD

There are four suicides mentioned in the Bible. They are:

- **Saul (I Sam. 31:4-5).**
- **Ahithophel (II Sam. 17:23).**
- **Zimri (I Ki. 16:18).**
- **Judas Iscariot (Mat. 27:5).**

Some would classify Samson as a suicide; he wasn't!

He died combating the forces of evil and, in effect, gave his life in the Work of God. He, no doubt, knew that his actions would mean certain death, yet he gave his life. His purpose was to destroy the enemies of God's People and, thereby, perform a tremendous service, which he did. It was not suicide.

As far as we know, the four people mentioned above, Saul, Ahithophel, Zimri, and Judas Iscariot, all died lost. There is no record that any of these people called out to God in their last minutes. Without exception, each of these suicides followed a long series of disobediences to God that climaxed in this deadly deed.

SATAN'S BUSINESS

It is Satan's business to destroy a person. He steals, kills, and destroys (Jn. 10:10). This is his ultimate goal — to drive

a person to the place where he would take his own life; therefore, Satan is the one behind this terrible act.

Consequently, I feel from my study of the Word of God that all suicides die lost, with one exception. I will explain that in a moment.

A suicide actually breaks many Commandments. The Sixth Commandment says, *"You shall not kill"* (Ex. 20:13). Suicide kills, actually, the person is committing his own murder, consequently, with no way to ask God's forgiveness. There are no second chances in eternity. First, second, third, and fourth opportunities, etc., are on this side of the grave.

FORGIVENESS?

That brings up the question that I basically touched on earlier. Can a person ask God for forgiveness, then commit suicide and the deed be forgiven by God? No, that cannot happen. Jesus said:

***"You shall not tempt the Lord your God"* (Mat. 4:7).**

Paul said:

***"Shall we continue in sin, that Grace may abound?"* His answer was to the point, *"God forbid!"* (Rom. 6:1). This is a fallacy that some people have been led to believe. An act of this nature cannot be perpetrated by premeditating the deed and asking for forgiveness before it is done. That is a frustration of the Grace of God, and it automatically negates itself.**

ONCE SAVED ALWAYS SAVED?

Here in Baton Rouge some time back, a young man asked a Preacher if it was true that when a person had truly been Saved, that they could never again be lost no matter what they did?

The Preacher replied in the affirmative!

A short time later the young man committed suicide, thinking, no doubt, that he could not be lost!

Unconditional eternal security is a false doctrine. It has

condemned untold numbers to Hell simply because they believed a lie and were lost.

There is one thing that gets us into the Grace of God, i.e., *"Salvation."* That one thing is Faith in Christ and what He did for us at the Cross. The Scripture says:

> **"For by Grace** *(the Goodness of God)* **are you Saved through Faith** *(Faith in Christ, with the Cross ever as its Object)***; and that not of yourselves** *(none of this is of us, but all is of Him)***: *it is* the Gift of God** *(anytime the word 'Gift' is used, God is speaking of His Son and His Substitutionary Work on the Cross, which makes all of this possible)***:**
>
> **"Not of works** *(man cannot merit Salvation, irrespective what he does)***, lest any man should boast** *(boast in his own ability and strength; we are allowed to boast only in the Cross [Gal. 6:14])***.**
>
> **"For we are His Workmanship** *(if we are God's Workmanship, our Salvation cannot be of ourselves)***, created in Christ Jesus unto good works** *(speaks of the results of Salvation, and never the cause)***, which God has before ordained that we should walk in them.** *(The 'good works' the Apostle speaks of has to do with Faith in Christ and the Cross, which enables the Believer to live a Holy life)***" (Eph. 2:8-10).**

If one abandons Faith in Christ, thereby, placing their Faith in something else, this constitutes a lost condition. It is Faith in Christ which got us in, and if Faith in Christ be abandoned, the person reverts to a lost condition. The Scripture says regarding that:

> **"For *it is* impossible for those who were once enlightened** *(refers to those who have accepted the Light of the Gospel, which means accepting Christ and His great Sacrifice)***, and have tasted of the Heavenly Gift** *(pertains*

to Christ and what He did at the Cross), **and were made partakers of the Holy Spirit** *(which takes place when a person comes to Christ)*,

"And have tasted the good Word of God *(is not language that is used of an impenitent sinner, as some claim; the unsaved have no relish whatsoever for the Truth of God, and see no beauty in it)*, **and the powers of the world to come** *(refers to the Work of the Holy Spirit within hearts and lives, which the unsaved cannot have or know)*,

"If they shall fall away *(should have been translated, 'and having fallen away')*, **to renew them again unto Repentance** *('again' states they had once repented, but have now turned their backs on Christ)*; **seeing they crucify to themselves the Son of God afresh** *(means they no longer believe what Christ did at the Cross, actually concluding Him to be an imposter; the only way any person can truly repent is to place his Faith in Christ and the Cross; if that is denied, there is no Repentance)*, **and put *Him* to an open shame** *(means to hold Christ up to public ridicule; Paul wrote this Epistle because some Christian Jews were going back into Judaism, or seriously contemplating doing so)*" **(Heb. 6:4-6).**

CHRISTIAN SUICIDES

There is an area where I believe some suicides are Saved and not lost.

It is a terrible thing for a person to be driven to this point of despair, but it is worse for a Christian. A Christian should cast all of his cares and anxieties on the Lord. Jesus came that we *"might have life, and . . . have it more abundantly"* (Jn. 10:10). There are problems, but God gives us victory over those problems if we walk in obedience to the Word of God and rely on Him. The sad fact is this: despite the great teaching of the Word of God and the Victory afforded by Jesus Christ, still, some Christians find themselves in perilous straits. If a Christian

becomes mentally disturbed, and due to temporary or total insanity, commits suicide, I believe that person would not be held responsible by God and would die in a Saved condition, simply because such an individual is not responsible for his action. And yet, the Lord, of course, would have to be the Judge of such a situation.

Now, some might say, *"Aren't all suicides either insane or at least temporarily so?"*

Even though a would-be suicide may be under great stress, I certainly do not agree that all are insane or even temporarily insane. We come back to the final conclusion. When it comes to a Christian, no one can answer that but God. No one knows the state of that individual's mind but God. And yet, we have this infallible Promise:

***"Shall not the Judge of all the Earth do right?"* (Gen. 18:25)**

CHAPTER SEVENTEEN

What Should Be The Christian's Position In Respect To Alcohol?

QUESTION:

WHAT SHOULD BE THE CHRISTIAN'S POSITION IN RESPECT TO ALCOHOL?

ANSWER:

"And he drank of the wine, and was drunken; and he was uncovered within his tent" **(Gen. 9:21).**

This is speaking of Noah.

The situation with Noah is the first mention of wine in the Bible, or any type of intoxicating beverage for that matter.

Some have claimed that the fermentation process didn't exist before the flood and that, consequently, Noah was not familiar with the possible product of the grape; however, there is no proof of such a thing and, in fact, the Hebrew language indicates that the Patriarch was familiar with what could be done with the grape as it regards fermentation. As well, Moses does not say this was the first occasion on which the Patriarch tasted fermented liquor (Moses wrote Genesis).

Since the sin of Noah, and it was sin, cannot be ascribed to ignorance, we can only ascribe it to the weakness of the human being.

Also, we find here that intoxication tends toward sensuality, inasmuch as Noah *"uncovered himself."* Ellicott says, *"It was no accident, but a willful breach of modesty."*

Inasmuch as the first mention of intoxicating beverage in the Bible revealed such a shameful episode, we cannot help but garner from this illustration as given by the Holy Spirit through Moses concerning Noah, the lesson that is being taught here.

- **What should our stand be as a Christian, as it regards alcohol?**
- **Is moderate drinking permissible?**
- **Is alcoholism a disease or a sin?**

Due to the seriousness of this matter, I think it would be

proper for us to give it a little more thorough treatment.

ALCOHOL

Back in the 1980's, the News Media seemed inordinately preoccupied with nuclear energy protestors, as if it was their civic duty to convince the American public that nuclear power was extremely dangerous. In view of this constant media barrage against this particular industry, which incidentally caused the stoppage of all construction of nuclear power plants, we are now experiencing a severe power shortage.

In view of this, I would like to focus on another subject of even more consequence — and I'd like to use the Media's rhetoric regarding nuclear power plants, as they then claimed such to be:

- What if 40-50 people were killed every day by malfunctioning nuclear power plants?
- What if such malfunction seriously injured 1,500 more every day?
- What if the presence and influence of nuclear plants caused 8-20 people per day to commit suicide?
- What if the secondary effects of nuclear power caused 200 broken homes each day?
- What if it caused 250 people each day to suffer permanent brain damage — besides the injuries already described?
- What if it caused some 3,000 parents to abuse their children, or to assault loved ones each day?
- What if it caused 50 billion dollars a year in direct damages, and an inestimable amount in indirect damages every year?

Awesome and disturbing statistics? Well, if you will *"double"* every figure I have just cited, you will have a fragmented picture of the effects of alcohol on American society today. In view of the fact that after decades of use, there hasn't been a single case of a person in the public sector being injured by nuclear power plants, one would have to question why the Media remains silent on alcohol's effects, while carrying on a

scathing campaign against other things. I can't answer that, but we can probe the reason behind the Media's silence on the alcohol question. But first, remember this.

Alcohol is responsible for:

- **50 percent of all automobile fatalities.**
- **80 percent of all home violence.**
- **30 percent of all suicides.**
- **60 percent of all child abuse.**

WHAT IS THE CAUSE OF ALCOHOLISM?

According to statistics, there are about 20 million alcoholics in this nation, a figure which is equivalent to two out of every five heavy drinkers. Actually, I find it hard to see the difference between the alcoholic and the heavy drinker. Think about it:

For every ten automobiles on the road, one is driven by a drunk. It's no wonder that 40,000 people a year are killed because of alcoholics behind the wheel. In addition, over one million are injured — some never to function normally again.

Incidentally, it is a scientific fact that if it takes ten beers to make a person drunk, one beer makes them one tenth drunk. That means, according to the amount of alcohol consumed, whether little or much, that a person is not in full control of his faculties. That's the reason for the accidents. Accidents?

SICKNESS OR SIN?

I picked up an article some time back written by a Minister. Unfortunately, his name wasn't credited, so I have no way of acknowledging him for his statement. What he said was excellent, however, and I want to share it with you. He asked the question, *"What is wrong with the drunkard?"* And then went on to say this:

"Years ago, while holding a city-wide Meeting in Salinas, California, I was attracted through an article in the daily paper,

to a Convention to be held in a Northern California town. Psychiatrists from all over America were coming out to the coast for this Convention.

"The object of the Convention was the thing that attracted me. They announced as their project . . . the discovery of what causes alcoholism, and then to suggest a cure. Here is the sum of the findings of this body.

"They stated that an alcoholic is not a moral degenerate, but a sick man. He can't help being sick anymore than an asthmatic or arthritic. (Notice the lack of personal responsibility.)

"He should not be picked up in a police car and thrown in jail, but should be picked up in an ambulance and put in a hospital. He shouldn't be treated as a moral degenerate, but a respected member of society who is sick.

"That was the trend of thought all through the deliberation, and not once during the Convention was whisky mentioned. The closest to it was the word 'alcoholism.' They never said if a man simply didn't drink, he would have no problem. No such ugly insinuations were made.

"The final session was the clincher. Headlines in the San Francisco paper stated: 'Psychiatrists decide,' then, in smaller print, 'alcoholism is caused by an unknown quantity that we shall choose to call "X" . . . until this unknown quantity can be isolated and defined, we have no suggested cure.'"

The Minister went on to state, *"I would hate to be an alcoholic depending on psychiatrists to help me!"*

I can only say *"Amen"* to that.

I am not a psychiatrist, but I know what makes men and women alcoholics. I'm certain it is not, as one alcoholic figured it: he railed against God for having done this to him. He shook his fist at his genes, at his heredity, at his father. He felt he had been programmed before birth to be a victim of alcohol.

No, the problem isn't a sickness, and it's not in the genes. It's not heredity, and it's certainly not God. The problem is *"sin"*— which results in an even more frightening word — bondage.

TODAY THE BIG EXCUSE FOR ALMOST EVERYTHING IS *"SICKNESS"*

Today, everyone is sick: the alcoholic, the thief, the child molester, the rapist, and the murderer. As one august Supreme Court Justice said some time ago, *"Everybody ought to be turned out of prison, because the prisoners are not really guilty; it's all of society that's responsible."* This statement might be humorous if it weren't so *"stupid."*

You see, the Bible says that men are liars, thieves, drunkards, immoral — and all the other things mankind is inevitably prey to — simply because they are sinners. They have turned their backs on God. Man is a product of the Fall. His Salvation lies not in treatment of a *"sickness,"* but in treatment of his sin — and Jesus took care of this at Calvary. Until men accept this treatment, they will not be cured. And, in fact, treatment is not really the correct word that should be used, but rather *"deliverance."*

Our Lord said concerning this: *"The Spirit of the Lord is upon Me, because He has anointed Me . . . to preach Deliverance to the captives"* (Lk. 4:18).

When Jesus died on Calvary's Cross, He addressed every sin, every bondage, every perversion, and every aberration that may attach itself to mankind, and did so by the giving of Himself as a Perfect Sacrifice, which was accepted by God. When the believing sinner places his Faith in Christ and what Christ did for us at the Cross, the Holy Spirit will then help such a person, Who, to be sure, has the Power, and because He is God. In fact, this is the only cure, the Deliverance afforded by Christ.

THE GREAT PROBLEM

But the problem is people want to escape the bondage of alcohol, without accepting Christ. I'm sorry, but there is no other answer to the ills of man. It is Jesus Christ and what He did for us at the Cross, and that is the only answer.

At least one of the reasons that the world of psychology labels alcoholism as a disease is the effort to escape responsibility. One of Satan's favorite ploys is to make someone else responsible!

But what does the Bible say?

It says, *"All have sinned and come short of the Glory of God."* Of course, man doesn't want to hear that. He doesn't want to admit he's a sinner and that he's lost. Most of all, he doesn't want to admit that unless he comes to God he will remain eternally lost. So we give it a new name. We call it a disease or a sickness. Well, listen to this. If it's a disease, it is the only disease . . .

- That is contracted by an act of the will.
- That requires a license for distribution.
- That is bottled and sold.
- That requires outlets for its sale.
- That produces revenue for the Government.
- That promotes crime.
- That is habit-forming.
- That is spread by advertising. (Can't you see this in the supermarket's ad? *"Get Coors, it's the best disease we have in the store."*
- For which we are fined and imprisoned when we exhibit its symptoms.
- Which brings death on the highway.
- Without a bacterial or viral cause, and for which there is no corrective medicine.
- Last but not least, alcoholism bars the patient from Heaven. For the Bible clearly states in I Corinthians 6:10 that no drunkard shall inherit the Kingdom of God (and I hasten to point out that while no drunkard will inherit the Kingdom of God, the Power of God can set the drunkard free and make him a fit subject for the portals of Glory — just as it can for anyone else).

No, alcoholism is not a disease. So this crutch that is being

used by the medical profession, the Psychiatrist, the Psychologist, and many others is merely that — a crutch. It serves to shift blame (and thus, remove the responsibility) from the one who is actually to blame, and that is the individual himself.

WHO PROMOTES ALCOHOL?

Constant attention is drawn to the terrible use of such mind-destroying drugs as heroin, marijuana, and cocaine, etc., and this should be done, but very little is being said about the most sinister drug of all — alcohol — the drug that is destroying our nation. It causes untold pain and suffering, and there is scarcely a word said against it. The newspapers are silent, newsmen seem unaware of the problem, and the pulpits (sad to say) are almost silent. As one realizes the tremendous amount of physical, financial, moral, and spiritual damage wrought by alcohol, one can't help but ask, *"Why?"*

Of course, the answer is obvious. Whereas cocaine, heroin, and other drugs are considered to be outside the limits of *"decent society,"* alcohol has been socially accepted. Why is this so?

- **Because it kills a little more slowly than the other type of drugs.**
- **Because there are vast amounts of money to be made from alcohol and the same people who control the distribution of alcohol control the dissemination of the information that influences people to use alcohol.**

TELEVISION AND MOVIES PROMOTE ALCOHOL

It is a sad fact that the image of alcohol is tremendously manipulated on Television. In one recent survey it was found that alcohol related violence was twenty-five times higher in real life than on Television dramas. In other words, the sinister aspects of alcohol are greatly downplayed on TV programming. Again, I ask why? Well, one should keep in mind that the TV Networks receive millions of dollars in revenues from

beer and wine accounts.

A short time ago one of our Telecasts was censored because we mentioned the name of a specific brewery on one of the programs. Should this shock us? Not if we consider beer and wine accounts that keep TV Stations operating in the black. No one who loves money will bite the hand that feeds him.

Dr. Thomas Radecki of the National Coalition on Television Violence recently stated, *"With the new research in the past two years, it is increasingly clear that TV advertising and program use of alcohol is playing a major role in the increasing abuse of alcohol."*

Radecki noted that the average child will see alcohol consumed 75,000 times on TV before he reaches the legal drinking age! When he must make his personal decision in regard to drinking, what will the subliminal influences tell him? That the *"in people,"* those who are bright, sophisticated, and successful on Television are almost inevitably seen holding a drink in their hands. In other words, as far as Hollywood and network television people are concerned, if you are bright and smart, you too will have a drink in your hand.

He also observed that on network programming the typical viewer sees 5,000 incidents of alcohol intake per year. Ninety-nine percent of these cases of drinking will be portrayed as favorable or at least neutral!

THE REAL WORLD

Another question must be asked. Is this what life is like in the real world? The facts show us that fifty percent of real-life balance is associated with alcohol consumption! On Television, only one percent of televised violence is associated with drinking. Dr. Radecki believes that TV's benign portrayal of alcohol consumption is one of the major reasons why alcohol abuse and violence are the two most rapidly increasing causes of death in the United States.

A total of seventy-six percent of those shown drinking any

kind of beverage on television will be shown drinking alcohol.

TV characters spend twice as much time drinking alcohol as tea or coffee. They consume fourteen times more liquor and beer than soft drinks, and they drink fifteen times more alcohol than water, or at least it is promoted as such, whatever is in the glass. Television viewers will see an average of three incidents of alcohol consumption for each hour they watch during prime time. Those watching daytime TV will see six instances of drinking per hour. (Obviously soap opera characters have a higher percentage of alcoholism than the evening characters have.)

Contrary to what one might expect (if TV is supposed to reflect the real world), it isn't the villains who do the most drinking. The heaviest TV drinkers are well-known stars appearing in regular series where they serve as role models for our children and young people. TV characters seldom refuse a drink — nor do they express disapproval of someone else's drinking. In situation comedies, excessive drinking is often used as a *"good natured"* way to get more laughs.

It is now understandable why over three quarters of all high school seniors use liquor regularly — with one-half getting drunk at least once a month. It's also easy to understand why the White House Drug Abuse Office states that pressure to drink begins as early as the fourth grade. It might be a fine thing if someone led a crusade to get wine and beer commercials taken from the air as cigarette ads were.

THE MAIN PROMOTERS OF BEER AND WINE

It certainly isn't hard to imagine the producers of a product as the main promoters of that product. They're in the business of selling the poison they produce; however, it's the manner in which they promote it that's despicable. Let's take a look at this.

We're told that beer in Australia is vitamin-enriched. Researchers at the University of Queensland report that chronic vitamin deficiencies in alcoholics could be offset if brewers

were to add vitamin B-1 to their products. They assert that *"A lot of heavy drinkers stand to benefit."* They also said, *"The average person in the northern Territory consume 60 gallons of beer yearly!"*

This will, of course, be yet another advertising plus for the breweries. They will suddenly be able to trumpet the nutritional benefits of drinking — trying to divert the consumer's attention from the bondage that comes along with the intake of a little vitamin B.

A California winery has introduced Red Life, a light wine aimed at these soda drinkers who want something *"a little stronger."* The main idea of course, is to get young people — even children — interested in drinking at an early age so they will then graduate to something stronger.

You must remember, the breweries help to manufacture customers — and they have to start with the children to do this. I'll give you another example.

In the Oklahoma City Times, containing the report of a speech William Coors (then Chairman of the Adolph Coors Company) made to a Convention of security analysts meeting in Denver — he described the advertising of his own company as well as other breweries as *"outrageous"* for its lack of ethics.

ADVERTISEMENT

He referred especially to the fact that his company pays 250 college students throughout the United States to promote its beer through campus *"Wet T-Shirt Contests," "Get Drunk,"* and *"Chug-a-lug"* parties. He said the other breweries did this so his company followed suit as something *"strictly defensive."*

Coors said, *"We do this — not because we think it is right — but because other brewers do it. They will steal our lunch — if we don't do it."* He added, *"I personally think it's outrageous, and everyone in the company thinks it's outrageous. One way or the other, the country is going to stop this because our industry doesn't have the ethics to stop themselves."*

In legal parlance, testimony against self-interest is the most damaging type possible in a court of law. Coors certainly testified against his own self-interest when he confessed the lack of ethics among the brewery owners and managers. And by the way, his company sold nearly 15 million barrels of beer in the first nine months of last year — 15 percent increase over the same period for the previous year.

At the same time Coors was confessing his sins, he also lashed out at do-gooders who were trying to raise the drinking age from 18 to 21 — questioning the motives of such crusades. He then went on to claim that only five percent of alcohol users are abusers.

However, what he neglected to add is that the other 95 percent of nonabusers are on the way to becoming abusers — in other words, drunks. They will eventually get there if they drink long enough. Simply stated, the 5 percent who are now abusers were not guilty of drunkenness when they started drinking!

Yes, the boys who make the alcohol are their own best promoters, and they do so in the most hypocritical, and perverse manner imaginable.

POLITICIANS

Legislators in the state of Wisconsin some time back argued recently whether milk or beer should be the state drink. Wisconsin is known for both its dairies and breweries (*"The Beer That Made Milwaukee Famous"*) so the competition was intense. One State Representative declared his choice was alcohol, because, in his words, *"Beer tempers the emotions of our hard-working adults."*

This Representative should be reminded that beer murders scores of Wisconsin motorists every year. Alcohol also compels some of those so-called *"hard-working adults"* to beat their wives and deprive their children. To my knowledge, milk has never been cited as a cause of broken homes or bruised bodies.

Since marijuana is the number one cash crop in several

sections of the United States, maybe it's only a matter of time before some political opportunists will nominate pot as the official drug for the state.

One cannot help but say and think that the Legislators of Wisconsin ought to have better sense.

One doctor stated the other day that the reason stiffer laws are not enacted for drunk driving (or stiffer sentences not imposed) is because too many of the Legislators and Judges are drunks themselves. This could well be true.

PREACHERS

Sadly, it is true, from the American pulpits, there is seldom heard a discouraging word — on the subject of alcohol.

As I write this, I am reminded of a religious periodical that stated (from a teletype news report) that one of the world's noted Evangelists said there was nothing wrong with an occasional drink. Talking to reporters, this particular Evangelist said he didn't believe the Bible taught teetotalism. *"After all* (this Preacher went on to say) *Jesus drank wine,"* and he pointed to the Biblical account in which Jesus is said to have turned water into wine at a wedding feast. And as the Evangelist put it, *"that wasn't grape juice, as some try to claim."* I wonder if this statement was made to please and excuse the cocktail-drinking friends of the Preacher.

(We will discuss momentarily the water that Jesus turned to wine.)

Not so long ago, one major Missionary Evangelist told me personally that in a great religious conclave (with thousands of Preachers present) he asked all the Preachers (who were Pentecostal incidentally) in the congregation to stand if they did — or would — take a public stand against any and all use of alcohol. He was startled at the number who would not stand!

I had a Preacher tell me just today that our institutions are the way they are because our Churches are the way they are — and our Churches are the way they are because our families

are the way they are. I wonder if our families are the way they are because the pulpits are silent.

I want to make a statement: any Preacher of the Gospel who won't take a public stand against any and all use of alcohol — and be vocal in that stand — is doing his people, his God, and his country a disservice. The position that many Preachers take, that they never mention alcohol because *"their people already know it's wrong,"* is a cop out. Many take this position because they don't want to offend the *"sipping Saints"* in the congregation.

The Preacher of the Gospel has always been the one to whip the nation into line. The Preacher of the Gospel is supposed to address the moral issues. It may not be popular at times but it is our business. And if we fail to do it — there's no one else to do it. You could be dead-level sure that the Media aren't going to do it, and you can also be sure that the politicians aren't going to do it. (Although, in the last couple of years, a few politicians have stood up and taken a stand on this matter — perhaps a reaction to the dead, dry sermonizing they hear from the pulpits.)

Preachers — no matter what it costs you — stand up before your congregation and make your position known. Warn the young people of the terrible ravages of alcohol. Make no bones about it, pull no punches, and quibble not. And if you don't have strong feelings about seeing death and carnage all around you as a result of America's worst drug — there's something wrong with you!

WHAT SHOULD BE THE CHRISTIAN'S POSITION IN RESPECT TO ALCOHOL?

Any true Christian in today's society, desiring to set a good example for the Cause of Christ will be a teetotaler. It's just that simple.

All types of arguments are offered to defend social drinking. Some say that it's the culture of some places, such as beer

in Germany and wine in France. But Believers must understand, when we come to Christ, we leave the culture of this world, whatever it is, and come into the culture of the Lord, which is Bible Culture.

We must remember, every alcoholic in this nation or anywhere in the world, didn't start out as an alcoholic. It started out as a lark, but it began with their first drink. Where it is true that some people do not become bound by alcohol and can stop with what is referred to as moderation; however, millions can't. And as a Believer, we certainly should desire to set a good example before the world, and setting an example that can lead to alcoholism, is certainly not a Biblical example. Considering the damage that alcohol does, to which we have enumerated, it would seem to me that Believers should desire to shun alcohol in any fashion, whether it be social drinking or whatever. What does the Bible say on this subject?

***"Wine is a mocker, strong drink is raging: and whosoever is deceived thereby is not wise"* (Prov. 20:1).**

***"Who has woe? who has sorrow? who has contentions? who has babbling? who has wounds without cause? who has redness of eyes? They who tarry long at the wine; they who go to seek mixed wine. Look not upon the wine when it is red, when it gives his color in the cup, when it moves itself aright. At the last it bites like a serpent, and stings like an adder"* (Prov. 23:29-32).**

***"Woe unto them who rise up early in the morning, that they may follow strong drink; who continue until night, till wine inflame them!"* (Isa. 5:11).**

***"Woe unto them who are mighty to drink wine, and men of strength to mingle strong drink"* (Isa. 5:22).**

***"Woe to the crown of pride, to the drunkards of Ephraim, whose glorious beauty is a fading flower, which are on the head of the fat valleys of them who are overcome with wine!"* (Isa. 28:1).**

"But they also have erred through wine, and through strong drink are out of the way; the Priest and the Prophet have erred through strong drink, they are swallowed up of wine, they are out

***of the way through strong drink; they err in vision, they stumble in Judgment"* (Isa. 28:7).**

ALCOHOL'S CONSEQUENCES

I was in a Midwestern city in a Meeting many years ago, and a tragedy had struck locally that riveted the attention of the whole area.

Services had ended for the night. After almost everyone had left, I walked back to the Pastor's office. I saw him sitting behind his desk, his head in his hands. I asked him what was wrong. He looked at me and asked me if I had heard about the tragedy that had taken place that very day. I had, and then he gave me this background.

The young lady who was murdered was raised in his Church. She had once been Saved and followed Jesus, but had turned her back on God. She and her boyfriend had been to a party and both had been drinking heavily. They left this particular party and then went to a bar — and then left it and were on their way to another bar. The boy made advances toward her, which she repelled. He grew incensed and started beating her with his fist.

He had a large ring on his finger, and in his anger and drunken delirium he beat her to death. She was beaten so badly that they were unable to open her casket for the service.

Some hours later, after he had sobered up, he wandered into a police station and gave himself up. He really didn't know why he did it. He said, *"I was drunk."*

Incidents like this are repeated many thousands of times every year. I can't comprehend how any Christian could see the misery and the heartache that alcohol has caused and not be a teetotaler. Of course, the contention we are told is always this:

It's the abuse of alcohol that is wrong. If you drink moderately, they say, it then becomes a question of *"social relaxation."*

However, who with any sense would question that those

who are now abusers (over 20 million in this country) started out as social drinkers, but wound up as falling-down drunks? No, that argument is too thin to skim. Let's go a little further with it.

As previously stated, I personally do not know how many beers it takes to make a person drunk (or shots of whisky or glasses of wine for that matter), and I suppose it's a different intake for different people. But if it takes ten beers to make a person drunk, then it is a scientific fact that one beer makes the person one-tenth drunk. The vision is impaired by that much, with the motor responses also impaired. The reaction time is also slowed. And this is not merely the conclusion of a Preacher — this is a scientific fact after exhaustive investigation. Even one drink will affect reflexes and will take two hours to leave the body. That's why it's dangerous to drive after only one drink!

Once again, and because it is so important, let us say it again: it is a scientific fact that after just one drink, your judgment is impaired and your reflexes are slowed. After only one drink, a person is *"a little drunk."*

No, alcohol has broken up more homes, murdered more human beings, made paupers of more people, starved more children, started more wars, wrecked more careers, broken more marriages, caused more crimes, sent more souls to Hell, and wrecked more lives than any single factor on the face of the Earth.

In view of this, I must ask the question again. How can any Christian justify even one drink? Alcohol is the most rotten, debilitating, damnable, despicable devil that ever fastened itself upon the human race.

WHAT IS THE ETERNAL FUTURE FOR THE USER OF ALCOHOL?

The Bible is crystal clear on the eternal Judgment of the drunkard. Galatians 5:19 begins a list of the works of the

flesh, and Verse 21 lists drunkenness among them. Then the conclusion of Verse 21 states, *"They which do such things shall not inherit the Kingdom of God."*

So the eternal destiny of those who engage in drunkenness is eternal Hell. The Bible is very clear in regard to this. Of course, the answer always comes back, *"But Brother Swaggart, I'm not a drunkard, I only take a social drink now and then, and I can't see where the Bible condemns it."* Let's look at it this way.

As we have mentioned, when a person takes just one drink, he is partially drunk. So the question we must ask ourselves is this, "Where will it lead in regard to the road we're traveling?" It's not so much the single drink as it is the path that one drink leads to — the example it sets.

When a Christian takes one drink, he's voting in favor of all the broken homes, twisted lives, and broken dreams caused by alcohol. He's declaring himself in favor of all the hell and horror that alcoholism has caused over the centuries. When you take one drink, you're saying you're in favor of all the world stands for, all the flesh stands for, and all the Devil stands for. No sir, no Christian who wants to serve his Lord as he should will countenance even one drink. But the Bible has more to say about it than even that.

***"Woe unto him who gives his neighbor drink, who puts the bottle to him, and makes him drunken also, that you may look on their nakedness! You are filled with shame for glory: drink you also, and let the foreskin be uncovered, the cup of the LORD's Right Hand shall be turned unto you, and shameful spewing shall be on your glory. For the violence of Lebanon shall cover you, and the spoil of beasts, which made them afraid, because of men's blood, and for the violence of the land, of the city, and of all who dwell therein"* (Hab. 2:15-17).**

ONE TRAGIC EXAMPLE

A lot of people have looked with great sorrow, and rightly so, on the terrible tragedies that have befallen the Kennedy

family. Despite untold riches, fame, power, and popularity, this family has suffered a jarring succession of tragedies.

Joe Jr. was killed in an airplane crash in WWII and one daughter was born with serious mental problems. Everyone knows the horror of the terrible assassinations of Jack Kennedy and Bobby Kennedy. Then there was the tragedy of the Chappaquiddick incident with Ted Kennedy — and then the untimely death of David Kennedy from a drug overdose. And then of late, the death of John Jr. in a plane crash with his wife and others.

Admittedly, all of these tragedies would not fall under the category of being alcohol induced. But I feel there were too many of them to just be chance. Let's look at the Kennedy background.

When prohibition ended, Franklin Delano Roosevelt told Joseph Kennedy, Sr. that the legislation of prohibition would be repealed. Once again, it would be legal to make and sell alcoholic beverages in the United States. Joseph Kennedy, Sr. bought up the great Haig & Haig Scotch Whisky Industries in England. The hour of prohibition ended — and it became legal to make and sell alcohol in the United States — Joseph Kennedy had a ready supply of alcohol stored in warehouses in many cities in the United States. He had received permission to store it under the guise of medicinal purposes. So, for a considerable period of time, a good portion of the whisky sold in the United States came from Joseph Kennedy. That was one of the ways in which multiplied millions of dollars were amassed, which later helped to finance the political aspirations of Jack Kennedy, and his election to the Presidency of the United States.

In short, one might say that whisky money at least helped buy the presidency for Jack Kennedy. What produced this money?

Multiplied millions of homes inflamed with violence, heartache, dissipation, pain, and death. Multiplied millions were started on the road to ruin. And God said plainly, *"Woe unto him who gives his neighbor drink, who puts the bottle to him."*

He also said in the first part of Verse 17 that *"Violence . . . shall cover you"* (Hab. 2:17). That identifies perfectly what has happened to one of America's most famous and powerful families.

However, this applies not only to people like the Kennedy's who amass great fortunes, but also the bartenders serving it, the grocery store owners selling it, the liquor store distributing it, and the brewery manufacturing it. It also holds for the restaurants that sell it. All are cursed by God. This could be one of the reasons America is the violence capital of the world. It could be the reason that violent crimes are increasing at an unprecedented rate.

LINCOLN'S WORDS

Abraham Lincoln delivered the following words in Springfield, Illinois, on February 22, 1842:

"Whether or not the world would be vastly benefited by total and final banishment of all intoxicating drinks, seems to me not now an open question. Three fourths of mankind confess the affirmity with their tongues, and, I believe, all the rest acknowledge it in their hearts . . . turn now to the temperance revolution. In it we shall find a stronger bondage broken; a viler slavery manumitted; a greater tyrant deposed. In it, more of want supplied, more disease healed, more sorrow assuaged. By it, no orphan starving, no widows weeping. By it, none wounded in feelings, none injured in interest.

"If the relative grandeur of revolutions shall be estimated by the great amount of human misery they alleviate, and the small amount they inflict, then indeed will this be the grandest the world shall ever have seen.

"And when the victory shall be complete — when there shall be neither a slave nor a drunkard on the Earth — how proud the title of that land, which may truly claim to be the birthplace and the cradle of both those revolutions, that shall have ended in that victory. How nobly distinguished that people, who shall have planted, and nurtured to maturity, both the political and moral

freedom of their species."

A DOCTOR SPEAKS OUT

A doctor wrote this to a newspaper some time ago:

"Recently we saw another preview of Hell in the Parkland Hospital Emergency Room. A woman was struck down by a drunken driver, a college student lying semi-conscious following a head-on collision with another drunken driver, who was himself critically injured. The drunk's companion was dead. Four other drunks, with lacerations and stab wounds, waiting to be treated.

Night after night, year after year, the same bloody trail of horror — major auto accidents, stabbings, rapes, and wife beatings. Nightly emergencies, treated and released, are admitted to the hospital or pronounced dead on arrival. And almost always the bloody trail is led to that honored man of distinction — the weekend drinker. Almost always this is the moderate drinker, not the alcoholic. I wonder if there is that much joy to be gained, from the total consumption of all the beers and whiskies made, to equal even a small fraction of the innocent suffering, the damaged bodies, the broken marriages, the discarded children, the total brutalities, and crimes that accompany its use.

"What a quiet place our Emergency Room would be if beverage alcohol were ever abolished from our city."

No, sir, alcoholism is not a sickness — it is a sin that results in bondage.

No, sir, the moderate drinker is not socially acceptable — for every alcoholic starts out drinking moderately.

No, sir, no Christian who wants to serve his Lord can even remotely accept the consumption of even one drink.

WAS THE WATER THAT JESUS TURNED INTO WINE IN JOHN CHAPTER TWO THE KIND OF WINE THAT WILL MAKE ONE DRUNK?

No, and I will explain why:

If the wine is understood to be intoxicating wine, our Lord is automatically placed in a position of providing who had already *"well drunk"* (Jn. 2:10) with more wine. If it was intoxicating wine, the Lord would have been breaking His Own Law against temperance. The total amount of water turned into wine that day was about 150 gallons. If this had been an intoxicating beverage, it would have served as an invitation to drink and would havc placed our Lord in the unsavory position of providing a flood of intoxicants for the people who had already consumed a considerable amount.

GOOD WINE

The word *"good"* was used to describe what the Lord had miraculously brought about. It was the Greek word *"kalos"* and is defined in *"Vine's Expository Dictionary of New Testament Words"* as denoting what is intrinsically good. Now the pure, sweet juice of the grape could rightly be denoted as *"intrinsically good"*; but the rotted, fermented, decayed, spoiled, intoxicating kind of wine could hardly be called good. It is easy to think of the term *"good"* in describing whatever the Lord makes. For example, in describing the Creation, Moses said, *"And God saw everything that He had made, and, behold, it was very good"* (Gen. 1:31).

It is unthinkable that our Lord would have made corrupted, fermented wine at Cana and called it *"good."* You see, fermentation is a kind of decomposition, just as are putrefaction and decay. It would be almost blasphemous to call that *"good"* in connection with our Lord.

Pliny (an ancient Greek scholar) said that *"good wine"* was a term used to denote the juice destitute of spirit. Albert Barnes says, *"The wine referred to here was doubtless such as was commonly drunk in Palestine."* That was the pure juice of the grape; it was not brandied or drugged wine. Nor was it wine compounded of various substances, such as people drink in this land. The common wine of that day, which was drunk in

Palestine, was the simple juice of the grape, i.e., *"grape juice."*

As well, it is tantamount to blasphemy, in my opinion, to suppose that the First Miracle performed after being filled with the Holy Spirit (compare Mark 1:9-12; Luke 4:1) with an act of creating an intoxicating wine for a crowd of celebrants, the kind of wine that would make them drunk, it is unthinkable!

Still another fact from the record in John, Chapter 2 is this: those men who had already drunk a considerable amount praised the bridegroom for having kept the *"good wine"* until the last. Now, it is a simple fact that alcohol drunk to any excess, will deaden the taste buds of the drinker. If the wine in Cana of Galilee, that the guests had already been partaking of was intoxicating wine (and they had already partaken of quite a bit at this point), then when the wine that Jesus miraculously made was given to them, they could not have detected its taste. Their taste buds would have been deadened. To be honest with you, they would have been drunk by this time, or almost so. Only if they had been drinking the form of the vine's fruit that we know as grape juice, and then had been provided some fresh grape juice would the Governor of the feast had been able to make the observation he did.

WINE IN BIBLICAL TIMES

There are several words in the Bible which describe wine; however, two of these words are the most commonly used. In the New Testament, it is the Greek word *"oinos,"* which can mean either fermented or unfermented wine.

Dr. Ferrar Fenton, a Biblical translator (The Holy Bible in Modern English), lists six different meanings of the word *"oinos"*:

- Grapes, as fresh fruit.
- Raisins.
- Thick grape syrup.
- A thick jam.

- Fresh grape juice.
- Fermented grape juice.

The last type is the only one which would make one drunk.

Dr. Lyman Abbott said that fermented wine in Bible times was the least common of all wines. Even in the fermented kind, the percentage of alcohol was small.

In the Old Testament, the Hebrew word for wine most commonly used is *"yayin."* That word is found 141 times in the Old Testament, and is used interchangeably, depending on the context. In other words, it can mean either grape juice or alcoholic beverage.

I think the reasons given are sufficient proof that Jesus did not change water to the kind of wine that would make one drunk. Instead, it was a sweet, pure grape juice.

Before prohibition *"wine"* was considered to be exactly what it was in Bible times. However, when prohibition was enacted in 1929, the term had to be defined more closely; consequently, *"wine"* was designated to mean something that will make you drunk. The other kind of non-intoxicating beverage was called by whatever name desired, grape juice or whatever; consequently, many people today confuse the simple word *"wine"* as it was used in the Bible without understanding of that word presently, but that is not universally true.

No, Jesus' First Miracle was not the making of wine that would make one drunk. It was pure, sweet, fresh grape juice; and I believe Scripturally, scientifically, and legally we have proof of that.

DID THE SAVIOUR USE INTOXICATING WINE IN THE LORD'S SUPPER?

In the description of the Lord's Supper, the Lord never used the word *"wine."* We are told, *"He took the cup and gave thanks, and gave it to them saying, drink you all of it"* (Mat. 26:27). Mark says, *"He took the cup, and when He had given thanks, He gave it to them"* (Mk. 14:23). Luke says, *"He took the cup, and gave thanks, and said, Take this, and divide it among yourselves"* (Lk. 22:17). Jesus called the drink, *"Fruit of the vine"* in Matthew 26:29 and also in Mark 14:25 and Luke 22:18.

It seems the Holy Spirit carried this directive right on through even into the Early Church. The Apostle Paul said, *"After the same manner also, He took the cup, when He had supped, saying, This cup is the New Testament in My Blood"* (I Cor. 11:25). Then, following, He mentioned *"this cup"* and then, later on, *"that cup."*

It becomes clear, when the Passages are read consecutively that God intended for us to use grape juice. I also think the Holy Spirit took particular pains not to use any words that could be construed as referring to any kind of intoxicating beverage. There's not a single reference in the Word of God that a person should use intoxicating wine for the Lord's Supper.

THE SYMBOL OF DECAY

The very meaning of fermented wine makes it unsatisfactory to represent the Blood of our Lord Jesus Christ, and that's exactly what the grape juice of the Lord's Supper is to represent. I do not know a whole lot about fermentation or the wherefores of making alcoholic beverages, but I do know that fermented wine is grape juice in which decay (or rot) has taken place. In other words, the process of fermentation is the breakdown of large molecules caused by the influence of bacteria or fungi. Wine, then, results from the degenerative action of germs on pure substances.

Fermented wine used in Communion would actually symbolize tainted, sinful blood and not the Pure and Perfect Blood of Jesus Christ that had to be made evident to a be a Perfect cleansing for our sins. Pure, fresh grape juice tends toward life, but fermented wine tends toward death. Alcohol use for drinking purposes is both a narcotic and a poison. It could hardly be used as a symbol for the Blood of the Lord Jesus Christ.

THE PASSOVER FEAST

To give an example, the Jews were required to use unleavened bread with the Passover Feast, and they were commanded that during that time, *"There shall no leavened bread be seen with you, neither shall there be leaven seen with you in all your quarters"* (Ex. 13:7). As early as this, bread that had been tainted with bacteria or yeast was considered unsuitable at the religious events celebrated by the Jews. Jesus also used unleavened bread in initiating the Lord's Supper. (Of course, the New Testament made no special issue of the unleavened bread; and as far as that is concerned, any bread made without yeast today would serve as unleavened bread.) Consequently then, from Exodus to the Gospels we are told to use only untainted, pure substances in Spiritual Celebrations.

Consequently, the point that I make is this: if the Lord specifically chose bread that had no bacteria, no fungus spores in it, to picture His Broken Body, do you honestly think He would choose alcoholic wine, fermented wine, which is directly the product of fungi and bacteria, to represent His Blood? I hardly think so! The pure Blood of Jesus Christ would be best represented by pure grape juice.

THE MORAL STATUTES

Next, even the High Priests were commanded, *"Do not drink wine nor strong drink . . . when you go into the Tabernacle of the congregation, lest you die: it shall be a Statute forever throughout your generations"* (Lev. 10:9).

You must remember, these Priests entering into the Tabernacle were types of the Lord Jesus Christ, Who is our great High Priest. Now I ask you a question. Would Jesus, the night He was betrayed, drink intoxicating wine before going to the Crucifixion and entering into His High Priestly Work? I think not. It would have been a rejection and a contradiction of His Own Word given in Leviticus.

I close by saying this, we must always remember that the word *"wine"* in the Bible simply means *"the fruit of the vine."* It can either mean unfermented grape juice or intoxicating wine. So, when the Word is read, whether it is New Testament or Old Testament, this distinction must always be kept in mind according to the context.

No, I do not believe the wine that Jesus used at the Lord's Supper was intoxicating wine, nor do I believe it is proper and permissible for us to use such wine in the Lord's Supper today. I think it is a travesty of His Word and a perversion of His Intent.

To sum up, and as we've already stated several times, every Christian should be opposed to alcohol in any form, even to the slightest amount, as it regards its consumption. As Believers, we are to set an example of Righteousness before the world. Being a moderate drinker of any type does not serve that purpose. Saying *"no"* to all alcohol, does!

CHAPTER EIGHTEEN
Is Abortion Wrong?

QUESTION:

IS ABORTION WRONG?

ANSWER:

First of all, abortion is sin. Absolutely and without question it is sin. In fact, it is the equivalent of murder, in this instance the murder of an unborn, but yet living infant.

For many centuries no decent person, and certainly no respected Christian, has advocated killing an unborn baby. Like any other act of killing in cold blood, it is murder. This used to be the law of civilized nations, and more important, it is presently the Law of God and, in fact, always has been.

Yet now, Godless people are saying, *"Kill the baby. It will be good for the mother's mental health. She doesn't want the child. She has become pregnant* (most of the time) *because of the sin of fornication or adultery. She doesn't want to feed, clothe, or rear the child."* She will then go to a doctor and pay him to kill the unwanted baby, and somehow greed will still the conscience.

However, let it ever be understood, laws passed by man, if those laws are wrong, do not make it right. This means that the conscience will still haunt the guilty party. As well, at any given time, the young lady will wonder, what would my baby have looked like? What color would their eyes have been? Would they have had my features?

Yet, any lady who reads this, who has suffered an abortion in the past, and will ask the Lord to forgive her, to be sure, He most definitely will hear and answer such a prayer. He will forgive and heal, but yet, the haunting memory remains.

ALL MURDER IS WRONG

In the Old Testament, even before the Law, God said, *"Whoso sheds man's blood, by man shall his blood be shed: for*

in the Image of God made He man" (Gen. 9:6). Under the Mosaic Law, God plainly commanded, *"He who smites a man, so that he die, shall surely be put to death"* (Ex. 21:12).

The death penalty for murder is also clearly implied in the New Testament (Rom. 13:1-7).

To God the killing of an unborn child is murder. No law made by man can make it otherwise.

A HUMAN BEING

Second, the unborn child, the fetus, is a human being — a person — from the time of conception. Some persons have foolishly said that the unborn child, up to the sixth or seventh month, is little more than a *"blob"* of flesh; but that is simply not true. The little unborn baby is not just a part of the mother's body. It is a separate life altogether. All of the child's particular traits have already been charted in its genes. The sex of the child, the color of the eyes and hair, the physical features, the special talents and gifts are all determined at the time of conception. Both the mother and father of the child have already, at this point, passed down to their baby every genetic characteristic they will contribute.

A LIVING SOUL

The Bible also teaches that the fetus, from conception, is a person and, consequently, a living soul. David was inspired to say, *"Behold, I was shaped in iniquity, and in sin did my mother conceive me"* (Ps. 51:5). When David said, *"I was shaped,"* it was his honest inference that from the moment of conception, he was the person who would later be known as David, the great king of Israel. Again, the Psalmist David was inspired to write, *"You have covered me in my mother's womb. I will praise You; for I am fearfully and wonderfully made"* (Ps. 139:13-14). From the moment of conception, and as the Holy Spirit gave the intent, David was, indeed, a person. It was David's body,

his very substance, in the womb of his mother.

We have the same kind of teaching concerning Jeremiah who said: *"Then the Word of the LORD came unto me, saying, Before I formed you in the belly, I knew you; and before you came forth out of the womb I sanctified you, and I ordained you a Prophet unto the nations"* (Jer. 1:4-5). God knew the Prophet Jeremiah before he was born. If, by abortion, the fetus had been murdered, it would have been Jeremiah the great Prophet who died. The mother would not have known his name, but God would have. The mother might not have known that this was to be the mighty Prophet of God, but God would have known that too.

Yes, a fetus is a person, a living soul, from the time of conception.

A CHILD, BORN OR UNBORN

John the Baptist was *"filled with the Holy Spirit, even from his mother's womb"* (Lk. 1:15). Mary, the Mother of Jesus, came to greet Elisabeth. *"And it came to pass, that, when Elisabeth heard the salutation of Mary, the baby leaped in her womb"* (Lk. 1:41). The fetus of John the Baptist, in the womb of his mother, may not have understood clearly why he leaped at the sound of the voice of Mary (the Mother of our Saviour), but God knew.

It is interesting to note the words of Jesus, *"Suffer the little children to come unto Me, and forbid them not: for of such is the Kingdom of God"* (Mk. 10:14). He was speaking in reference to the infants brought to be blessed by Him. The term used for *"infants"* in the Greek is *"brephos,"* which Young's Analytical Concordance defines as *"a child born or unborn."* Does that mean, then, that all the little ones who died either as a baby or as a small child, had an immortal soul (*"Of such is the Kingdom of God"*) and that they will meet us in Heaven, that is, if we are privileged to be there? Well, certainly it is implied if not fully stated in this Passage of Scripture.

QUESTIONS . . .

Some have asked the question, if the girl is unmarried, would not abortion be permissible?

Others have asked, *"If the girl is raped, and becomes pregnant, would not abortion under those circumstances be permissible?"*

The answer is *"no"* on both counts!

However the pregnancy came about, the child is still a living person in the mother's womb. Under no circumstances, does anyone have the right to kill the child.

Another question that is often asked, *"Would it not be proper for an abortion to be carried out, if the life of the mother was at risk?"*

I suppose that in a few rare cases, a doctor would have to choose between saving the life of the baby and saving the life of the mother. In such a case, the life of the mother would come first. However, this so rarely happens that really it's not worth the sake of argument.

In the Eyes of God, human life is very, very precious. It should be very precious in our eyes as well.

A MORAL QUESTION

Abortion is a moral question, meaning it's not really a legal question. It is essentially the same thing as murdering the incompetent, the retarded, the handicapped, and the aged, or senile. If we are going to kill the unwanted, possibly there are many 1-, 2-, 5-, 10-, even 50 — year olds who are unwanted. Why not just kill them too? You see how horrendous this terrible crime becomes when carried to its ultimate conclusion. To slay the innocent because he cannot protest is a sin of the worst sort. And the Scripture says, *"Be sure, your sin will find you out"* (Num. 32:23). There is a God to be sure, Who cares for the weak, the unloved, and the unprotected. Ultimately, He will bring Judgment. *"God's mills may grind slow, but they*

grind exceedingly fine, meaning they miss nothing."

Previously it was abortion at conception. Now, some are trying to get laws passed in each State that will allow abortion up to the time of birth. The horror of that knows no bounds.

Where do we go from there?

If you remember, Nazi Germany enacted a law permitting the elimination of *"useless members of society;"* consequently, 18 million people were slaughtered (among them, 6 million Jews) because they represented a category that was considered useless.

We have the same pattern before us in America today, in which a whole category of human beings — unborn babies who cannot yet speak for themselves — are to be slaughtered at the whim of a mother or a doctor who decides that the mother is somehow unable or unwilling to have a baby.

As asked, where do we go from here? What is the next class of humanity to be destroyed?

No, abortion is a grievous sin. It is totally ungodly; a terrible case of man's inhumanity to man, and one day man will answer to God for this terrible sin.

CHAPTER NINETEEN

Are Homosexuals Born That Way?

QUESTION:

ARE HOMOSEXUALS BORN THAT WAY?

ANSWER:

No!

We will address ourselves to that to a greater degree momentarily.

There are several places in the Word of God which addresses itself to this perversion (Gen. 19:1-13; Lev. 18:22; 20:13; Deut. 23:17-18; Judg. 19:22; Rev. 22:15); however, we will address ourselves primarily to Romans 1:24-28. Hopefully in these Passages given by the Holy Spirit to the Apostle Paul, your questions will be answered.

SEXUAL UNCLEANNESS

Paul said, *"Wherefore God also gave them up to uncleanness through the lusts of their own hearts, to dishonor their own bodies between themselves"* (Rom. 1:24).

The phrase, *"Wherefore God also gave them up to uncleanness through the lusts of their own hearts,"* presents mankind not merely drifting toward, but actually, in a sense, being shoved by God in that direction.

Since men chose to give up God and worship the creature, God could do nothing but give men into the control of the sinful things they preferred. In other words, God would not violate man's will and force him to do something he did not want to do. When men persisted in following their totally depraved natures, God allowed them free rein. The natural result was immorality of the vilest kind.

Alford says of God's Act of delivering mankind over into the control of utter human depravity, *"Not merely permissive, but judicially, God delivered them over. As sin begets sin, and darkness of mind, deeper darkness, Grace gives place to Judgment,*

and the Divine Wrath hardens men, and hurries them on to more fearful degrees of depravity." **God, in other words, delivered man to uncleanness.**

The word *"lusts"* is *"epithumia"* in the Greek Text, and means, *"a passionate craving, longing, desire,"* and in this sense, an inordinately sinful one.

Alford again says, *"Not by or through the lusts; the lusts of their heart were the field of action, the department of their being in which the dishonor took place."* In other words, this was what their hearts wanted.

The phrase, *"To dishonor their own bodies between themselves,"* carries with it more than mere profligacy in the satisfaction of natural lusts, but rather bestiality, which refers to impurity in the physical, and not only in the social and religious sense. In other words, man is grossly immoral.

It speaks of adultery, fornication, pedophilia (sex with children), bestiality (sex with animals), lesbianism, and homosexuality. In other words, this *"dishonor"* includes all of these things mentioned.

CHANGING THE TRUTH OF GOD INTO A LIE

Paul said, *"Who changed the Truth of God into a lie, and worshipped and served the creature more than the Creator, Who is blessed forever. Amen"* (Rom. 1:25).

The phrase, *"Who changed the Truth of God into a lie,"* refers back to Verse 23, which speaks of spiritual and sexual uncleanness.

In the realm of idolatry, it refers to the images of men, birds, cattle, dogs, crocodiles, frogs, and snakes, which are common among all idolaters.

Such idolatry has been the root of all the abominable immoralities of the heathen. The idols have been the patrons of licentiousness.

When they formed their gods in human shape, they endowed them with passions and represented them as slaves to

disgraceful sex perversions and as possessing unlimited powers of sexual gratification.

However, this condition of men's hearts in purposely refusing the Truth of God, led to the Lord using no restraining force over man whatsoever, allowing him without restraint to push headlong into this lie of darkness, which, in effect, is the same as God giving man a push. Considering man's already depraved condition, the slide even further downward was terrible, to say the least!

As we see here, the words, *"God also gave them up,"* as given in Verse 24, is a restraining force exercised by God even on unregenerate mankind, unless refused, which it was and continues to be.

As well, there is far greater restraining force on Believers as should be obvious (Job 1:10; Ps. 91; Rom. 8:28).

However, this restraining force even on Believers can be removed, as well, through disobedience and rebellion.

The phrase, *"And worshipped and served the creature more than the Creator,"* (Rom. 1:25) presents that of which Paul spoke in his Message to the Athenians (Acts 17:29-30).

For man to worship and serve the creature, means he is doing such to something he has made with his hands and is, therefore, less than him.

Regarding the *"creature,"* even if man worships himself or other men and women, which most of the world does, still, what good does that do him?

The phrase, *"Who is blessed forever,"* should have been translated, *"bless-ed,"* because it refers to God.

The word *"blessed"* refers to one receiving a blessing, in which, as should be obvious, God needs nothing.

The two syllable word *"bless-ed,"* in effect, refers to the One doing the Blessing, in this case, the Lord.

The idea is all True Blessings come exclusively from the Lord, with idols or anything else for that matter, able to produce none at all.

The word *"Amen"* means that this is anchored in the Word

of God, and, as such, will not change.

WOMEN AND HOMOSEXUALITY

"For this cause God gave them up unto vile affections: for even their women did change the natural use into that which is against nature" (Rom. 1:26).

The phrase, *"For this cause God gave them up unto vile affections,"* presents once again the people purposely and with forethought rejecting God, desiring instead a way of gross evil, with the Lord removing His restraints and, therefore, giving them unimpeded access to their desires. It must be remembered that the way down picks up speed as it goes, therefore, making it more and more difficult to stop or turn around, even though desire to do so may ultimately come about.

I speak of the untold millions who are hooked on alcohol, drugs, immorality, gambling, or any vice one may name. It begins oftentimes as a lark, but as the acceleration downward increases, it becomes more and more difficult to stop, actually impossible without the help of God.

DISHONOR

The word *"vile"* in the Greek Text is *"atimia,"* and means *"dishonor, ignominy, and disgrace."*

The first word in this meaning is *"dishonor,"* and looking at the meaning of its opposite *"honor,"* means to evaluate the worth of a person and to treat him with the consideration, respect, and love due his character and position.

Conversely, to dishonor a person is to either put an incorrect appraisal upon his worth and treat him accordingly, or, having properly evaluated his character, to refuse to treat him with the respect and deference that are his due.

Paul is using this in the sense of the world putting an incorrect estimate upon the sacredness, dignity, and purity of the physical body which was made by God and, in effect, in God's

Image, and thus, using it in a way which dishonors it.

In that this is what the world wanted, they were given over to a *"condition,"* and not merely to an evil desire. It is one thing for an individual to do something which is very evil, but something else altogether for that person to *"become"* what they do, which is always where sin leads one. As stated, the problem can only be rectified by the Saving Grace of the Lord Jesus Christ.

LESBIANISM

The phrase, *"For even their women did change the natural use into that which is against nature,"* in short, speaks of lesbianism — unnatural sexual relations between women (homosexuality). Several things are said here:

- **The word *"women"* as used here is not the word used as in John 4:9, which simply speaks of designation, but rather the Greek word *"thelus"* which means *"a female."* In other words, the Holy Spirit through Paul is pointing to the gender, meaning that it is to stay that way.**
- **That women tried to *"change"* the purpose of their gender, is the reason that Paul used the Greek word for *"female."* They were not trying so much to change the gender, but rather its purpose respecting the sexual sense.**

Consequently, they were changing what God had designed, and doing so in a rebellious, base, and ignominious way. They went from a far higher use down to a far lower use.

Even though this is one of the worst, or possibly the very worst example, still, this is the great sin of man, changing God's Ways for man's ways, and in every capacity.

- **The *"natural use"* presents that intended by God, in this sense, the way sexually that women were originally created.**

The word *"natural"* in the Greek is *"phusis,"* and means *"the nature of things, the force, laws, order of nature, as opposed to that which is monstrous, abnormal, perverse."*

- **That which is *"against nature"* respects that which is against Nature's laws, or God's Laws, which are one and the same.**

MEN AND HOMOSEXUALITY

Paul said, *"And likewise also the men, leaving the natural use of the woman, burned in their lust one toward another; men with men working that which is unseemly, and receiving in themselves that recompense of their error which was meet"* (Rom. 1:27).

The phrase, *"And likewise also the men,"* presents the word *"men"* used in the same fashion as the word *"women"* in the previous Verse.

The Holy Spirit through Paul is not pointing out the mere designation of man, but rather the male as distinguished from a female. These terms are used because only the distinction of sex is contemplated.

The phrase, *"Leaving the natural use of the woman"* speaks of the sex act which is to be performed between the man and his wife. This natural way formed and made by God, is set aside, in favor of that which is far, far lower.

Let it ever be understood, man can never improve upon that which God has done. He cannot add to it, or take away from it, at least with any positive results. He always drops down to a lower level, which is the problem with the world, and always has been since the Fall.

The Holy Spirit through the Apostle is using this example of lesbianism and homosexuality, because it portrays in the most glaring way, the obvious truth of these statements. In other words, this example portrays in the worst way the folly of changing God's Designed Direction, and designed, I might quickly add, for our good and not harm. Actually, this is one of Satan's greatest ploys, even as he tempted Adam and Eve in the Garden. He tried to make them think that God was withholding some good things from them, exactly as men think today; however, let it ever be known, that all good things are found in the Ways of God, and not outside those Ways. Satan has no good ways, only bondage. While he is able to offer some pleasure and can titillate the flesh somewhat, without exception, his efforts will lead to destruction. In other words, the Marlboro man dies of cancer.

The phrase, *"Burned in their lust one toward another,"* refers to that which is terrible in its intensity.

The word *"burned"* in the Greek is *"ekkaio,"* and means *"to burn out,"* and can be explained as *"the rage of lust."* Robertson defines it as, *"to inflame with lust."*

In other words, this type of lust satiates or consumes the entirety of the individual. It is an all-out endeavor to satisfy their totally-depraved natures. Once again, we are speaking here of homosexuality.

The phrase, *"Men with men working that which is unseemly,"* specifies its direction.

PEDOPHILES

The word, *"working"* taken from Verse 27 in the Greek is *"katergazomai,"* which means *"to perform, accomplish, achieve, to do that from which something results, to carry to its ultimate conclusion."* It is a *"lust"* which will not be satisfied until it obtains its desired results.

Many would ask as to how a man could take advantage of a little boy, sexually molesting him, when the man knows in his heart the child will be greatly affected mentally and emotionally?

The answer is obvious, it is *"lust"* which drives the person and will not quit until it is momentarily satisfied. As well, each act takes the man lower and lower in its depravity.

At this stage, it is not why the man does such a thing, but that he has reached the point to where he has no choice in the matter. That is the reason that many pedophiles openly state, if given the opportunity they will do such again. They are right! Within themselves it is not possible for the situation to be changed.

At this stage and even long before, the favorite word used, and even by the Church is, *"they need professional help!"* Of course, they are speaking of psychological counseling, etc.

However, I must remind the Reader, that there is no *"professional help"* for something of this nature or any sin for that matter, be it great or small.

I would ask the reader to think back to the Catholic situation, where scores of Priests have been exposed as being pedophiles. The Catholic system has the greatest psychologists in the world. As well, many, if not most, of these Priests have undergone untold hours of psychological counseling, but with no positive effect. To be sure, if psychological counseling was the answer, it would have worked in those situations. It didn't work, because it cannot work.

CHRIST AND HIM CRUCIFIED

The only answer is Jesus Christ and what He did for us at the Cross (Rom. 6:1-14; 8:1-2, 11; I Cor. 1:17-18, 23; 2:2; Col. 2:14-15).

As we have previously said, and will continue to say over and over again, if, in fact, man has the answer for these problems in the realm of psychoanalysis, or any other way, Jesus Christ made an unnecessary trip down to this sin-benighted world to die on Calvary, thereby, paying a terrible price to redeem humanity. Once again I remind the reader, man's problem is sin, not environment, association, or education, even though these things certainly may have some affect. And once again I say, man's solution is Jesus Christ and Him Crucified, and that alone! In other words, there is no other answer.

Also, I remind the reader, Jesus needs no help in this capacity, for, in effect, He has already effected the cure, which is His Shed Blood coupled with His Power. For the Church to look elsewhere, to do otherwise, to think otherwise, is not just sin, but actually, rank, raw, ignominious blasphemy.

ALTERNATE LIFESTYLE?

The word *"unseemly"* as used in the Twenty-seventh Verse, in the Greek is *"aschemosune,"* and means *"want of form, disfigurement, deformed, one's nakedness, shame."*

It does not matter that modern man may attempt to label

homosexuality as merely an *"alternate lifestyle,"* insinuating that there is nothing wrong with this direction, the Truth is the opposite, and irrespective of what type of erroneous laws that Congress may make, or the Supreme Court may judge. Man's law in no way changes God's Laws, i.e., that which God has deemed will happen! The awful results will always come about, irrespective of how much man may attempt to apply a seal of approval to this issue, or any other issue pertaining to Life and Godliness.

ERROR

The phrase, *"And receiving in themselves that recompense of their error which was meet,"* refers to the penalty that is attached to wrongdoing, and if persisted, will always be brought about.

***"Recompense"* in the Greek is *"antimisthian,"* and means *"a reward given in compensation, requital, recompense."* The word here refers to that natural result of their sin which pays them back for what they have done. The evil consequences are necessary as ordained by Divine Law. When one violates the Laws of Nature (God), one must pay the price.**

The word *"error"* in the Greek is *"palne,"* and means *"a wandering, roving, or wrong action."* It carries the idea of an individual leaving the natural instincts created by God and forcing those instincts into perversion. The *"wandering, roving, wrong action"* steadily gets worse and worse, with the *"error"* becoming more and more pronounced.

An excellent example is the many homosexuals and lesbians who have had their mental, emotional, and even physical appearances changed, and for the worst. In other words, their homosexuality shows in their mannerisms, which again are unnatural and repulsive.

THE SIN OF HOMOSEXUALITY

The Bible has much to say about this sin, as it does all sin.

Historically, according to the Bible, homosexual behavior was linked with idolatrous cult prostitution (I Ki. 14:24; 15:12; 22:46). However, the stern warning against this practice is included in Levitical Law, and upheld under the New Covenant as well, even respecting these Passages in Romans, which we are now studying (Lev. 18:22; 20:13).

In this Chapter, to which we have already alluded, Paul greatly condemns homosexual acts, lesbian as well as male, putting them in the same breath, in a sense, as idolatry. However, his theological canvas is broader than the expression of the homosexual act regarding idolatry, but is rather held up as the terrible exchange fallen man has made in departing from his Creator's intention. Seen from this angle, every homosexual act is unnatural, not so much because it cuts across the individual's natural sexual orientation, or even infringes Old Testament Law, which it definitely does, but rather because it flies in the face of God's Creation Plan for human sexual expression.

OTHER WARNINGS

Paul makes two more references to homosexual practices in other Epistles. Both occur in lists of banned activities and strike the same condemnatory note. In I Corinthians 6:9, practicing homosexuals are included among the unrighteous who will not inherit the Kingdom of God; however, Paul then adds a redemptive note, saying, *"And such were some of you"* (I Cor. 6:11). In other words, the Lord Saved these once practicing homosexuals, cleansing them of their sin, and made them new creations in Christ Jesus.

The idea is, as should be obvious, that the Lord does not save in sin, but from sin.

A newsman asked me once if God would save homosexuals. My answer to him was very clear and concise: *"Yes, God will save homosexuals, or anyone who comes to Him for that matter. Actually, that is the very reason Jesus came and died on Calvary."*

"However,"* I quickly added, *"But that means they will have

***to give up their sin of homosexuality, just as the drunkard gives up his drink,"* etc.**

In I Timothy 1:10, Paul again speaks of the sin of homosexuality, and by inference, declares the lost condition of those who practice this sin as well as other sins.

It has been suggested that the meaning of *"arsenikoites"* in I Corinthians 6:9 and I Tim. 1:10 may be restricted to that of *"male prostitute."* However, Greek linguistic evidence to support this view is lacking.

It is beyond reasonable doubt that Paul intended to condemn homosexual conduct in any capacity, but not homosexual people. As Creator, Law-giver, and King, the Lord's condemnation of such behavior is absolutely plain, but yet He loves the sinner.

Following are some questions respecting homosexuality with some answers, which hopefully will be helpful.

ARE HOMOSEXUALS BORN THAT WAY?

In a word, *"No!"*

While it is true that the seed of original sin carries with it every type of deviation, aberration, perversion, and wrongdoing, the homosexual cannot claim to have been born that way any more than the drunkard, gambler, killer, etc. However, I think it correct to say that the gene pool which constitutes the character and personality make up of every individual is more predisposed toward some aberrations in certain persons than others. In the spiritual sense, the perverted or abnormal number of genes in any particular direction is not the cause of these situations, but rather the results. The genes are that way because of man's fallen condition in a spiritual sense. So, even if scientists one day can find a way to control the genes, the problem will still not be solved, because that which feeds the genes, which is the soul and the spirit of man, cannot be changed by medical or psychological procedures, but only by the Power of God. It is called the New Birth, and is referred

to in the Word of God as *"Regeneration."* The actual Passage says, *"Not by works of Righteousness which we have done, but according to His Mercy He Saved us, by the washing of Regeneration and renewing of the Holy Spirit"* (Titus 3:5).

The word *"Regeneration"* in the Greek Text is *"Plaiggenesia,"* and means *"once more or again,"* in other words, *"re-gened."*

The Lord Jesus Christ and Him Alone can change the person, i.e., *"Re-gene the individual, hence, Regeneration."*

To further prove the point, when identical twins are born, the gene pool is identical, at least to a greater degree, in these twins. At times one has become a homosexual, while the other one did not. If, in fact, they were born that way, if one was homosexual, the other would be likewise. The very fact that both seldom turn out to be that way proves that they are not born in that manner.

Again we stated, that even though there are greater propensities toward certain proclivities in some people than in others, does not mean the thing is set in concrete, but only that there is a lean toward a certain direction. In fact, the Lord does not condemn the sinner for what he is, but rather for refusing to accept God's Way out of the situation, which is the Salvation afforded by Christ at Calvary. That goes for every sinner, homosexuals included!

WILL GOD SAVE HOMOSEXUALS?

Actually, this is a question we have already answered.

Yes, the Lord will save homosexuals, or anyone who comes to Him, irrespective as to who or what they may be. That is the very reason Jesus came to this world, *"to save sinners"* (I Cor. 6:9-12).

However, the homosexual, upon coming to Christ, must abandon the former lifestyle immediately, and that goes for the drunk, gambler, or anyone for that matter.

When a person comes to Christ, he leaves something (the old lifestyle), and comes to something, and more particularly to someone, the Lord Jesus Christ. As such, we take upon ourselves,

and by His Help, His Lifestyle.

WILL PSYCHOLOGICAL COUNSELING HELP THE HOMOSEXUAL?

Biblical Counseling will help, but not Psychological Counseling. The problem is Spiritual, and the Bible alone deals with such.

Biblical Counseling will simply direct the person to the Lord Jesus Christ and the price that He paid at Calvary, so that one may be Saved. It must be understood, that Jesus atoned for every sin at the Cross. This means that Satan and all of his cohorts of darkness were defeated at Calvary (Col. 2:14-15). Sin is that which gives Satan the legal right to hold man in bondage. With all sin atoned, he has no more right to do such.

That being the case, how is it that he keeps most of the world in bondage?

He does such simply because men will not take advantage of what Christ has done for us at Calvary. Untold millions in the world are lost without God, but it's because they will not avail themselves of the opportunity of accepting Christ.

Regrettably, many in the Church, if not most, fall into the same category. They do not understand that it was at the Cross that all victory was won. This means that the Cross of Christ must ever be made the Object of our Faith (Rom. 6:1-14; 8:1-2, 11; I Cor. 1:17-18, 23; 2:2; Gal., Chpt. 5; 6:14; Eph. 2:13-18; Col. 2:14-15).

When the Believer places his Faith exclusively in Christ and the Cross, and maintains his Faith exclusively in Christ and the Cross, the Holy Spirit, Who Alone can effect what is needed in our lives, will work grandly on our behalf. However, the Holy Spirit will not work outside the parameters of the Finished Work of Christ, which necessitates our Faith in that Redemption Plan. Paul said:

***"For the Law of the Spirit of Life in Christ Jesus has made me free from the Law of Sin and Death"* (Rom. 8:2).**

The Cross of Christ is God's Way, and His only Way, because that is all that is needed.

In order for the person to be set free, there has got to be a power greater than the powers of darkness, and the homosexual spirit is one of the most powerful spirits of darkness in the world. The greater Power is in the Holy Spirit, Who works exclusively, as stated, within the parameters of the Cross. This is God's Way, the Way of the Cross, and it does not need the help of the ways of the world.

In fact, psychology holds no help at all for the homosexual, or anyone else for that matter, only harm. It is harm because it attempts to make the person believe a lie, and it keeps them from their only Source of help, the Lord Jesus Christ.

THE WISDOM OF THE WORLD

Psychological counseling, for the most part, attempts to make the homosexual *"feel good about himself,"* in other words, to accept his orientation, as it is called. If the truth be known, many psychologists claim that the guilt felt by homosexuals (or anyone for that matter), is the real problem, and is present because of certain myths, they say, called the Bible, etc.

While it is true that the *"Law"* of the Bible does point out man's terrible sins, still, if the Bible did not exist, the guilt of man's fallen condition would remain. The guilt can only be removed by Jesus Christ. The Bible did not originate the guilt — sin being the fault — it only defines it.

Concerning guilt Paul also said:

***"There is therefore now no condemnation* (guilt) *to them who are in Christ Jesus, who walk not after the flesh but after the Spirit"* (Rom. 8:1).**

ARE ALL HOMOSEXUALS INSTANTLY DELIVERED AT THE MOMENT OF SALVATION?

In fact, yes! Actually, it can be no other way, if Salvation

is to be Salvation (II Cor. 5:17-18); however, whereas this terrible bondage, as with other problems such as temper, alcohol, nicotine, etc., are at times broken immediately, with some, certain things regarding particular victory does not come quite so quickly. In other words, at times there is a struggle.

However, the Lord does not throw us out if we fail or slip back, but, in fact, instantly forgives us as we ask for such (I Jn. 1:9). Consequently, the new Believer must continue to believe God, making certain that his Faith is strictly in Christ and the Cross, which, as stated, will then give the Holy Spirit latitude to work within his life, which will ultimately bring victory. In fact, the struggle may continue for a period of time, but if the Believer keeps his Faith in Christ and the Cross, and doesn't allow it to be moved to something else, ultimately, that sin will no longer have dominion over that person, whatever type of sin it might be. Paul said:

> **"For sin shall not have dominion over you** *(the sin nature will not have dominion over us if we as Believers continue to exercise Faith in the Cross of Christ; otherwise, the sin nature most definitely will have dominion over the Believer)*: **for you are not under the Law** *(means that if we try to live this life by any type of law, no matter how good that law might be in its own right, we will conclude by the sin nature having dominion over us)*, **but under Grace** *(the Grace of God flows to the Believer on an unending basis only as long as the Believer exercises Faith in Christ and what He did at the Cross; Grace is merely the Goodness of God exercised by and through the Holy Spirit, and given to undeserving Saints)*" **(Rom. 6:14).**

WILL HOMOSEXUALITY CAUSE ONE TO BE ETERNALLY LOST?

Yes, that is if the person does not repent and, thereby, forsake that lifestyle. Of course, the same can be said for alcoholism,

drug addiction, or religion for that matter (Gal. 5:19-21).

The age-old problem of mankind is the desire to live in sin and have Salvation at the same time; however, those who would attempt such a thing have not truly been Born-Again.

When the person truly comes to Christ, making Him the Lord of one's life, affections change totally and completely. Actually, the Scripture is rather implicit about this, saying, *"Old things are passed away; behold, all things are become new"* (II Cor. 5:17). In other words, the new Believer does not want the old sinful lifestyle any longer, even though he may at times sense its pull. He is now a *"new creation in Christ Jesus."*

WHAT ABOUT THE LAWS OF CERTAIN STATES LEGALIZING HOMOSEXUAL MARRIAGES?

The Courts legalizing something, does not legitimize it in the Eyes of God. The Word of God does not change irrespective of what others may do. That is the reason it is referred to as Objective Truth, which means it is the same Standard forever and for everyone.

The recognition of homosexual marriages by the Courts is an abomination in the sight of God.

As well, the allowing of homosexual couples to adopt children is again, an abomination. Putting a child in such an abnormal environment, can do nothing but have an adverse effect on that child, which will affect them negatively for the rest of their life. In fact, a study was recently done in England concerning this very thing. They found after exhaustive surveys, that irrespective what the world of psychology said, that the children who were placed in homosexual homes did not fare near as well as otherwise. In fact, there was such a negative influence on these little hearts and lives, that most of them, if any of them, outside of Christ, would ever get over the situation.

Regrettably, this is also the case in many so-called straight homes and for the simple reason that most do not know Jesus. Only Jesus can make a marriage, and He definitely will not do

so with such an unscriptural, perverted lifestyle of homosexuality, irrespective of claims to the contrary.

However, if a home does have Christ, it has the only solution for its problems and the only guarantee for success.

HOW SHOULD CHRISTIANS REACT TOWARD HOMOSEXUALS?

To which we have alluded elsewhere in our comments on this subject, the Lord loves the homosexual just as much as He does anyone else. When He died on Calvary, He died for these people just as well as He died for you and me. In fact, His Atonement is no different for them than for us.

Likewise, Christians must show kindness and the God kind of Love toward homosexuals, as they do for others. That means, at least as far as possible, to treat them as human beings, and that means with respect and dignity; however, the Believer must never leave the impression that such a lifestyle is condoned, while at the same time not leveling condemnation on the person. No one has ever brought people to Christ with a club, but millions have been brought to the Saviour because they felt somebody cared for them.

At the same time, I do not think it is possible that Believers could be close friends with a homosexual, or anyone outside of Christ for that matter! The Believer and the unbeliever have absolutely nothing in common, at least on which to build and sustain a friendship. One serves Christ, while the other serves himself.

THE REPROBATE MIND

The Scripture says, *"And even as they did not like to retain God in their knowledge, God gave them over to a reprobate mind, to do those things which are not convenient"* (Rom. 1:28).

The phrase, *"And even as they did not like to retain God in their knowledge,"* carries the idea of the human race putting God

to the test for the purpose of approving or disapproving Him.

They wanted a God to their liking, and finding that He did not meet those specifications, the world refused to approve Him as the God to be worshipped, or have Him in its knowledge.

The *"knowledge"* spoken here, in the Greek is *"epignosis,"* and means *"full and precise knowledge."* In other words, their knowledge of God, due to their rebellion against Him, and, therefore, going into deep sin, was only a dim and perverted memory!

If one wants to know what is wrong with the modern School System in America, despite the fact of hundreds of billions of dollars being thrown at this ever-worsening situation, it is because educators *"did not like to retain God in their knowledge."* So, and speaking of the Public School System, we have Godless schools, which means that the schools are filled with Satan. We have Godless education, which means that what knowledge the students do have is largely warped and twisted, ill-preparing them for life. We have Godless direction, consequently we have erroneous ways.

The phrase, *"God gave them over to a reprobate mind,"* presents the third time such a statement is used (Rom. 1:24, 26, 28). Once again, humanity wanted that which was licentious and evil and the Lord took away the restraining forces, allowing them to have what they desired.

The words *"reprobate mind"* in the Greek Text is *"adokimon noun."* It carries the idea of the human race putting God on trial, and because it rejected Him, God gave it a *"trialless"* mind, in other words, one incapable of discharging the functions of a mind with respect to the things of Salvation.

As they did not think it fit to keep God in their knowledge, God gave them over to a mind which has no way to comprehend God. In other words, Light rejected is Light withdrawn. The one thing answers to the other.

Virtually, they pronounce the True God disapproved and would have none of Him, and He in turn gave them up to a disapproved mind, a mind which actually is no mind, and cannot

discharge the functions of one, a mind in which the Divine distinctions of right and wrong are confused and lost, so that God's condemnation cannot but fall on it at last.

This speaks of people who are completely perverted. As the Canaanites of old who did their abominations unto their gods, the last depth of evil has been reached.

There were three terrible sins pandemic in the great empires of the past, which contributed greatly to their fall. They are:

1. **Homosexuality;**
2. **Pedophilia (child molestation); and,**
3. **Incest.**

Regrettably, America is heading down the same path.

The only answer for the homosexual and anyone for that matter is the Lord Jesus Christ. When He comes into the heart, this bondage of darkness will cease, and it will only cease if He comes into the heart. There is no answer other than *"Jesus Christ and Him Crucified."*

CHAPTER TWENTY

Is "Infant Baptism" A Scriptural Doctrine?

QUESTION:

IS "INFANT BAPTISM" A SCRIPTURAL DOCTRINE?

ANSWER:

No!

Infant baptism is not a Scriptural doctrine; and more probable, infant baptism is responsible for sending more people to Hell than perhaps any other doctrine or religious error.

It's a terrible thing when a person has been led to believe that being baptized as a baby constitutes his Salvation and, consequently, he is on his way to Heaven. Untold millions down through the centuries have believed that lie and, thereby, perished without the Lord. There is nothing worse than a false way of Salvation, and infant baptism into particular Churches definitely falls under the heading of a false way.

JESUS AND THE CHILDREN

The fact that Jesus loves children very much was made evident when He stated, *"Suffer little children, and forbid them not, to come unto Me"* (Mat. 19:14).

We believe that all babies and children below the age of accountability are protected by the Lord respecting their eternal soul, meaning that if they die in that state, they instantly go to be with the Lord. This means, that there are no babies or children in Hell.

A child does not have the capacity to reason; therefore, it cannot make a rational decision, especially something as weighty as the Salvation of the soul.

WHAT IS THE AGE OF ACCOUNTABILITY?

It would vary with different children. There are some children that would probably reach the age of accountability at

the tender age of six, because they are raised in a Christian home, raised in Church, and, thereby, have understanding. But for other children who are not so privileged, the age of accountability might reach up to eleven or twelve. Only the Lord would have the answer to that question as it regards each child, and to be sure He most definitely does.

The Lord began to deal with my heart when I was eight years old, which is when I came to Christ. If I had said no to Him at that time, even though only eight years of age, and had been killed in an automobile accident or in some way, I would have died eternally lost. I had the privilege of being raised in a Christian home, at least from the age of five. To be sure, a child can absorb much if they are in Church, and I should say, the right kind of Church.

I might quickly add, that even though a little baby was baptized as an infant into a particular Church, and if that child would die before reaching the age of accountability, they most definitely would be Saved. The child has no choice in that which is proposed by the parents, as should be obvious. But the tragedy is, millions have thought and do think that because they were baptized as an infant, that that means they are Saved. It doesn't! In fact, such baptism has absolutely nothing to do with one's Salvation, at least that is positive. It most definitely can have a negative effect, even as we've already stated, if the person, upon reaching the age of accountability places their faith in such.

THE HISTORY OF INFANT BAPTISM

Infant baptism appeared in Church history about the year A.D. 370. It came about as a result of the doctrine of baptismal regeneration — the teaching that baptism is essential to Salvation; or if you want to turn it around, that water baptism saves the soul (or at least is a part of a person's Salvation). So, consequently, as the teaching of baptismal regenerations began to be propagated, it was natural for those holding to this doctrine

to believe that everyone should be baptized as soon as possible. Thus, the baptism of infants still in the innocent state (and as yet unaccountable for their actions) came into vogue among many of the Churches. Once again I state: these two grievous errors (baptismal regeneration, which teaches that water baptism saves, and infant baptism) have probably caused more people to go to Hell than any other doctrine.

THE EARLY CHURCH

Incidentally, the Church that we read about in the Book of Acts, and referred to as the Early Church, was that which was founded, so to speak, by the Holy Spirit. In fact, the Lord used the Apostle Paul to serve as the masterbuilder of the Church (I Cor. 3:10). Even though Satan tried repeatedly to insert false doctrine into the New Covenant, with the true meaning given to the Apostle Paul (Gal. 1:12), still, Satan little succeeded. In fact, this particular Church touched much of the Roman world of its day.

It basically stayed true to the Lord, which means it stayed true to the Word of God, throughout the lifetime of the original Apostles, and even those who followed them. However, about a hundred years after the founding of the Church, incidentally, by the Holy Spirit, the Church began to apostatize. Gradually it began to adopt false doctrine and finally emerged into what is presently known as the Catholic Church. If I remember correctly, it was the year 607 that the title *"Pope"* was given to the Bishop of Rome. So that means that the Catholic Church was not begun by Simon Peter as our Catholic friends claim! To be blunt that particular Church is the result of apostasy.

MORE HISTORY

The professed conversion of Emperor Constantine in A.D. 313 was looked upon by many persons as a great triumph for Christianity. However, it more than likely was the greatest

tragedy in Church history because it resulted in the union of Church and State and the establishment of a hierarchy that ultimately developed into the Roman Catholic system. There is great question whether Constantine was ever truly converted. At the time of his supposed vision of the sign of the Cross he promised to become a Christian. He was not baptized in water until near death, having postponed the act in the belief that baptism washed away all past sins, and he wanted all his sins to be in the past tense before he was baptized. In other words, he wanted the freedom to sin as much as he wanted; and then when he was too old or too sick to care, he would have them all washed away by the act of baptism.

In A.D. 416 infant baptism was made compulsory throughout the Roman Empire. Naturally this filled the Churches with unconverted members who had only been *"baptized into favor."* So, whatever power the Church had in the past relative to actual conversions was now null and void. Consequently, the world was plunged into the gloom of the Dark Ages, which endured for more than twelve centuries, actually until the Reformation.

During this time God had a remnant who remained faithful to Him; they never consented to the union of Church and State, to baptismal regeneration, or to infant baptism. These people were called by various names, but probably could better be summed up by their generic name, *"Anabaptists,"* meaning, re-baptizers. These people ignored infant baptism and re-baptized those who had truly been Saved through personal Faith. They also had a generic name for themselves, *"Anapedobaptists,"* meaning *"against infant baptism."*

THE STRANGE THING

The strange thing about these two diabolical doctrines of baptismal regeneration and infant baptism is that the great reformers (Martin Luther, for one) brought with them out of Rome the two dreaded errors: the union of Church and State

and infant baptism. Strangely enough, in those days, not only did the Roman Catholic Church persecute those who were not conformed to its ways, but after the Lutheran Church became the established Church of Germany, it persecuted the nonconformists as well — of course, not as stringently so, and not in such numbers as those before them.

John Calvin, as well as Cromwell in England and John Knox in Scotland, all stuck to the union of Church and State and infant baptism and used their power, when they had power, to seek to force others to conform to their own views.

Unaware to a lot of people, this thing came to the Americas as well in the early days of this republic. Before the Massachusetts Bay Colony was twenty years old, it was decreed by statue that, *"If any person or persons within this jurisdiction shall either openly condemn or oppose the baptizing of infants, or go about secretly to seduce others from the approbation or use thereof, or shall purposely depart from the congregation at the administration of the ordinance — after due time and means of conviction — every such person or persons shall be subject to banishment."*

Religious persecution existed even in the early days of the United States of America. Roger Williams and others were banished (when banishment meant to go and live with the Indians) because they would not submit to the doctrine of baptismal regeneration or the baptizing of infants.

However, it was the constitution of the Rhode Island Colony (founded by Roger Williams, John Clark, and others) that established religious liberty by law for the first time in 1,300 years (over the world). Thus, it was that Rhode Island, founded by a small group of Believers, was the first spot on Earth where religious liberty became the law of the land. The settlement was made in 1638, and the colony was legally established in 1663. Virginia followed, to be the second, in 1786.

As you can see, the doctrine of infant baptism has a long and bloody history, and it has been one of Satan's chief weapons to condemn untold millions of people to Hell.

FURTHER EXPLANATION

What does the above have to do with us today? A great deal!

You see, the union of Church and State continues today in most countries of the world. In these State Churches Pastors and leaders christen babies, which means they make them *"Christians"* by baptizing them; thus, the person having been christened as a baby believes he is on his way to Heaven simply because he was christened (or baptized) in infancy. Having been taught all his life that this Saved him, he naturally considers himself saved by the act of infant baptism. The Roman Catholic Church teaches baptismal regeneration and practices infant baptism. Its statement of doctrine says, *"The Sacrament of baptism is administered on adults by the pouring of water and the pronouncement of the proper words, and cleanses from original sin."*

The Reformed Church says, *"Children are baptized as heirs of the Kingdom of God and of His Covenant."*

The Lutheran Church teaches that baptism, whether of infants or adults, is a means of regeneration.

Because of the following declaration I believe the Episcopal Church teaches that Salvation comes through infant baptism. In his confirmation the Catechist answers a question about his baptism in infancy by saying, *"In my baptism . . . I was made a member of Christ, a Child of God, and an inheritor of the Kingdom of God."* (This is printed in the prayer book and can be read there by anyone interested enough to look for it.)

Most people who practice infant baptism believe the ceremony has something to do with the Salvation of the child. These are traditions of men, so we can follow the Commandments of God, or follow after the traditions of men; it is up to us.

CLEAR BIBLE TEACHING

The Word of God is clear regarding the matter of Salvation. Jesus said, *"He who believes on the Son has Everlasting*

***Life: and he who believes not the Son shall not see life; but the Wrath of God abides on him"* (Jn. 3:36). *"He who believes on Him is not condemned: but he who believes not is condemned already, because he has not believed in the Name of the Only Begotten Son of God"* (Jn. 3:18).**

Basically, there are two groups of people in the world today: those who believe on the Son and those who do not. Those who believe are not condemned; they have Everlasting Life (whatever Church they may belong to). Those who believe not on the Son are condemned already, and they shall not see Life, but the Wrath of God abides on them.

This is the clear, unmistakable teaching and language of the Bible.

If you will notice, the Word of God never says simply believe and be Saved, but rather believe *"on the Lord Jesus Christ"* and be Saved. The Word of God always identifies the Object of Faith, which is the Lord Jesus Christ Himself. *"For God so loved the world, that He gave His Only Begotten Son, that whosoever believeth in Him should not perish, but have Everlasting Life"* (Jn. 3:16). It is not enough just to believe; a person must believe *"in Him."*

When the Philippian jailer asked, *"Sirs, what must I do to be Saved?"* Paul answered, *"Believe on the Lord Jesus Christ, and you shall be Saved"* (Acts 16:30-31). It was not enough simply to believe; such belief, such trust, such dependence had to be *"in Him."*

TRUST IN THE LORD

If a person is trusting in baptism for Salvation, he cannot be trusting *"in Him."* Christ is not one Way of Salvation; He is the only Way of Salvation (Jn. 14:6; 10:1, 7, 9). There is no Promise in the Word of God to those who believe partially in Christ. In other words, a person cannot trust the Lord Jesus Christ ninety percent and water baptism ten percent, or Jesus fifty percent and baptism fifty percent, or Jesus ninety five

percent and a church five percent, etc. As a matter of fact, there is no such thing as partially trusting Christ, which means there is no such thing as a partial Justification. The man who is partially trusting is not trusting at all. Yet, the sad fact is that the majority of people in Churches in the United States and the world today are not trusting Christ at all — because they are trusting Him partially.

It is even sadder to realize that more people are going to Hell through religious organizations than any other way. That is a shocking and startling statement, but it is true. Jesus said, *"Many shall say to Me in that day, Lord, Lord, have we not prophesied in Your Name? and in Your Name have cast out devils? and in Your Name done many wonderful works? and then will I profess unto them, I never knew you: depart from Me, you who work iniquity"* (Mat. 7:22-23).

You see, any works offered to Christ for Salvation are called by Jesus Himself, *"works of iniquity."*

There is an old song that expresses my feelings totally. It says:

"My hope is built on nothing less,
"Than Jesus' Blood and Righteousness;
"I dare not trust the sweetest frame,
"But wholly lean on Jesus' Name.

"On Christ, the solid Rock I stand;
"All other ground is sinking sand,
"All other ground is sinking sand."

(Portions of source material for this article were derived from a message by the late Dr. William Pettingill, entitled *"Infant Baptism."*)

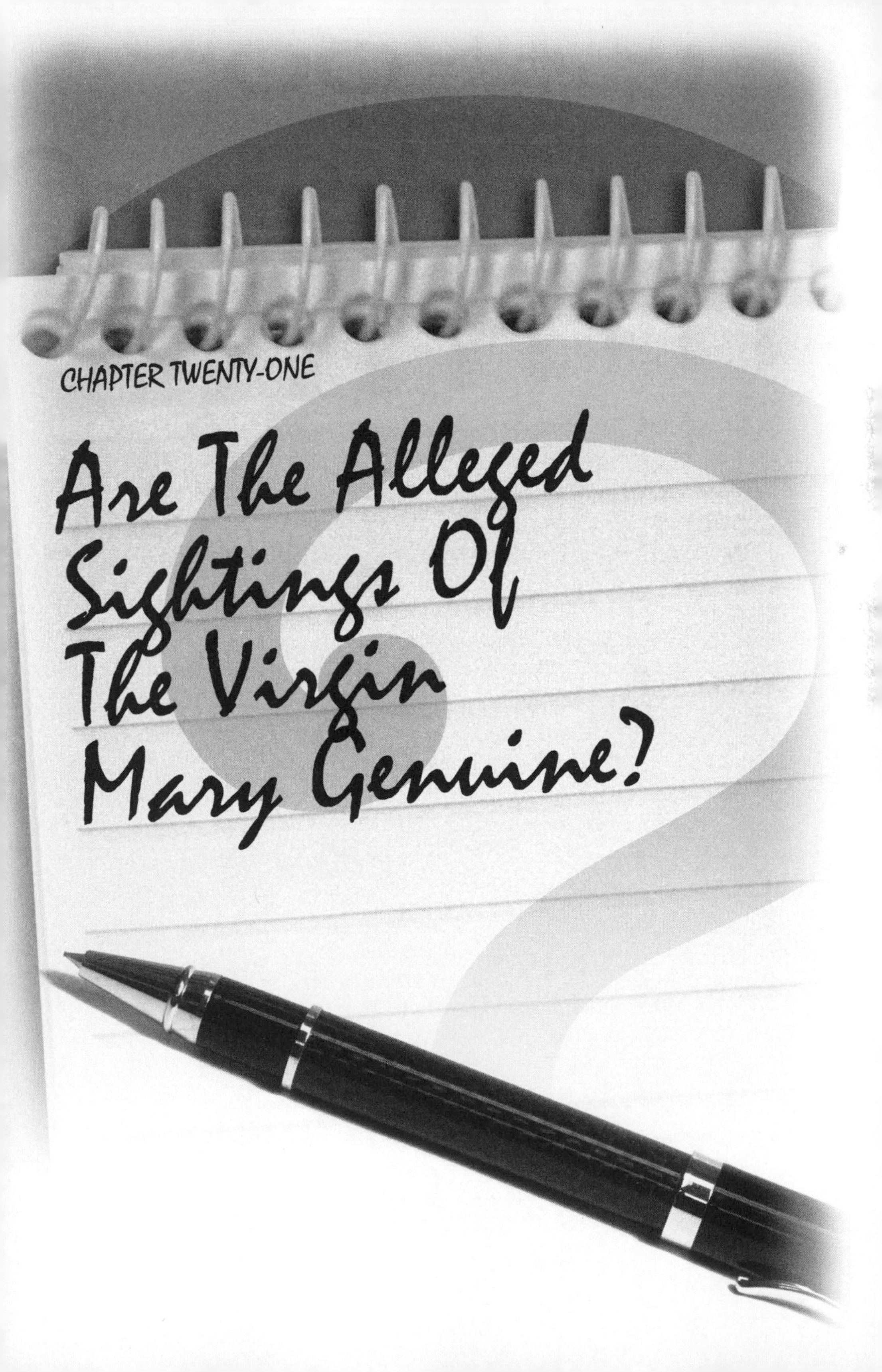

CHAPTER TWENTY-ONE

Are The Alleged Sightings Of The Virgin Mary Genuine?

QUESTION:

ARE THE ALLEGED SIGHTINGS OF THE VIRGIN MARY GENUINE?

ANSWER:

In a word, no!

In fact, there have been scores of alleged sightings of Mary virtually all over the world. The frequency of the alleged sightings has risen and fallen throughout the many, many years in which they have been reported.

I remember seeing over Television a short time back, of an alleged sighting of Mary in a Catholic Church in a small town in Kentucky. The mayor of the town was making plans to handle the crowds as a result of this event. They were apparently receiving phone calls about it from all over America.

Some time back, someone reported seeing a vision of Mary in one of the south Louisiana parishes which is heavily Catholic. Thousands of cars converged on the area as people went to ogle the place of the alleged sighting.

I'm sure that many are acquainted with Medjugorje, Yugoslavia; at least that's what it was formally called, where over a period of time several little girls were supposed to have held conversations with Mary. Until the war in that region stopped the visits, literally hundreds of thousands of people climbed that particular hill to observe this place. Quite a number of tours originated from all over America, Baton Rouge, and New Orleans included, with Catholics traveling to the area and, thereby, seeing the place where Mary is supposed to have appeared numerous times to the young girls.

POPE JOHN PAUL II

The late Pope John Paul II claimed that he owed his position as the Pope to Mary. He claims to have been visited by

her some time in the past and given varied instructions, with her telling him that he would one day be Pope. As a result, when he gained this position, he strongly encouraged and even greatly increased the Mary cult. Since then, the alleged sightings have multiplied.

Actually, Pope John Paul II did all that he could do to have Mary elevated to the position of a co-redemptress with Christ. Wiser heads prevailed, which kept him from issuing such a decree. There is no greater blasphemy than someone attempting to elevate Mary, or anyone for that matter, to be equal with Christ, especially in the Redemption process.

The Catholic Church has always venerated Mary in an unscriptural manner, such as the *"Immaculate Conception,"* as well as *"praying to Mary,"* and *"looking to her as an intercessor,"* and in other ways, however, and, as stated, this unscriptural conduct has multiplied many fold since the advent of John Paul II. In the thinking of many Catholics presently, Mary is deified.

DID THE POPE ACTUALLY HAVE A VISION OF MARY?

No!

I do not doubt that he had a vision, but it was not of Mary, but rather a familiar spirit.

FAMILIAR SPIRITS

Concerning this, the Bible says:

> ***"Regard not them who have familiar spirits, neither seek after wizards, to be defiled by them: I am the LORD your God"* (Lev. 19:31).**

The Lord said through the Prophet Isaiah:

> **"And when they shall say unto you, Seek unto them who have familiar spirits, and unto wizards that peep, and that mutter: should not a people seek unto their God? for the living to the dead?** *(Isaiah was speaking of those in Judah who were attempting to contact departed loved ones and claiming communication with the dead.*
>
> **"***The question is: should not these individuals seek a Living God rather than dead people?)***" (Isa. 8:19).**

The great Prophet then said:

> **"To the Law and to the Testimony: if they speak not according to this Word, it is because there is no light in them.** *(The great question should always be, and about any situation, 'Is it Biblical?')***" (Isa. 8:20).**

Some would say, inasmuch as this man became Pope, doesn't that prove that it was actually Mary who appeared to him?

No!

It was a familiar spirit impersonating Mary, in which they can do such in a convincing way.

John wrote, *"Beloved, believe not every spirit, but try the spirits, whether they are of God: because many false prophets are gone out into the world"* (I Jn. 4:1).

There is no such thing as communicating with the dead. There is not one single instance in the Word of God of Mary or any of the Apostles appearing to anyone after their deaths. On the Mount of Transfiguration Moses and Elijah appeared to Christ, with Peter, James, and John present. They viewed the event; however, they were not included in the exchange of conversation (Lk. 9:27-36).

Actually, when Peter suggested that they *"make three tabernacles; one for You* (Christ)*, and one for Moses, and one for Elias* (Elijah)*,"* the Scripture says he didn't even know what he said.

Then the Word says:

"And there came a Voice out of the cloud, saying, This is My Beloved Son: hear Him" (Lk. 9:35).

The purpose of the statement is clear. Peter was putting Moses and Elijah on the same par with the Lord Jesus Christ, and the Heavenly Father was quick to correct his presumption. Jesus was the One they were to listen to and to no other.

The validity of any *"spiritual experience"* must be established by the Word of God. It cannot be established by the Pope, a Church Denomination, a Preacher, or anything else, even the actual fact of the vision itself. I repeat, it must be established by the Word of God, or else it is not valid.

THE WORD OF GOD

As stated, there is no record in the Word of God of any appearance of Mary to anyone after her death. Therefore, if the precedent was not established in the Bible, then the alleged appearances are not Scripturally valid and, consequently, it is not actually Mary who is appearing to these individuals. If it's not Mary, then what is it?

Most of the sightings are fabrications; however, the possibility definitely exists that some could be real; nevertheless, and as stated, it is not Mary, but a familiar spirit impersonating Mary.

If it's not clear cut, Scriptural foundation, then it's not of God, but rather of Satan. Paul said this:

"And no marvel; for Satan Himself is transformed into an angel of Light" (II Cor. 11:14).

There are many *"angels of light"* impersonating that which appears to be of God.

Visions, Dreams, or actual Visitations by the Lord are real because they are Scriptural. Still, we must be careful not to arbitrarily accept anything that claims to be of God, but we must, as stated, *"try the spirits"* to determine their Scriptural validity, whether it's a dream, or a so-called vision, etc.

THE PROTESTANT CHURCH WORLD

Most of the alleged Mary sightings or visions are associated with the world of Catholicism; however, the Protestant world, especially the Pentecostal and Charismatic segments, is little better. By and large, the Christian Church is so Scripturally illiterate that if anything is claimed to be a miracle, it is eagerly embraced. We who are Protestants smile at the unscriptural claims of the sightings of Mary and other phenomenon. Yet, at the same time, we follow and loudly proclaim that which purports to be a miracle from God when, in reality, most of the time it is not. Yes, God performs Miracles today, but He needs no false claims of false miracles to validate His Miracle-working Power. Too often the claims are not meant to praise the Lord at all, but to praise man.

The same scrutiny must be applied to all so-called miracles as we apply to the alleged sightings of Mary. They must have Scriptural validity.

- **There is Scriptural validity for *"anointing with oil"* and *"praying for the sick"* (James 5:14).**
- **There is Scriptural validity for the use of *"handkerchiefs or aprons"* taken from the person of a man or woman of God, regarding the healing of the sick or evil spirits being cast out (Acts 19:11-12).**
- **There is Scriptural validity for using the Name of Jesus in casting out demons, speaking with Tongues, taking up serpents, with the words *"take up"* (in the Greek, *"airo"*) meaning the removing of demon spirits (and having no reference to the handling of snakes), and the drinking of any deadly thing without hurt, with the latter never referring to presumptuous exhibitionism, but to accidental ingestion (Mk. 16:17-18).**
- **There is Scriptural validity for *"falling out under the Power of God,"* for the Apostle John said, *". . . I fell at His Feet as dead . . ."* (Rev. 1:17). Also, at the dedication of Solomon's Temple, *". . . the Priests could not stand to minister because of the cloud . . ."* (I Ki. 8:11).**

• There is Scriptural validity for the laying on of hands for healing (Acts 28:8).

• There is Scriptural validity for taking someone by the hand and lifting them up after prayer (Acts 3:7).

• There is Scriptural validity for the *"place being shaken"* as a consequence of prayer and the moving of the Holy Spirit (Acts 4:31).

• There is Scriptural validity for one's shadow passing over someone and they were healed (Acts 5:15).

• There is Scriptural validity for mixing spittle and clay and anointing the eyes of the blind with the mixture (Jn. 9:6); however, it should be noted that the Lord Jesus Christ is the only One Who ever did this, with no record in the Word of the Apostles or anyone else ever attempting to do such.

• There is Scriptural validity for praying for the dead to be raised (Acts 9:36-41).

• There is Scriptural validity for one being miraculously transported from one place to another without the means of transportation or conveyance (Acts 8:39-40).

• There is Scriptural validity for the visitation of Angels (Acts 5:19); however, as stated, we must make sure it's an Angel from the Lord and not an *"angel of light."*

• John 20:22 speaks of Jesus breathing on the Disciples, saying, *". . . Receive you the Holy Spirit."* There is no record that He did this at any other time or in any other capacity. I feel it would be a serious presumption or even sin to think that any frail mortal could breathe on anyone and have them receive the Holy Spirit.

• The Scripture does say, *"And by the hands of the Apostles were many signs and wonders wrought among the people"* (Acts 5:12).

THE LAST DAYS

In these Last Days proceeding toward the advent of the Antichrist and the Great Tribulation, miracles from the spirit world

are going to become numerous. When the Antichrist makes his debut, it will not only be political, but also spiritual. He will be accompanied by the False Prophet who will perform miracles, and they will be genuine miracles. The Apostate Church will, no doubt, fall in with him, claiming that the Antichrist is the Messiah. The Antichrist, the Scripture says, will come with "*. . . power, signs, and lying wonders . . .*" (II Thess. 2:9). His tactics will be amazingly successful. He will deceive many "*. . . because they received not the love of the Truth, that they might be Saved*" (II Thess. 2:10).

As these days swiftly approach, we must be very careful that what we accept is totally Scriptural. The Bible is the foundation — it is the criteria — there is no other.

Just because something purports to be a miracle (or actually seems to be one) does not necessarily mean that it is genuine.

As the Prophet of old said:

"*To the Law and the Testimony . . .*" (Isa. 8:20).

CHAPTER TWENTY-TWO

Can A Person Believe In Creationism And Evolution At The Same Time?

QUESTION:

CAN A PERSON BELIEVE IN CREATIONISM AND EVOLUTION AT THE SAME TIME?

ANSWER:

No, he cannot. If a person says he can, evidently he does not know the meaning of Creation and the Bible, nor does he understand evolution. Thomas Henry Huxley (a contemporary of Darwin) said, *"It is clear that the doctrine of evolution is directly antagonistic to that of creation . . . evolution, if consistently accepted, makes it impossible to believe in the Bible."*

Spencer (another teacher) said that evolution is purely mechanical and anti-supernatural.

Ernest Haeckel said, *"It entirely excludes the supernatural process — every prearranged and conscious act of a personal character."*

Others could be named also, but I think that it is clear that no true evolutionist can be a Christian or a Believer in the Bible. There's no place for God in evolution; hence, there is no need of a belief — in sin or a Saviour, Heaven or Hell. Those in the Church who try to harmonize evolution with the Bible rule out God despite themselves and are enemies of both God and the Church, at least the True Church.

Not one single branch of organic evolution has ever been proved, much less the main theory. Actually, evolution is a bankrupt, speculative philosophy — it has never been, and is not now a scientific fact.

SOME FALLACIES OF EVOLUTION

- **Evolution accepts —**
  . . . heathen and pagan philosophers in preference to God, Christ, the Holy Spirit, and the Bible.

- **Evolution nullifies —**
  . . . the idea of Biblical Creation by God. Blind force is substituted for the Creative Power of the Personal God Who created all things (Gen. 1:1).
- **Evolution degrades —**
  . . . God's Image to nothing more than a mere beast.
  . . . man from Creation by God in the Image of God to a monkey ancestry.
- **Evolution does away with —**
  . . . the Fall of man, for how can a mere beast that has evolved steadily from a molecule to an intelligent being go backward and have a fall?
  . . . Bible Miracles and the supernatural in all its forms. The only miracle of power in evolution is the inherent force of molecules.
  . . . the virgin birth, making it both impossible and unnecessary. It makes Christ a product of evolution in the same sense that it does all other men.
  . . . the authority of the Bible as a real Revelation from a Personal and a Living God, making it a lie in regard not only to Creation, but other Doctrines as well.
- **Evolution denies —**
  . . . the bodily Resurrection of Christ, which declares that it is contrary to the process of evolution.
  . . . the Atonement; for, according to evolution, there was no Fall of man and, therefore, no sin for which to make Atonement.
  . . . the Second Advent of Christ and the final Restoration and preservation of all things by the Personal Act of God.

For a person to argue that the Christian can accept evolution on the grounds that the Bible is not to be taken literally presents a surrender to the foes of Christ, the Holy Spirit, the Bible, and all Christian teachings. This particular theory (and it is doubtful that it can even be referred to as a theory) is anti-God, anti-Christ, anti-Bible, anti-Christian, and actually anti-intelligence.

WHAT A CHRISTIAN BELIEVES

The Christian must believe —

. . . that the Bible is the Word of God — not that it merely contains the Word of God, but that it is the Word of God (Jn. 1:1; Mat. 4:4).

. . . that God is a Person Who creates (brings into existence all material and Spiritual substance) and that out of the created material He Personally formed the worlds and each creature therein (Jn. 1:3; Heb. 11:3).

. . . that God created man in His Own Image and Likeness in one day, fully mature and highly intelligent, not that he descended from molecules through the lower forms of life to monkey and finally man (Gen. 1:26-27).

. . . that all Angels and spirit-beings were created by God fully mature and intelligent (Ps. 104:4; Ezek. 28:15; Col. 1:15-18; Rev. 4:11).

. . . that God created man, animals, fish, fowls, and plants to reproduce themselves after their own kind (Gen. 1:20-31; 2:5-7, 19-25).

. . . that Jesus Christ is the Son of God and, as such, no other man is. The Christian must also believe that Jesus is the Only Begotten of the Father, not that He is a Son of God, in the sense that all men are, but that He is the Son of God (I Tim. 3:16; Heb. 1:1-3; Rev. 1:8-11).

. . . that the Holy Spirit is a Person, separate and distinct from both the Father and the Son, and that all three Persons of the Godhead have Their Own Personal Body, Soul, and Spirit, and make up the Divine Trinity (I Jn. 5:7).

. . . that man is a sinner fallen from original righteousness and that he fell from an intelligent and responsible place as head of the present creation (Gen. 3:1-24).

. . . that except for God's Redemptive Grace, man is lost. Man is not the unfortunate victim of environment, but rather, is like he is as a result of the Fall (Rom. 3:10-19).

. . . that man is justified by Faith in the Atoning Blood of

Jesus Christ, resulting in a supernatural Regeneration from above (Mat. 1:21; Jn. 3:18; Rom. 5:1; II Cor. 5:17; Eph. 2:8-9).
. . . that the death of Christ was expiatory, not exemplary. He died for all men. His Blood is the only Atonement for sin and by His Stripes we are healed (Gal. 1:4).
. . . that Jesus Christ rose bodily from the dead, not spiritually or as a spirit-being. He is alive forevermore in His earthly, Resurrected, flesh-and-bone Body and represents men before God as their High Priest and Saviour (Lk. 24:30; Jn. 10:17-18; Acts 1:3).
. . . that all men who accept Christ and have conformed to God's Plan for man will be Saved, will be Resurrected from the dead to immortality, and will help God administer the affairs of the Universe forever (Jn. 3:16; I Cor. 6:2; II Tim. 2:12; Rev. 1:6; 22:4-5).
. . . that all men who reject Christ and do not conform to God's Plan will pay the eternal death penalty for sin, will be resurrected to immortality, and will be punished eternally in the Lake of Fire (Mk. 16:15-16; Jn. 3:16; Rev. 14:9-11; 22:15).

A person cannot know the statements of both the Bible and evolutionists and believe both, nor can he be neutral. A stand must be taken, either for God and the Bible or for evolution and all that evolution produces — which is only unbelief.

SOME FACTS ABOUT EVOLUTION

The Bible —
. . . condemns the theory of both cosmic and organic evolution.
. . . declares that God created the heavens and the Earth — in fact, all things were created by Him (Rev. 4:11).
. . . declares (ten times in the First Chapter of Genesis) that everything created by God was given power to reproduce its own kind. Not one thing could break this

Law and produce any other kind. Since that Law was written, thousands of years ago, it has never been broken, not even once. Now, after nearly 6,000 years, the Law of Reproduction is the same. The sponge is still a sponge and has not become an oyster. No lowly earthworm has ever turned into a spider; and no lizard, a crocodile. No bug or bird has ever been able to reproduce another kind except its own.

• It is a Natural Law that nothing reproduces anything greater than itself.

• No monkey has ever produced a man, and the missing link is still missing — and actually the link is all the way from *"A"* to *"Z."* This is quite remarkable in view of the fact that there are over two million species of plant and animal life. Each species proves the Law of Reproduction (each after its own kind) established by God.

• Science has proved that dead matter cannot generate life.

• Darwin's argument that plants and animals have within themselves tendencies to vary of their own accord in many and all direction to an unlimited degree has been disproved many times.

• Some persons have mentioned the cavemen of past ages as proof of evolution. Actually, there has never been any proof that cavemen existed. Of course, I am certain that some men have lived in caves in the past as some live in caves today. But as far as animalistic, crawling primates, uttering some guttural language — half-man, half-monkey — there is not one iota of proof that such ever existed. These things have been created out of the fertile minds of unbelief and supported by so-called specimens created, at times, out of plaster of Paris. The movies, television, and much of literature suggests such — but it is only a suggestion. There is not one scintilla or iota of scientific proof; rather, the facts are that such never existed.

NO PROOF

Most of the manufactured bones of prehistoric men are

fakes. The Piltdown man, for example, was no man at all. It was made from two or three bits of a skull bone, a piece of a jaw bone, and a tooth. It was finally acknowledged that these scraps did not belong to the skull and were those of a chimpanzee. The Java man was built in Java from a skull bone, a leg bone, and two molars. The rest was a concoction of plaster of paris. The Peking man of China was made from human skull fragments found in a cave. The Nebraska man was made from a single pig's tooth and said to be one million years old.

Such are the hoaxes in the name of science which are being passed upon our innocent boys and girls by many educators.

THE THEORY OF EVOLUTION

The theory of evolution is that all forms of life are derived by gradual modification from earlier and simpler forms or from one rudimentary form. It teaches a process in which something complex is developed by itself from a simple beginning. It accepts the existence of the cause or causes of the first substance and the force or forces working successive transformations from a lower to a higher form of matter and life.

Cosmic evolution claims that the vast material suns, moons, planets, and universes were formed by themselves from lower units of matter (atoms and molecules) through random chants, not the intervention of God.

Organic evolution teaches that the vegetable and animal kingdoms evolved from lower forms of life to what they are today. Evolutionists do not say from where the lower forms of life came. Their theory begins with matter or substance already in existence. They do not try to account for how these came to exist or how molecules got their inherent powers or how they came to be definite laws governing them so that they could produce without failure all things as we now have them. These theories do not show why there is such bitter hatred against the God of the Bible as being the Creator of all things.

FALSE TEACHING

The evolutionists teach that hair is but elongated scales of prehistoric animals. They teach that legs of all animals developed from warts on aboriginal amphibians. They teach that eyes are but an accidental development of freckles on blind amphibians who responded to the sun. They also teach that ears came about by the airwaves calling to spots on early reptiles. They teach that man came from monkeys. They teach that the vast Universes came from a few molecules. They actually teach that nothing working on nothing by nothing through nothing for nothing of nothing begat everything!

No, a person cannot believe in evolution and creationism at the same time.

***"In the beginning God created the heaven and the Earth"* (Gen. 1:1).**

***"And God said, Let the Earth bring forth the living creature after his kind, cattle, and creeping thing, and beast of the Earth after his kind: and it was so"* (Gen. 1:24).**

"And God said, Let Us make man in Our Image, after Our Likeness: and let them have dominion over the fish of the sea, and over the fowl of the air, and over the cattle, and over all the Earth, and over every creeping thing that creeps upon the Earth.

***"So God created man in His Own Image, in the Image of God created He him; male and female created He them"* (Gen. 1:26-27).**

***"And God saw everything that He had made, and, behold, it was very good. And the evening and the morning were the sixth day"* (Gen. 1:31).**

CHAPTER TWENTY-THREE

What Does The Term "Judge Not" Refer To?

QUESTION:

WHAT DOES THE TERM "JUDGE NOT" REFER TO?

ANSWER:

Jesus said:

"Judge not, that you be not judged *(this statement by Christ harks back to Verses 25 through 34 of the previous Chapter; the idea is, God may permit poverty to test His Child, but fellow Believers are not to err, as Job's friends did, and believe the trial to be a judgment for secret sin; as well, the word, 'judging,' as used here, covers every aspect of dealing with our fellowman)***.**

"For with what judgment *you* judge, *you* shall be judged *(whatever motive we ascribe to others, such motive will ultimately be ascribed to us)***: and with what measure you mete, it shall be measured to you again** *(a double emphasis is given here in order to proclaim the seriousness of the Words of our Lord; when we judge others, we are judging ourselves)***.**

"And why do you behold the mote that is in your brother's eye *(the Believer is not to be looking for fault or wrongdoing in the lives of fellow Believers)***, but consider not the beam that is in your own eye?** *(We have plenty in our own lives which need eliminating, without looking for faults in others. The 'mote' and 'beam' are contrasted! The constant judging of others portrays the fact that we are much worse off than the one we are judging.)*

"Or how will you say to your brother, Let me pull out the mote out of your eye *(the seriousness of setting ourselves up as Judge, Jury, and Executioner)***; and, behold, a beam *is* in your own eye?** *(Once again draws attention to the fact that the person doing the judging is in far worse spiritual condition than the one being judged.)*

> **"You hypocrite** *(aptly describes such a person)*, **first cast out the beam out of your own eye; and then you shall see clearly to cast out the mote out of your brother's eye** *(the very fact that we do not address ourselves, but rather others, portrays the truth that our personal situation is worse; when we properly analyze ourselves, then, and only then, can we 'see clearly'; this is speaking of character assassination and not the correction of doctrine)***" (Mat. 7:1-5).**

MOTIVES AND FAILINGS

It is obvious here that the Lord is telling us, in no uncertain terms, not to judge the motives of others and, as well, not to judge their failings. We are to pray for them, love them, and help them in any way we can, but not judge them. The idea is this.

None of us have any room to criticize others in this capacity. We have enough failings in our own life, in our own living, to keep us busy, so to speak. Once we understand that, as we should, that is, that we see ourselves as we should see ourselves, then we will quickly realize we have no right to judge others.

SELF-RIGHTEOUSNESS

I think one can say without fear of contradiction, that the type of judging that Jesus described, is that produced by self-righteousness. This sin, and a gross sin it is, is a so-called righteousness, which is produced by man. In other words, he thinks he is righteous, because of certain bad things he hasn't done or certain good things he has done. To be sure, it's a righteousness that God will in no wise accept.

It was self-righteousness that nailed Christ to the Cross. And it is the sin, I think, that the Lord hates more than any other, and for all the obvious reasons.

When one truly understands the Righteousness of Christ, which is a perfect Righteousness, one at the same time will begin to understand himself, realizing that he has nothing good

that he can present and, as well, will begin to understand the Lord, at least as far as a poor human being can understand the Lord. When we see ourselves as we really are, and no matter how consecrated we may consider ourselves to be, we will then realize how much we need the Righteousness of Christ, and how much we don't deserve it.

***"Righteousness"* simply means *"that which is right;"* however, it is God's Standard of that which is right and not man's. But to repeat the statement, I think it can be said that it is self-righteousness that loves to judge the motives and the failings of others.**

WHAT ABOUT JUDGING DOCTRINE?

If it is to be noticed, our Lord in His earthly Ministry, said very little of that which was negative to the unsaved; however, He scathingly rebuked the Pharisees, and did so publicly. To conserve space, I will only quote a little of what He said, which is as follows:

> **"But woe unto you, Scribes and Pharisees, hypocrites!** *(The first of eight woes, and said to their faces. There could be no greater insult to them than being called 'hypocrites'!)* **for you shut up the Kingdom of Heaven against men** *(is the first scheme of Satan, and is carried out through religion)*: **for you neither go in *yourselves,* neither suffer you them who are entering to go in** *(they refuse to accept Christ, and stood in the door to bar access to any and all who would attempt to come in)*.
>
> **"Woe unto you, Scribes and Pharisees, hypocrites! for you compass sea and land to make one proselyte** *(working zealously to draw people to themselves, instead of the Lord)*, **and when he is made, you make him twofold more the child of Hell than yourselves** *(religious people are the hardest of all to bring to the Lord)*.
>
> **"You blind guides, which strain at a gnat, and**

swallow a camel *(this is self-righteousness taken to an ultra extreme)*" **(Mat. 23:13, 15, 24).**

Paul wrote:

"Let the Prophets speak two or three *(speaks not only of those who have the simple Gift of Prophecy, but also of those who stand in the Office of the Prophet)*, **and let the other judge.** *(This refers to the fact that all preaching and teaching should be judged according to Scriptural validity)*" **(I Cor. 14:29).**

Not only is it <u>not</u> wrong to judge doctrine, it is incumbent upon us, that is, if we are to be faithful to the Lord to do so. Millions are in Hell today, simply because they blindly followed what they heard, which, in fact, caused them to be eternally lost.

THE WORD OF GOD

The criteria for all things is the Word of God. ***"Is it Scriptural?"*** **must be that which is asked of all things.**

That being the case, should a member of a congregation rebuke a Pastor for false doctrine?

PROPER BEHAVIOR ON THE PART OF THE BELIEVER

The answer to the question would depend on several things.

If a rebuke is done kindly and with diplomacy, and it is felt that the Pastor was of such a frame of mind that he would accept such a correction, then it might be possible; however, such is very rare.

Unless the Believer is awful sure of his ground, in other words, that the Pastor will accept what is being said, he had best hold his peace.

If what is being preached is grossly erroneous, which at times is the case; it would be best that the Believer try to find another place of worship. The truth is, it seldom does any good to approach a Pastor about false doctrine that he is preaching, if, in fact, that is the case, and for many and varied reasons. To keep from having trouble, even though it's a very difficult thing to do, as stated, it would be best to try to find another Church.

***"Hear the Word of the LORD, you who tremble at His Word; Your brethren who hated you, who cast you out for My Name's sake, said, Let the LORD be glorified: but He shall appear to your joy, and they shall be ashamed"* (Isa. 66:5).**

***"Hear the Word of the LORD"* is an admonishment to the Church to not hear the word of man. The words, *"You who tremble at His Word,"* refer to those who are of a *"poor and contrite spirit."* The prideful never *"tremble at His Word,"* but rather substitute their own word. *"Your brethren who hated you, who cast you out for My Name's sake,"* refers to a formal excommunication, or at least to a renunciation of fellowship. This speaks of persecution by an apostate Church.**

***"Let the LORD be glorified,"* is actually a sarcastic statement from these false brethren! This was the sarcastic challenge of the Pharisees. It means, *"Let Jehovah manifest His Power and favor in Your behalf."* This, in effect, is what they said to Christ when He was hanging on the Cross.**

***"But He shall appear to your joy, and they shall be ashamed,"* refers to the fact that God, even though He tarry long, will ultimately vindicate your trust in Him.**

CHAPTER TWENTY-FOUR

What Is The Role Of The Husband And The Wife In The Family?

QUESTION:

WHAT IS THE ROLE OF THE HUSBAND AND THE WIFE IN THE FAMILY?

ANSWER:

To address this very important question, I will begin the answer by quoting from THE EXPOSITOR'S STUDY BIBLE. While it is somewhat lengthy, I think it is necessary in order that the answer be based strictly on the Word of God.

> **"But I would have you know, that the Head of every man is Christ** *(refers to authority)*; **and the Head of the woman *is* the man** *(pertains to the Creation model)*; **and the Head of Christ *is* God** *(speaks here of two separate and distinct Persons [I Tim. 2:5])*.
>
> **"Every man praying or Prophesying** *(refers either to the Gift of Prophecy or Preaching [I Cor. 12:10])*, **having *his* head covered, dishonors his Head** *(dishonors Christ; such portrays a covering other than Christ)*.
>
> **"But every woman who prays or Prophesies** *(tells us that women did pray and preach in the Church, or wherever)* **with *her* head uncovered dishonors her Head** *(portrays the fact that, due to the Creation model, the woman should have long hair, at least longer than that of the man)*: **for that is even all one as if she were shaven.** *(Refers to the fact that some women in those days had their heads shaved as a punishment for whoredom or adultery. The Apostle is saying that Christian women should not insist upon their rights so much that they begin to look like the worst of the world.)*
>
> **"For if the woman be not covered, let her also be shorn** *(in effect, says, 'if the woman wants to wear her hair short like a man, why not go all the way and be shorn')*: **but if it be a shame for a woman to be shorn or shaven,**

let her be covered. *(This refers to the fact that if she does not want to look like an adulteress, let her be covered, i.e., 'have long hair.')*

"For a man indeed ought not to cover *his* head *(while praying or preaching)*, **forasmuch as he is the Image and Glory of God: but the woman is the Glory of the man.** *(This refers to the fact that Eve was not 'God's Image and Glory' in the same sense as Adam.)*

"For the man is not of the woman *(Adam was not in any way derived from woman)*; **but the woman of the man.** *(In fact, the woman was derived from man by the Power of God.)*

"Neither was the man created for the woman; but the woman for the man. *(This probably would have been better translated, 'for also man was not created on account of the woman; on the contrary, woman on account of the man.')*

"For this cause *(refers again to the creation model that 'the woman is for the man')* **ought the woman to have power on *her* head** *(long hair, i.e., 'authority')* **because of the Angels.** *(This has to do with her submission to God's Plan as a constant reminder to the fallen Angels, who rebelled against God's Plan and the Revolution led by Lucifer, which took place long before Adam.)*

"Nevertheless neither is the man without the woman *(needs the woman)*, **neither the woman without the man** *(the woman also needs the man)*, **in the Lord.** *(This refers to the fact that this is the manner in which the Lord created the original model, and demands that it continues.)*

"For as the woman *is* of the man *(refers to the fact that Eve was originally created from Adam [Gen. 2:21-22])*, **even so *is* the man also by the woman** *(by or through the medium of natural birth)*; **but all things of God.** *(This puts everything on an even keel, meaning that men are no more important than women, or women than men.)*

"Judge in yourselves *(refers to common sense)*: **is it comely that a woman pray unto God uncovered?** *(This* *doesn't refer to a hat nearly so much as it refers to long hair, or at least hair that's longer than that of a man.)*

"Does not even nature itself teach you, that, if a man have long hair, it is a shame unto him? *(A man wearing long hair is really not in accord with the nature of a man.)*

"But if a woman have long hair, it is a glory to her *(is a way of saying that such manifests woman's voluntary submission to God's Will)*: **for *her* hair is given her for a covering.** *(This points to the idea that man is the head or covering of the woman under Christ.)*

"But if any man seem to be contentious *(refers to both men and women, who were insisting on conducting themselves wrongly)*, **we have no such custom** *(we have no custom other than what I have said)*, **neither the Churches of God.** *(What I have said is being done in all the other Churches)*" **(I Cor. 11:3-16).**

According to the Word of God, which we have just quoted, God has established in the home very distinct roles for the husband and the wife.

THE HUSBAND IS THE HEAD OF THE WIFE

Again, according to Paul, *"The husband is the head of the wife, even as Christ is the Head of the Church: and He is the Saviour of the Body"* (Eph. 5:23). A man, as head of the home, has a special position and responsibility assigned to him by God. To note the importance of this position is not to be chauvinistic or to minimize the tremendous devotion and influence of all good women. That would be foolish indeed!

Women do mighty works within the Kingdom of God. They are pillars of strength in countless areas of Christian activity. How many Churches would literally fall by the wayside if it were not for the Godly women within those Churches! A woman plays a tremendously important part in a man's life, and man, in fact, is incomplete without her. That is the reason

God said, *"It is not good that the man should be alone; I will make him an helpmeet* (suitable) *for him"* (Gen. 2:18).

But, it is the husband who is to be the leader in the home, directing the family Godward. The Lord imposed duties and responsibilities on the man, and he fitted man's personality and body so that he would be able to meet these responsibilities. When God gave directions, if it is to be noticed, He gave them to Adam. He commanded Adam not to eat the forbidden fruit. Adam named the animals and had various responsibilities. When Adam and Eve sinned, it was Adam whom God sought out and reproached, even though it was Eve who sinned first. It was to Adam that God said, *"Cursed is the ground for your sake. In the sweat of your face shall you eat bread"* (Gen. 3:17, 19). Notice that the woman was guilty and she was included in the curse, but it was the man who was held accountable.

Leadership and government have traditionally been male roles; however, there definitely are women in executive positions today, and even leaders of nations, and rightly so; but God intended that men lead in the home.

The Bible teaches that man is to rule the home with love. The Bible has a system; it has an order. God has a system and an order for everything that He does. After sin had come into the world, God said to Eve, *"Your desire shall be to your husband, and he shall rule over you"* (Gen. 3:16). These are strong words. The Apostle Paul again reminded the Children of God, *"For the husband is the head of the wife, even as Christ is the Head of the Church"* (Eph. 5:23).

LEADERSHIP AND RESPONSIBILITY

Does this imply a form of slavery for the wife then? God forbid! God took Eve out of the side of Adam, not out of his head or his feet. Adam, therefore, has no cause to lord it over Eve or to walk on her. God took Eve out of Adam's side, from under his arm. This means that they are, therefore, equal and Adam is to protect her. A husband is not meant to be a despot

or a tyrant. This is the opposite of what God is!

The husband is to be the head of the home. He is to rule over it and preside over it, leading it in love. It is God Who establishes relationships and authority. Going contrary to God's Plan will eventually lead to difficulty and heartache. The woman has a specific role under God, and the man too has a specific role under God. Whenever we seek to avoid the position God has assigned us, the result is, almost without exception, anarchy and chaos.

THE ROLE OF THE WIFE IN THE HOME

According to Scripture, as stated, the husband is to be the *"head"* of the home. It is interesting to note, however, that the wife is to be the *"manager"* of the household. We read, *"I will therefore that the younger women marry, bear children, guide the house, give none occasion to the adversary to speak reproachfully"* (I Tim. 5:14). Paul suggested that young women marry and thus live within the framework of a family. He suggested that they have children and *"guide the house."* The Greek word for *"guide"* means *"management and direction of household affairs."* In some newer studies and translations of this particular Scripture, *"guide the house"* is rendered *"manage their homes."* It is evident, however it is translated, that the wife is to be the manager of the household. This is her responsibility and she should be allowed to do so.

Women are much more suited for this than men. In fact, most of the time, women are far better managers of the budget than are men. They give more attention to detail and are more intuitive than men.

The following will again be quite lengthy, but I think it will contribute much to our answer.

THE VIRTUOUS WOMAN

"Who can find a virtuous woman? for her price is

far above rubies. *(The word 'virtuous' is not limited in Hebrew, as in English, in its meaning; it is a covering term suggesting character and ability. Spiritually, the dialogue concerning the 'virtuous woman' can also apply to the Church and what it ought to be.)*

"The heart of her husband does safely trust in her, so that he shall have no need of spoil. *(He has absolute confidence in her faithfulness.)*

"She will do him good and not evil all the days of her life. *(He is blessed by her tireless and unfailing industry, which will last all the days of her life.)*

"She seeks wool, and flax, and works willingly with her hands. *(She goes to every length to save money, even 'working willingly with her hands.' There is no hint of laziness about her.)*

"She is like the merchants' ships; she brings her food from afar. *(If she buys something, she does so with the idea in mind of using some of it and selling the other to pay for that which she has used.)*

"She rises also while it is yet night, and gives meat to her household, and a portion to her maidens. *(She takes the lead in guiding the house, and expects all who are in the household to follow her example, which they do.)*

"She considers a field, and buys it: with the fruit of her hands she plants a vineyard. *(She is constantly planning as to how to provide for her growing family.)*

"She girds her loins with strength, and strengthens her arms. *(She keeps herself and her family in good health with proper food and clothing.)*

"She perceives that her merchandise is good: her candle goes not out by night. *(She produces quality product.)*

"She lays her hands to the spindle, and her hands hold the distaff. *(All of this was a part of the spinning wheel, showing her industriousness and ability.)*

"She stretches out her hand to the poor; yes, she reaches forth her hands to the needy. *(Even though she* *works hard for her money, she does not fail to help the 'poor' and the 'needy.' She does so because she knows that God honors such.)*

"She is not afraid of the snow for her household: for all her household are clothed with scarlet. *(She has prepared for the coming winter with suitable clothing for all of her household. She thinks ahead. Coming difficulties do not catch her shortsighted.)*

"She makes herself coverings of tapestry; her clothing is silk and purple. *(Even though she is very conservative, still, money is not her God. Therefore, she does not skimp in providing the furniture for her home, or for her own personal clothing. It is such that befits her station in life, as one who is blessed by God and is a Child of God.)*

"Her husband is known in the gates, when he sits among the elders of the land. *(As her husband was guided in his choice of her, likewise, she was guided by the Holy Spirit in her choice of him. He is a leader in the community.)*

"She makes fine linen, and sells it; and delivers girdles unto the merchant. *(Once again, her business ability places her on a par with her husband. The Holy Spirit gives her no lesser position. She is capable of being a captain of industry and a maker of excellent decisions.)*

"Strength and honour are her clothing; and she shall rejoice in time to come. *(All that she manufactures is done so with quality. Her goods are sought the world over.)*

"She opens her mouth with wisdom; and in her tongue is the law of kindness. *(Even though this virtuous woman, whose price is far above rubies, is said by the Holy Spirit to be a captain of industry with striking and startling abilities, still, her 'mouth' is a mouth of 'Wisdom.' Despite all her qualities and riches, still, her 'tongue' is not harsh, but always 'kind.')*

"She looks well to the ways of her household, and eats not the bread of idleness. *(Even though she is now greatly blessed, still, there is no place for 'idleness' in her* *thinking or doing. In essence, industry never stops.)*

"Her children arise up, and call her blessed; her husband also, and he praises her. *(Such women could not be praised too highly. Bath-sheba was truly led by the Holy Spirit and inspired greatly to write the instruction that she did for her son Solomon. She was quite a lady!)*

"Many daughters have done virtuously, but you excel them all. *(It seems that the husband of this 'virtuous woman' speaks in this Verse. He claims that many have done 'virtuously,' but that this one whom God has given him, his lovely wife, 'excels them all.'*

If this is to be carried to its conclusion, David spoke these words about Bath-sheba. Such is God; such is Grace.)

"Favour is deceitful, and beauty is vain: but a woman who fears the LORD, she shall be praised.

"Give her of the fruit of her hands; and let her own works praise her in the gates. *(These two closing Verses of this Chapter are the Holy Spirit's conclusion, not only to the Chapter itself, but to the Message of the entirety of the Book of Proverbs. That Message is: the fear of the Lord secures abiding favor, moral beauty, public approbation, and eternal recompense)*" **(Prov. 31:10-31).**

NO RANK BASED ON GENDER

Emphasis on submission within the Word of God does not in any way infer inequality. For those who are in Christ, there is no preference on the basis of race, class, nationality, career, business, education, or gender.

***"There is neither Jew nor Greek, there is neither bond nor free, there is neither male nor female: for you are all one in Christ Jesus"* (Gal. 3:28). There is no rank based on gender.**

Throughout God's Word, there are illustrations of dedicated women as well as men. Men and women have complementary roles in society, and it is not a question of importance or of position that determines the structure of the family or

society. God has a Divinely established pattern and He has assigned specific responsibilities to the husband and to the wife. The two are complementary — a partnership — and together they comprise a unit. This is the reason Scripture can say that they become one.

THE DOCTRINE OF SUBMISSION

There is a teaching that says that Christian wives should submit to their husband in everything, even though he is unsaved. In other words, if he asks her to go to a nightclub with him, she should go. If he asks her to drink alcoholic beverages with him, she should drink. If he asks her to lie or bear false witness, she should do that, too, because in doing this — according to this teaching — she is obeying the Scriptures; however, this is blatantly and obviously error. Let's quote from THE EXPOSITOR'S STUDY BIBLE:

> **"Wives, submit yourselves unto your own husbands** *(the Holy Spirit, through the Apostle, is relating to the Spiritual Leadership of the family)*, **as unto the Lord.** *(First of all, the submission is to be to Christ as Lord and Master, and not to the husband. If the husband's supremacy had been in view, it would have been expressed in a different manner, so say the Greek Scholars. If the wife properly submits to the Lord, she will properly submit to her husband as it regards Spiritual Leadership, that is if he knows the Lord. If he doesn't know the Lord, such submission cannot be tendered, as would be obvious.)*
>
> **"For the husband is the head of the wife, even as Christ is the Head of the Church** *(suggests the obedience the wife renders to her husband is to be regarded as obedience rendered to Christ, which she can do if her husband is properly following the Lord)*: **and He is the Saviour of the Body.** *(This refers to the Lord being the Saviour of Believers, who make up the Church. While the husband*

cannot be the Saviour of his wife in redemptive terms, he can be her protector and provider.)

"Therefore as the Church is subject unto Christ *(as its Head)*, **so *let* the wives *be* to their own husbands in everything.** *(This presupposes that the husband is conducting himself even as Christ)*" **(Eph. 5:22-24).**

GOD NEVER CONTRADICTS HIS OWN WORD

The Word of the Lord tells us to *"not bear false witness"* (Ex. 20:16), and for a wife to do such for an ungodly husband, would be disobeying the Word, which the Lord can never sanction.

Second, any law that is given by a husband (or even the State, for that matter) always is subject to a higher law; namely, the Law of God. We are also told to *"render . . . unto Caesar the things which are Caesar's"* (Mat. 22:21; Mk. 12:17; Lk. 20:25) and to *"obey them who have the rule over us"* (Heb. 13:17); however, thousands of Believers in the Early Church died before they would obey those in authority, yet they were not breaking God's Laws or contradicting them. Caesar simply stated that those early Christians had to do obeisance to him, recant their faith in the Lord Jesus Christ, and proclaim Caesar as god. The early Christians chose to die rather than do this, and rightly so. They would have lost their souls if they had obeyed.

Likewise, millions of Christians from the time of the Early Church until now have died because they would not obey those who had power over them. The Word of the Lord comes first in all things.

Were these Believers, literally millions of them down through the years, breaking the Laws of God by refusing to yield to the demands of ungodly leaders? Certainly not! These commands given by the Lord Jesus Christ and the Apostle Paul were not, and are not, to be taken out of context. The Lord was speaking of money (taxes) that was owed Caesar, when

he spoke of rendering to Caesar . . . He was simply telling the Jews that they should pay their taxes because they received certain benefits from the State and consequently owed something to it in return.

The Apostle Paul meant that just because a person is a Christian does not mean he is above the Law. Christians must obey the Laws as anyone else, providing those laws do not disavow the Word of God or violate our conscience. But even then, as many of the Early Christians, failure to obey ungodly laws would also be to suffer consequences.

The same application may be made to Christian wives obeying ungodly husbands. They should strive to do everything they can that he asks if it does not violate the Word of God. But if anything he demands violates the Word and their conscience as well, those things they cannot do.

AS CHRIST LOVED THE CHURCH

What Paul was saying in Ephesians was that a wife's obedience to the husband in all things is based upon the husband loving his wife as Christ loved the Church. No husband who is an imitator of the Lord Jesus Christ will demand that his wife do something that is unscriptural, unholy, or ungodly. Any husband who is Christlike in conduct and attitude should be reverenced by his wife; and she should submit to him as unto the Lord. She should submit in everything knowing that everything he demands will be Scriptural, Godly, and Christlike.

HOW CAN A MARRIAGE BE IMPROVED?

Before we address this question, we should probably note that a marriage is a dynamic relationship. This means that it is a living, ever-changing association involving give and take on both sides. Although *"marriages are made in Heaven,"* they must be lived out on Earth, and men and women are responsible for the upkeep. The successful marriage requires daily

maintenance and dedication.

Marriage is most of all a relationship. The word *"relationship means an interaction between partners."* And interaction implies activity on both sides. Unless there is communion, fellowship, mutuality, and reciprocity, there can be no relationship. Many marriages founder on the shoals of separation or divorce simply because the partners stop interacting and begin to withdraw into their own separate interests and preoccupations. This leaves the two partners single although married. They live under the same roof, they may sleep in the same bed, they may even engage in sexual intercourse together from time to time, but they do not feel like they are *"one."* They feel like strangers living two distinct lives.

All too often, the husband or the wife makes demands of their partner that only the Lord can provide. If such is done, the strain will become quickly obvious, with the situation speedily deteriorating.

THE CROSS OF CHRIST

Every believing husband and believing wife should understand that every answer, and irrespective as to what it might be as it regards relationships, is found in the Cross of Christ. If the Believer places his or her faith exclusively in Christ and the Cross, the Holy Spirit will then become very active in one's life and, thereby, very active in one's marriage. Unfortunately, all too often, Christian marriage seminars are based upon the same advice given by the world, which is a loser from the very beginning. Let us say it again.

The answer to marriage problems between Christians and, in fact, any other type of problem that the Believer might have, is found exclusively in Christ and the Cross.

Most may wonder as to how our Faith in Christ and what He did for us at the Cross can have a bearing on marriage problems? The answer is simple; it is the Holy Spirit Who makes the difference.

THE HOLY SPIRIT AND HOW HE WORKS

Every husband and every wife should conduct themselves with an attitude of placing their mate first. This is the opposite of selfishness, and is the Christlike spirit. And one can do that, if one has the help of the Holy Spirit.

All too often, we place the Holy Spirit in a position that is totally divorced from needs such as problems which arise in a marriage. But please understand the Holy Spirit is given to us as our constant, ever abiding Helper. In fact, He is referred to by Christ as the *"Comforter,"* which in the Greek means *"Parakletos,"* which means *"One called to the side of another to help"* (Jn. 14:16). The help He provides covers every avenue of our needs, including marriages. In fact, one might say that the Holy Spirit is the greatest marriage counselor of them all. But His Help is predicated solely on our Faith in Christ and the Cross. That is what gives Him the legal right to do all the things that He does. It only remains for the Believer to place his faith exclusively in Christ, and what Christ has done for us at the Cross, and do so on a daily basis (Lk. 9:23).

Considering that, and obeying the command of our Lord, a marriage can be strengthened and even restored. In fact, this is the only way that it can truly be restored.

HUSBANDS

> **"Husbands, love your wives** *(with a God kind of love)*, **even as Christ also loved the Church** *(presents the qualifier; if a husband conducts himself accordingly toward his wife, she will have no problem whatsoever submitting to him, even as she should)*, **and gave Himself for it** *(presents the great Sacrifice which characterizes the God kind of love; the answer for marriage problems is not marriage seminars, but rather that both husband and wife place their Faith and confidence totally in Christ and what He has done for us at the Cross; in other words, the Cross alone,*

which refers to what Jesus did there, is the answer);

"So ought men to love their wives as their own bodies *(is proclaimed in this manner because 'they are one flesh,' even as Paul will say in Verse 31)*. **He who loves his wife loves himself** *(proclaims the oneness of the Sacred union of marriage)*.

"For we are members of His Body, of His Flesh, and of His Bones. *(We are visible parts of that Body of which He is Head, and this is the reason He nourishes and cherishes the Church. 'His Flesh' and 'His Bones' speak of the Incarnation, and the giving of Himself on the Cross, which made it possible for us to become part of Him [Rom. 6:3-5].)*

"For this cause shall a man leave his father and mother *(while he certainly continues to love his father and mother, his primary love is now for his wife)*, **and shall be joined unto his wife, and they two shall be one flesh.** *(The union that is meant to symbolize Christ and the Church)*" **(Eph. 5:25, 28, 30-31).**

WHAT IS THE PURPOSE OF SEX? HOW IS THE BIBLICAL VIEW DIFFERENT FROM THE WORLD'S VIEW?

God has created in human beings a physical passion that presses men and women toward marriage. This is normal and proper. The sex drive is something that should be considered holy in the sight of God. Of course, as in everything else in this fallen world, man has found innumerable ways to pervert that which God has created.

Physical attraction and mating are ordained by God. Men and women are made for marriage. In fact, God performed the first marriage, which was, of course, between Adam and Eve. In all of this, he intended that the sex drive be satisfied in the holy communion of wedlock. Men and women have been made with an innate desire for one another. This drive is by design very strong. Paul said, and concerning this very thing:

"Now concerning the things whereof you wrote unto me *(the Apostle will now address things he was asked in a letter; the previous Chapters addressed things he had been told)*: ***It is*** **good for a man not to touch a woman** *(it is not wrong for a man not to marry, providing the Lord desires this for the man's personal life)*.

"Nevertheless, *to avoid* fornication, let every man have his own wife, and let every woman have her own husband *(this is a rule, not merely permission)*.

"Let the husband render unto the wife due benevolence *(it refers to the husband respecting the sexual needs of his wife, and to meet them accordingly; of course, we speak of legitimate needs)*: **and likewise also the wife unto the husband** *(proclaims the same duty imposed upon the wife regarding the husband)*.

"The wife has not power of her own body, but the husband: and likewise also the husband has not power of his own body, but the wife *(refers to the fact that the husband and wife belong to each other, meaning neither has the right to refuse normal demands)*.

"Defraud you not one the other *(it seems that some married couples in that day were refraining from sexual activity, which they erroneously thought enabled them to live more spiritual lives; man seems to go from one extreme to the other!)*, **except *it be* with consent for a time, that you may give yourselves to fasting and prayer** *(not mandatory, but given as a suggestion)*; **and come together again, that Satan tempt you not for your incontinency** *(the idea is that the Believer not unnecessarily place himself or herself into a self-tormenting repression beyond what God demands)*.

"But I speak this by permission, *and* not of Commandment. *(The Holy Spirit, through Paul, leaves the details of lives, whether celibate or married, to the individual consciences, though with large-hearted wisdom and charity. He would emancipate them from human and* *unauthorized restrictions)"* **(I Cor. 7:1-6).**

As the Word declares, sexual desire is natural and proper; however, it is supposed to result in love and marriage.

TO AVOID TEMPTATION

Later, Paul declared that *"If they cannot contain, let them marry: for it is better to marry than to burn"* (I Cor. 7:9).

He was repeating the exhortation that people ought to marry, as a general rule, to avoid unrest and temptation. The sin of fornication often occurs when people are frustrated in their natural sexual urges. This is not to imply that a Christian cannot live a happy, normal life without being married. He most definitely can do so with the help and Grace of God. But, for the most part, men and women are meant to be together.

THE PROCREATION OF THE HUMAN RACE

One important reason for men and women coming together in marriage is for the procreation of the race. God told Adam and Eve in the Garden of Eden, *"Be fruitful, and multiply, and replenish the Earth"* (Gen. 1:28). God also commanded Noah and his descendants, *"Be fruitful, and multiply, and replenish the Earth"* (Gen. 9:1). So a major factor in the sexual union of husband and wife is to bring children into the world.

The sex act is not just for procreation, however. It is also essential in creating an intimate bond or relationship, in love, between husband and wife. It is a provision of God and a blessing of marriage. In fact, the union of a husband and wife who love each other dearly, in intercourse, is a physical symbolism, of the spiritual union between Christ and the Believer (Rom. 6:3-5).

THE WORD OF GOD

According to God's Word, the husband is to have authority

over his wife's body, and she is to satisfy permissible sexual needs. Those needs are to be limited to the guidelines God has laid down. Likewise, the husband is to satisfy the needs of the wife within God's guidelines. *"Marriage is honorable in all, and the bed undefiled: but whoremongers and adulterers God will judge"* (Heb. 13:4).

There are, however, perversions of sexual activity and other practices that certainly would be considered unclean. Scripture does not by any means assert that any kind of sexual activity is permissible, simply because individuals are married. Such sexual activity as oral-genital or anal sex can be considered unclean or a kind of perversion. Paul spoke of uncleanness wherein sexual partners *"dishonor their own bodies between themselves." ". . . Without natural affection"* (Rom. 1:24, 31). These are unholy desires and unnatural experiences between adulterers, homosexuals, or even legally married couples who debase the human body.

PERVERSION

Satan tries to pervert sex drives that were intended to be good. These sex desires go all the way from natural sexual acts to unnatural sexual acts such as homosexuality, lesbianism, bestiality, incest, and even such sexual acts that involve murder. The Child of God must always remember that his body is the Temple of the Holy Spirit (I Cor. 3:16-17) and the body is never to be given over to perversion or uncleanness.

It was these unnatural sex acts that Paul warned against in Romans, Chapter 1. Because of the growing tenacity of sin, he said, any perverse indulgence will require more and more deviance to satisfy man's lust. From the beginning, the Lord warned against perversion. He said:

"None of you shall approach to any who is near of kin to him, to uncover their nakedness (incest). *Moreover you shall not lie carnally with your neighbor's wife* (adultery). *You shall not let any of your seed pass through the fire to Molech* (infanticide).

***You shall not lie with mankind as with womankind* (homosexuality)*: it is abomination. Neither shall you lie with any beast to defile yourself therewith* (bestiality). *Defile not you yourselves in any of these things: for in all these the land is defiled . . . the land itself vomits out her inhabitants"* (Lev. 18:6, 20-25).**

IMMORALITY

With all the emphasis on sex and pornography in our society today, and with all the perversions Satan has brought out into the open, is it any wonder that some people are inclined to think that any sexual activity is bad? The fact is though, God created men and women as sexual beings — as well as mental, physical, and spiritual beings. There are sexual needs, wants, and desires built into the human body that are perfectly legitimate. It's just that God intended that these desires be satisfied between husband and wife.

Marital sex should be a beautiful act that binds and draws two people together. And it is, if it is done in the proper manner with the proper attitude. *"Rejoice with the wife of your youth . . . let her breasts satisfy you at all times; and be thou ravished always with her love"* (Prov. 5:18-19).

CHAPTER TWENTY-FIVE

What Do Preachers Mean When They Speak Of Having Other Preachers Or A Denomination As Their "Covering"?

QUESTION:

WHAT DO PREACHERS MEAN WHEN THEY SPEAK OF HAVING OTHER PREACHERS OR A DENOMINATION AS THEIR "COVERING"?

ANSWER:

Some time ago I was watching a particular Christian Television Network, which was featuring a prominent Preacher and a Christian entertainer.

The entertainer had just made a rock album, which, of course, presented some difficulties. It was not Christian rock, but rather the type of music recorded by the rockers, etc. He was trying to defend his actions on this Christian Television Network.

As I observed the proceedings, even as the host proceeded to ask him some particular questions, which were softball so to speak, it quickly became obvious that the audience was not exactly agreeing with his position.

At a particular point in the program, the Pastor spoke up and stated words to this effect, *"If anyone has any doubt about his consecration to the Lord, I am his covering, and I will vouch for him."*

Now I suppose that was supposed to make everything right.

THE WORD OF GOD

The criteria for any and every situation in the heart and life of any Believer, is not what someone else says, or even a Church or a denomination, it is what the Word of God says. Unfortunately, the Church has departed from the Word of God to such an extent, that it hardly matters anymore.

The *"covering teaching"* has become very prominent in the last few years. In its most simplistic form, it means that a Preacher will submit himself to a group of Preachers who, in

turn, will vouch for him, and so forth.

Denominations are used in the same context, with Preachers submitting themselves to the denomination which then provides their covering, etc.

It is generally taught that those who will not yield to such are, in effect, *"lone rangers,"* who are trying to hide something.

To be frank, the very opposite is true. Preachers, who do this, or anyone for that matter, claiming that some Preacher is their covering, or even a denomination, are themselves most of the time trying to hide something.

If, as a Believer, I am living for God and, thereby, conducting myself in such a way, simply because of what other people might think, then I don't have very much Christianity. I serve God because I love Him.

Irrespective as to who is looking or not looking, who is observing or not observing, I want to please the Lord. That is the overriding factor in all that I do, and should be the overriding factor in the hearts and lives of every Believer.

CARNALITY

Even though this idea of *"covering"* seems good to the carnal mind, there is no Scriptural validity for this found in the Word of God. It must always be remembered, even as we've already stated, that the Bible must be the criteria and the foundation of all that we do. If it's not Biblical, then it's either wrong or of no worthwhile consequence.

Actually, this *"man covering belief"* is not only of no worthwhile consequence, but it is also, in effect, unscriptural. This is what the Bible says about covering:

"Woe to the rebellious children, says the LORD, who take counsel, but not of Me; and who cover with a covering, but not of My Spirit, that they may add sin to sin:

"That walk to go down into Egypt, and have not asked at My Mouth, to strengthen themselves in the strength of Pharaoh, and to trust in the shadow of Egypt!" (Isa. 30:1-2).

As is obvious from the Word of God, the only covering that we have that is of any consequence, is the Precious Shed Blood of the Lord Jesus Christ. Anything else is of man's doing and is facetious. True, all of us need the counsel, prayers, and support of our Brethren in the Lord. True, it is very helpful to have fellow Ministers (or anyone) to confide in regarding weaknesses, problems, or anything that Believers can help us pray about.

To look to mere mortals, denominations, or any type of man-made structure as a covering, however, is to deny the covering of the Shed Blood of Christ, and the Holy Spirit, and, instead, to resort to man. One will then receive only the help that man can give, which is precious little to say the least!

ONE CAN LIE TO MEN; ONE CANNOT LIE TO THE HOLY SPIRIT

One cannot successfully lie to God, but one can lie to men, and many often do. The idea that one is safe if he has some type of man-made covering is foolishness. This teaching stems from psychology, which denies the Word of God as our source of strength and direction, and, instead, calls for leaning on the frail arm of man. What difference does it make if all the men in the world vouch for an individual, and God doesn't? Conversely, what difference does it make if all the men in the world will not vouch for an individual, and God does?

We should seek earnestly the well-wishes, the prayers, and approval of our Brethren in the Lord; however, it is not man's approval or well-wishes that make the difference; it is God's approval and His Alone. Paul said this:

***"Do we begin again to commend ourselves? or need we, as some others, Epistles of commendation to you, or letters of commendation from you?"* (II Cor. 3:1).**

Paul also said:

***"For not he who commends himself is approved, but whom the Lord commends"* (II Cor. 10:18).**

AN EXAMPLE

Some time ago in a Christian magazine, there was a write-up by one of the editors concerning a particular Evangelist. He had submitted himself to a group of men, and they became his covering. It was ballyhooed as an example of an honest ministry.

The truth was this Evangelist lived in Texas. One of the Preachers who claimed to be his covering lived in California, and if I remember correctly, another one lived in New England, and the third one lived in London, England.

These Preachers might see this Evangelist once a year, if that! How silly can we be?

Once again, I come back to the idea, that the *"covering situation,"* as it is presently proposed, is no more than a joke. And if the truth be known and, as stated, the Preachers who submit to such are in reality trying to hide something.

AND FINALLY . . .

We can either have the covering of the Lord or the covering of man; we cannot have both. If we opt for man's so-called covering, then in reality, we receive no covering at all. The Holy Spirit will simply step aside and allow us to trust the ways of Egypt. I love my Brother in the Lord. I seek his counsel and his help – and I need all the help I can get! But to proclaim a poor, frail individual or poor, frail denominational head as my *"covering"* is grossly unscriptural.

How far has the Church drifted from the Ways of God? Today one is ridiculed if he says, *"The Lord is my covering."* He is praised if he says, *"Man is my covering."*

I will say as Joshua said a long time ago:

". . . but as for me and my house, we will serve the LORD" (Josh. 24:15).

CHAPTER TWENTY-SIX

Does The Bible Teach "Capital Punishment"?

QUESTION:

DOES THE BIBLE TEACH "CAPITAL PUNISHMENT"?

ANSWER:

Yes, it does, but only under very limited circumstances.

The first Command, as far as we know, that was given by God concerning capital punishment for the capital crime of murder, was given immediately after the flood, some 1,600 years from the time of Adam and Eve. In this Covenant with Noah and his sons, the Lord said:

> **"Whoso sheds man's blood, by man shall his blood be shed** *(in this Covenant, we actually have the institution of Government; the Passage speaks of cold-blooded murder; that being the case, the State has the right to take the life of such a murderer)*: **for in the Image of God made He man** *(capital punishment is not meant by God to serve as a deterrent, but rather to portray the inherent worth of man)*" **(Gen. 9:6).**

About 900 years after Noah, the Lord gave the great Law to Moses, which was for a particular people (the Israelites), and for a certain time frame — to the time of Christ, a period of approximately 1,500 years. In the Law, the Lord commanded: *"He who smites a man, so that he die, shall be surely put to death"* (Ex. 21:12). But yet, the Lord placed a caveat, so to speak, in the instructions. He said:

***"At the mouth of two witnesses, or three witnesses, shall he who is worthy of death be put to death; but at the mouth of one witness he shall not be put to death"* (Deut. 17:6). That means if there was only one eyewitness to a capital crime, and no matter how reliable that person was, while the criminal could be incarcerated, he could not be put to death. For the death sentence to go into force there had to be two or more eyewitnesses**

to the crime; consequently, there were not too very many executions under the Law.

THE NEW TESTAMENT

Concerning the New Covenant, and as it regards capital punishment, Paul said and I quote from THE EXPOSITOR'S STUDY BIBLE:

> **"Let every soul be subject unto the higher powers** *(refers to Human Government)*. **For there is no power but of God** *(refers to the fact that God has ordained Government)*: **the powers that be are ordained of God** *(refers to Human Government being a permanent institution, brought into being by God for the regulation of human affairs)*.
>
> **"Whosoever therefore resists the power, resists the Ordinance of God** *(anarchy is not of God)*: **and they who resist shall receive to themselves damnation** *(the Law of the Land is always to be obeyed, providing it does not offend our conscience or the Word of God; the 'damnation' mentioned here does not necessarily refer to such coming from God, but rather from men)*.
>
> **"For rulers are not a terror to good works, but to the evil** *(concerns the Divine right of Government to oppose crime and to protect its citizens)*. **Will you then not be afraid of the power?** *(This means that Civil Government should be respected, and all should fear breaking the Law.)* **do that which is good, and you shall have praise of the same** *(refers to obeying the Law, as all Christians ought to do; as well, it assumes that the Laws are right and just)*:
>
> **"For he** *(the Civil Magistrate)* **is the minister of God to you for good** *(proclaims Government as a Divine Institution)*. **But if you do that which is evil, be afraid; for he bears not the sword in vain** *(the sword is the symbol of the right of the State to inflict Capital punishment for Capital*

crimes): **for he is the minister of God** *(not a Preacher of the Gospel, but a servant of the State)*, **a revenger to *execute* wrath upon him who does evil** *(proclaims the right of the State, as ordained by God, to use whatever force is necessary to stop 'evil,' i.e., crime)*.

"Wherefore *you* must needs be subject *(plainly tells us that Christians are subject to the Law of the Land; that is, if it does not violate the Word of God)*, **not only for wrath, but also for conscience sake** *(refers to the fact that the Believer has a higher principle than that of the unbeliever)*.

"For for this cause pay you tribute also *(refers to the paying of taxes)*: **for they are God's ministers, attending continually upon this very thing** *(refers to public servants)*.

"Render therefore to all their dues *(means that it is proper and right for all people to pay taxes, Christians as well!)*: **tribute to whom tribute *is due*** *(refers to that which is owed, and should be paid)*; **custom to whom custom** *(addresses hidden taxes, which we should pay as well)*; **fear to whom fear; honour to whom honour** *(Government is an Institution to be respected, extending to all Civil servants from the lowest to the highest)*" **(Rom. 13:1-7).**

HUMAN GOVERNMENT

As we've already stated, human government was instituted by God Himself, in what is referred to as the *"Noahic Covenant"* (Gen. 9:1-17). As we've already given in the above Text, Christians are commanded in the New Testament to pay taxes and to support government. Law, as a part of Government, will continue as the rule of right in all eternal societies. If the right to govern is based upon the best public interest, then the right and duty to use any necessary means to attain this end must be recognized by all. It is somewhat absurd to

believe that rulers have a right to govern, yet have no right to use the necessary means to enforce that government. Making the same error, many Christians object to the right of capital punishment, the right to deal with mobs, the right to suppress rebellions, and the right to make war, that is, if such is necessary. Erroneously they think that under all circumstances Government can be carried on without resorting to any means that would take life. Others go so far as to maintain that Government can be carried on without force to sustain the authority of the Law. But these positions cannot be maintained with any degree of logic, and they are not backed by God and Scripture.

It is absurd to hold that rulers have a right to rule as long as their subjects voluntarily obey, but then when they refuse to obey, Government should cease to exist. It is impossible for the right to govern to exist when the right to enforce obedience does not exist.

THOU SHALT NOT KILL?

The Sixth Commandment given by God under the Law is, *"You shall not kill"* (Ex. 20:13). It should have been translated, *"You shall do no murder."* God, in His Holy Word, commands Magistrates to put evil men to death. Such is not murder. To *"kill"* and to *"commit murder"* are two different verbs in the Hebrew Text.

In fact, in Exodus, Chapter 21, the Lord levels the punishment of execution for several things: murder being one, the smiting of parents by their son or daughter being another, and kidnapping, etc.

But again, we go back to the ruling that stated there had to be two or more witnesses to these capital crimes before the sentence of execution could be carried out. As we also stated, considering this rule, there were not many executions in Israel.

Under the New Covenant, while capital punishment is still in force, I personally, feel as it regards the caveat given

in Deuteronomy 17:6, that no sentence of execution should be imposed upon anyone, if there is the slightest hint of a lack of mental equilibrium. Incarceration, yes, execution no, except in rare cases.

There were reasons that the Lord gave for this prohibition of having two or more witnesses to a capital crime before capital punishment could be instituted. One person claiming to be a witness could have a grudge against the person and, thereby, lie about the situation. While this can happen with two or more witnesses, it is not nearly as likely to do so.

As well, at times the evidence, even as D.N.A. has proven, even though it seems to be ironclad, sometimes is proven to be otherwise. It's a terrible thing to have to execute anyone, but the horror of being executed for something that one did not do, is beyond comprehension.

There are, according to Scripture, and experience, at times when certain individuals should be executed; however, for all the obvious reasons, such a sentence should be rarely handed down.

CHAPTER TWENTY-SEVEN

How Did Our Bible Come Into Being?

QUESTION:

HOW DID OUR BIBLE COME INTO BEING?

ANSWER:

For a more detailed account of this question, please see the article at the back of THE EXPOSITOR'S STUDY BIBLE entitled, *"Introducing The Bible."*

At the end of the First Christian Century, the Jewish Rabbis, at the Council of Jamnia, closed the Canon of Hebrew Books — those Books considered as authoritative by the Jews. Their decision resulted from:

1. The multiplication and popularity of sectarian apocryphal writings.

2. The fall of Jerusalem (A.D. 70), which created a threat to the religious tradition of the Jews.

3. The disputes with Christians over their interpretation of the Jewish Scriptures in preaching and writing.

There never was any doubt about the five Books of the Law — the Pentateuch — but beyond that various sects of Judaism disagreed. The prophetic collection was generally agreed upon by 200 B.C., but the major problem concerned the other writings. Four criteria operated in deciding what Books should occupy a place in the authoritative Old Testament Scriptures:

1. The content of each Book had to harmonize with the Law.

2. Since Prophetic inspiration was believed to have begun with Moses (1450 B.C.) and ended with Ezra (450 B.C.), to qualify for the Canon and to be considered inspired, a Book had to have been written within that time frame.

3. The language of the original manuscript had to be Hebrew.

4. The Book had to have been written within the geographical boundaries of Palestine, with the exception of Daniel and possibly Esther.

THE CANON OF SCRIPTURE

On this basis the thirty-nine Books of the Old Testament were selected for the Palestinian Canon of Scriptures. Failing these criteria, the rest of the ancient Jewish writings came to be classified as *"Apocrypha"* or *"Pseudepigrapha"* literally, *"false writings."*

A number of Christian writings, other than those that came to be accepted for the New Testament, appeared early and were considered by some authorities to be worthy of Canonical status. The Didache, the Epistle of Barnabas, I and II Clement, the Shepherd of Hermas, the Apocalypse of Peter, and the Acts of Paul were some of the more popular ones. By the beginning of the Third Century, twenty-two of the Books comprising our present New Testament had become widely accepted. Four principles or considerations operated in determining which Books should occupy a place in the authoritative New Testament Scriptures:

1. Was the Book written by an Apostle or by someone associated with an Apostle?
2. Was the Book's content of a Spiritual Nature?
3. Was the Book widely received by the Churches?
4. Was there evidence in the Book of Divine Inspiration?

As far as is known, it was the Easter letter of Archbishop Athanasius of Alexandria in A.D. 367 that first listed the twenty-seven Books of our New Testament as authoritative. Jerome, by his Latin translation of these same twenty-seven Books (A.D. 382), further established this list as Canonical for the Churches.

DOES THE BIBLE HAVE ANY ERRORS IN IT?

One of the most basic tenants of the Christian Faith is that the Scriptures are inerrant. Because the Bible is God's Word, and is the only Word of God in the world, it is entirely error-free. Of course, this does not mean that all translations are

error-free. The King James translation, and all the modern translations since, are just that — translations. So, while the Bible's original Text is without error, mistakes may have crept into the many copies that were made, from which the translated Versions were derived. Because of age, there are no original manuscripts left; however, scholarship states that if there are ten exact copies of the original, then the copies are deemed to be authentic. Actually, there are more copies of the various Books of the Bible or parts thereof, some 10,000 total, than any other book of antiquity in the world. So, whenever you hold the King James Version in your hands, you can be confident that you are holding in your hands the Word of God.

Some so-called scholars have said that the Bible is filled with historical, chronological, and doctrinal contradictions. But a close examination of their objections reveals that the problem lies, not with the Bible, but with our limited perspective.

CONTRADICTORY PASSAGES EXPLAINED

For instance, there are several seemingly contradictory Passages about what happens when men gaze upon the Face of God, etc. St. John 1:18 says, *"No man has seen God at any time"* and Exodus 33:20 says, *"And God said, You cannot see My Face: for there shall no man see Me, and live."* Yet, in Genesis 32:30 it says, *"And Jacob called the name of the place Penial: for I have seen God face to face."* Further, Exodus 33:11 says, *"And the LORD spoke unto Moses face to face, as a man speaks unto his friend."* Which is correct?

What most of us fail to realize is that the word *"seen"* or *"see"* also means *"to comprehend"* or *"to understand."* So, the Verse in St. John does not contradict the Verses in Genesis and Exodus at all. What John was saying was that no man has ever comprehended or understood everything about God — not at any time. We use the same kind of terminology in our conversations today. For instance, we will explain something to someone and then say, *"Do you see?"* But we don't really

mean *"see,"* as to look with the natural eye. We simply mean, *"Do you understand?" "Do you comprehend?"* So, there is clearly no contradiction here.

Another so-called *"inconsistency"* along this line appears in Exodus 33:20 where God says, *"No man can see My Face and live."* Yet Genesis 32:30 says that Jacob saw God face to face. Again what must be understood is that God was not talking about appearance only. He was not talking about Moses looking upon His Face as we would look upon someone's face. The word *"see"* in Exodus 33:20 pertains to more than outward features. Here God was talking about His Glory, because He said in Exodus 33:22, *"And it shall come to pass while My Glory passes by, that I . . . will cover you with My Hand."* Moses wanted not just to see God's Face, but to see it in His usual Glory — in the Light in which He dwelt — *"which no man has seen, nor can see"* (I Tim. 6:16). Actually, God has appeared a number of times to individuals, according to the Word of God, and they did look upon His Face. They did not, however, behold His Glory.

ANOTHER WORD EXPLAINED

Another apparent contradiction that scholars wrestle over concerns Jesus' warning against calling anyone a fool. In Matthew 5:22, Jesus said that if a person called another a fool, he would be in danger of Hell fire. Yet, Jesus Himself repeatedly called people fools in Matthew and in Luke. In Matthew, Chapter 5, where Jesus forbade the use of that kind of accusation, the Greek word translated fool is *"moros,"* which means a wicked reprobate, destitute of all spirituality. This, in effect, consigned a person to Hell. No one but God has the right to pass that kind of Judgment. But, in Luke, Chapter 11, as well as in Matthew, Chapter 23, the word *"fool"* in the Greek is a totally different word — *"aphron"* — which means *"senseless ones without reason; foolish; stupid; acting without intelligence,"* so I think it's fairly obvious that Jesus was not saying

the same thing in Matthew, Chapter 5 as He was in Matthew, Chapter 23, and Luke, Chapter 11.

Our English word *"fool"* was used in each instance, but it meant two different things altogether in the Greek. The problem then comes with the translation from one language to another. Often the only way to resolve these complex difficulties is to study the Text of Scripture in the original Greek and Hebrew languages. We may have trouble understanding the context of a Passage, or a translator may have been imperfect in his choice of words, but the Bible itself is error-free.

WHAT IS MEANT BY THE TERM *"APOCRYPHA"*?

This group of Books, numbering about fourteen, is believed to be spurious, or at least, noncanonical. This in no way implies that the books in question do not contain some good things, nor does it mean they were written by evil men. It simply means they were believed not to be inspired; consequently, they were not placed in the Canon of Scripture.

Eleven of these Apocryphal books have been accepted by the Catholic Church, included in Roman Catholic Canon, and placed in the *"Douay Version"* of the Bible.

Why were these books not considered inspired or Canonical by the rest of the Church? Some of the reasons relate specifically to the Old Testament; some to the New Testament.

THE REASONS

- **As far as the Old Testament was concerned, these particular books were not included in the Hebrew Canon of Scripture.**
- **The Lord Jesus Christ, the Apostle Paul, or any other writer in the New Testament ever quoted from these writings. Yet they quoted frequently in the New Testament from the Books that were included in the Hebrew Canon of Scripture.**
- **Josephus, the Hebrew historian, expressly excluded**

these as *"false writings."*

• None of the Apocryphal books claimed Divine Inspiration.

• The Apocryphal books have historical, geographical, and chronological errors.

• As literature, they are considered to be myth and legend.

• Their Spiritual and even moral stance is generally far below both the Old and the New Testaments.

• Most of these books were written much later than the Books that were considered to be authoritative and inspired.

DIVINE INSPIRATION

As we saw in an earlier question, in order for the New Testament writings to be Canonized, a Book had to have been written by an Apostle or someone associated with an Apostle. The Book had to be Spiritual, had to have been widely received by the Churches, and had to show evidence of Divine Inspiration.

Satan has done everything within his power to hinder, destroy, dilute, and outright do away with the Word of Almighty God. But through the Power of God, the Bible as we have it today — all sixty-six Books, both Old and New Testaments, from Genesis to Revelation — is the Word of God. Nothing else can be added to it.

When any person or any Church claims that other writings, other books, other so-called inspirations should be included in the Canon of Scripture, we can be sure that the Evil One has been at work. Paul put it aptly when he said:

"Though we, or an Angel from Heaven, preach any other gospel unto you than that which we have preached unto you, let him be accursed. As we said before, so say I now again, If any man preach any other gospel unto you than that you have received, let him be accursed" (Gal. 1:8-9).

CHAPTER TWENTY-EIGHT

Why Do The Wicked Prosper?

QUESTION:

WHY DO THE WICKED PROSPER?

ANSWER:

Asaph, David's praise and worship leader faced this same dilemma. He said, *"As for me, my feet were almost gone, my steps had well nigh slipped. For I was envious at the foolish, when I saw the prosperity of the wicked"* (Ps. 73:2-3).

We must remember that Satan is *"the god of this present world system"* (II Cor. 4:4); consequently, he will help some people to get rich to further his kingdom. He wants people to believe that sin and following evil pays. This is the reason millions today are blinded. They look at wicked people who have land, houses, fame, and popularity. Deceived by this, millions of young people think it is smart to learn how to drink, smoke, gamble, and engage in the things that God has forbidden. Many of the so-called famous people of this world are heralded far and wide for doing these things, which makes many think that such is smart. Young and old alike are led to believe that emulating these individuals will bring happiness. But Jesus said, *"A man's life consists not in the abundance of the things which he possesses"* (Lk. 12:15). Proportionally, there are more up-and-outers than down-and-outers who commit suicide. A man who sets his heart to seek only riches is in for a rude awakening.

AS IN A MOMENT!

I remember years ago a co-worker I knew and respected, made the statement that when he was living for the Devil it seemed that everything he touched turned to money. Now, it seems he could not make the proverbial ends meet. The Devil had allowed him to prosper, even as he allows millions to prosper. In so doing, Satan can keep millions of people in

bondage. They think they are doing well when they are actually selling their soul for a few baubles and trinkets. When people trust in riches and walk in wickedness, *"How are they brought into desolation, as in a moment! they are utterly consumed with terrors"* (Ps. 73:19). I read some time ago that the heir of one of the great fortunes of America died of an overdose of sleeping pills; actually it was suicide. Having everything money could buy did not bring him peace and satisfaction.

BELIEVERS CAN PROSPER

Christians must remember that if they will believe God and use their faith, they can, as well, be prosperous in the Lord Jesus Christ. One of the great myths that Satan has perpetrated is that to be Godly, a person has to be poverty-stricken. That isn't so; God blesses, and blesses greatly those who believe Him, thereby, standing on His Promises. Conversely, those who allow Satan to persuade them that living an evil life brings prosperity are living in a fool's paradise. The only true way to enjoy prosperity and use it for the benefit of others is through the Lord Jesus Christ.

ENJOYMENT COMES FROM WICKEDNESS?

Why does it seem that those who deal treacherously are happy? The answer is simple; their enjoyment comes from the wickedness in which they are involved. Naturally, they are happy; however, happiness has to do with our present surroundings. Lasting temporarily, it has nothing to do with real and everlasting joy. Joy comes from within; consequently, one of the big stumbling blocks for the Child of God is seeing people who consistently live an evil life, yet, it seems, are so happy and carefree. Satan allows this, but again Psalm 73:19 applies here too. *"How are they brought into desolation as in a moment! they are utterly consumed with terrors."*

CHRISTIANS AND HAPPINESS

Some time ago, a survey was conducted in the United States to determine which group of people is the happiest? Much to the pollsters' amazement, it was found that Born-Again Christians who believe entirely in the Word of God and do their best to live for the Lord Jesus Christ are the most contented, joyful, and happy people in America. Of course, I did not have to read the article to know this to be a fact. Overcoming Christians are the happiest people in the whole world. Jesus said, *"The thief comes not, but for to steal, and to kill, and to destroy: I am come that they might have life, and that they might have it more abundantly"* (Jn. 10:10). Living for God now and for eternity is still the happiest life man has ever known.

MERCY

I know some Christians have thought and probably even vocalized their feelings that God should clear the Earth of all rebels; He should annihilate every person who is living in wickedness and evil. At times they wonder why He does not do it. There are several reasons.

First of all, God is merciful. *"His Mercy endures forever"* (Ps. 106:1) and *"is from everlasting to everlasting"* (Ps. 103:17). We have all lived in sin and ungodliness, but God's Mercy spared us, and we came to the saving knowledge of the Lord Jesus Christ. We ceased to be enemies of the Gospel and became Born-Again Christians.

Sometimes enemies of God change. It would have been easy for God to have stricken a man by the name of Saul. He made havoc of the Church, dragging Christians from their homes and throwing them in jail. He stood by while other enemies of God stoned Stephen; one of the greatest men of God who ever lived (Acts 7:58). He was probably the most notorious enemy of the Church of the Lord Jesus Christ of that day; but at high noon outside the city walls of Damascus, Saul, later called Paul, met the Lord Jesus Christ. A great light shone about him and Saul fell to the ground as one stricken dead. He was actually blinded by the brilliant light. The Lord Jesus spoke to him and changed his name to Paul. This Apostle of hate became the greatest Apostle of love the world ever knew (read for example, Acts, Chapter 26).

ENEMIES OF GOD

I stood in Rome, Italy, some time ago and looked at the great coliseum where the blood of multiple thousands of Christians had stained the soil. Rome, with all of its power, had done everything within its grasp to eliminate the memory of the Lord Jesus Christ. Yet, for every Christian who was snatched from the ranks, their body torn to pieces by wild beasts in the Roman arena, ten stepped in and took their place.

I stood there looking at it. What and where is Rome today? She is nothing but a drowsy beggar watching the hands of a broken clock. Her Caesars are peanut vendors; her mighty military generals are organ grinders. On the other hand, where is Christianity today? Rome perished, but Christianity survived, and greatly so!

We must also remember that one day every enemy will be defeated. After sufficient mercy has been expended and God has given every opportunity to every enemy to kneel at the foot of the Cross, then Satan will be *"cast into the Lake of Fire and brimstone"* along with *"the Beast and the False Prophet"* (Rev. 20:10). Every enemy will be vanquished. Victory, power, glory, honor, and above all love will reign when Jesus Christ comes back.

THE DAY OF GRACE

Ours is the day of Grace. God does not pour out fire and brimstone or issue execution for millions of people, simply because He is striving for the Salvation of all men. He is *"not*

willing that any should perish, but that all should come to Repentance" **(II Pet. 3:9). It is not His desire to see one single person lost. There is no joy in Heaven over the death of a sinner (compare Lk. 15:7).**

MAN, THE FREE MORAL AGENT

Another factor that must be reckoned with is this: man is a free moral agent. God does not force His Will on anyone; neither does He force anyone to be evil. Man has the power of choice. He can choose to curse God or to praise Him. He can choose to disobey God or to obey Him. He can choose to follow the Lord's Commandments, or he can break these Commandments. He has all the powers accorded a free moral agent. Actually, this is the primary cause of all the problems in the world today. God is not at fault; man is. Although we realize that Satan is the author of all sin and evil, man does not have to choose to follow him. He can choose to follow God if he so desires!

EYES ON THE WICKED

Psalm 73 is the story of Asaph, as stated, David's praise and worship leader. I think it would be profitable at this juncture for us to quote from THE EXPOSITOR'S STUDY BIBLE the entirety of the Seventy-third Psalm. I think that doing such would throw more light on this subject than anything else, and because it was given by the Holy Spirit for the very purpose of showing us that the prosperity of the wicked is fleeting, if at all, but that the prosperity of the Child of God is eternal. Asaph said:

> **"Truly God is good to Israel, even to such as are of a clean heart.** *(This is the third Book of the Psalms, referred to as 'The Leviticus Book.' Its subject is the Sanctuary, as that of the first Book was the Blessed Man [Christ], and that of the second, Israel [His People].*

"Israel, as a worshipper in her future time of trouble, is the subject of this Book, rather than the Messiah and the Remnant, which are that of the first two Books. Most definitely, God was good to Israel.)

"But as for me *(Asaph)*, **my feet were almost gone; my steps had well nigh slipped** *(Asaph was the leader of the choral worship under David [I Chron. 16:4-5]. So he held a very high Spiritual Position in Israel.)*

"For I was envious at the foolish, when I saw the prosperity of the wicked. *(Asaph, perplexed with the problem that the ungodly prosper and the children of the Kingdom at times suffer, learns the lesson that outside the Sanctuary, the mind is distracted and the heart fermented, but that inside, all is peace. Looking in confounds; looking out confuses; looking up comforts.*

"Asaph's problem was 'self.' Preoccupation with 'self' always leads to spiritual distraction. Men have ever tried to improve self; men have ever failed. Even Christian man fails, when endeavoring to improve 'self.' 'Self' can only be conquered when it is hidden in Christ [Jn. 14:20].)

"For there are no bands in their death: but their strength is firm. *(When one becomes enamored with 'self,' then one's Spiritual Judgment becomes flawed. Asaph fell into the age-old trap. First of all, 'prosperity' is not the purpose of Redemption; Salvation is.*

"Second, Asaph is wrong about the 'death' of the wicked. It is anything but positive.)

"They are not in trouble as other men; neither are they plagued like other men. *(The truth is, the system of this world is not of God, but of Satan; consequently, the Child of God is constantly 'plagued' by that system.*

"But considering that, still, the life of the follower of Christ is, by far, the most rewarding life there is. If there were no eternity, living for God would still be, by far, the greater choice.)

"Therefore pride compasses them about as a chain,

violence covers them as a garment. *(Asaph is saying that 'the wicked' constantly engage themselves in 'violence,' with few negative results. They are filled with 'pride,' and, instead of it bringing destruction, it seems to reward them.)*

"Their eyes stand out with fatness: they have more than heart could wish. *(These statements show that Asaph has given this much thought. Due to his preoccupation with 'self,' Satan has made great inroads to his soul. One of Satan's greatest weapons is to make the Christian think that, by living for God, he is truly missing out. However, we must always remember that Satan is a liar and the father of lies. Actually, the opposite is true.)*

"They are corrupt, and speak wickedly concerning oppression: they speak loftily. *(The speech of the wicked is lofty concerning how they will oppress people, and no harm seems to come to them.)*

"They set their mouth against the heavens, and their tongue walks through the Earth. *(Everything they say is in opposition to the Word of God. They boast of what they will do, evil as it may be, and they seem to be able to do it without hindrance.)*

"Therefore his people return hither: and waters of a full cup are wrung out to them. *(They cause men who have been converted from a life of covetousness to return to it.)*

"And they say, how does God know? and is there knowledge in the Most High? *(In other words, they laugh at God, thinking they are getting by with their wickedness.)*

"Behold, these are the ungodly, who prosper in the world; they increase in riches. *(It is true that some of the ungodly 'prosper' [financially], but, as a whole, it is not true. In fact, it is seldom true. Taking the whole world into consideration, for every one prosperous wicked man there are ten thousand who are the very opposite.)*

"Verily I have cleansed my heart in vain, and washed my hands in innocency. *(Every attack that Satan levels* *against a Believer, irrespective of its direction, is for one purpose: to destroy the faith of the individual. In other words, Asaph is saying that there is no profit in living for God.*

"*How wrong he is! The rewards of the wicked, such as they are, are fleeting and temporal. The rewards of the righteous are eternal.)*

"For all the day long have I been plagued, and chastened every morning. *(The Lord is sorely displeased with complaints. This is the opposite of faith and appreciation for what the Lord has done for us. And yet, so many of us are guilty of this sin — thanklessness.)*

"If I say, I will speak thus; behold, I should offend against the generation of Your children. *(He knew that the evidence was against him. Wickedness was not profitable, and living for God is.)*

"When I thought to know this, it was too painful for me *(now Asaph realizes he is wrong; he knows he is sliding down a path that leads only to destruction; still, he does not know the answer to his dilemma);*

"Until I went into the Sanctuary of God; then understood I their end. *(How could the Sanctuary give him the answers? Because the Sanctuary is where God dwelt. Now, he no longer sees the alleged prosperity of the wicked, but the Glory of God. Then and only then do the flaws of the wicked become obvious. As well, when he sees the Lord, he no longer sees himself.)*

"Surely You did set them *(the wicked)* **in slippery places: You cast them down into destruction.** *(On the surface, the road of the wicked may look prosperous; however, upon closer inspection, it is easy to see that it is 'slippery.' Being so, they will fall to their own 'destruction.')*

"How are they brought into desolation, as in a moment! they are utterly consumed with terrors. *(Now Asaph begins to see what the situation really is. The wicked look as though they are so prosperous, and then, all of a sudden, they are bankrupt and 'brought into desolation'*

— 'as in a moment!'

"Now he sees that all of their boasting and clamor against God is but a façade. In a moment, they are 'utterly consumed with terrors.')

"As a dream when one awakes; so, O Lord, when You awake, You shall despise their image. *(At times, it may seem as though the Lord is asleep; however, after a short period, the Lord will 'awake.' Then He will intrude into their 'evil dream.')*

"Thus my heart was grieved, and I was pricked in my reins. *(Now that Asaph has seen the Lord, he has come under Holy Spirit conviction. He is 'grieved,' because of his sin. What he has done now dawns upon him, and he is cut to the core of his being.)*

"So foolish was I, and ignorant: I was as a beast before You. *(The Holy Spirit causes Asaph to see that the direction he has been traveling was foolish indeed! In fact, one of the chief Ministries of the Spirit is to smite with conviction. Were it not that, the Christian would too often get off course, and would not know how to get back on course.)*

"Nevertheless I am continually with You: You have held me by my right hand. *(The Lord does not cast us off when we begin to go astray. Rather, He deals with us, speaks to us, and attempts to pull us back to the right direction. In doing so, He will literally, spiritually speaking, hold us by the hand.)*

"You shall guide me with Your counsel, and afterward receive me to Glory. *(Asaph had previously been listening to the 'counsel' of self-will. Now he tells the Lord, 'I will listen to Your counsel.' God's 'counsel' is His Word.)*

"Whom have I in Heaven but You? and there is none upon Earth that I desire beside You. *(After seeing the Lord and receiving a fresh touch from Glory, he realizes that his Salvation is not money, place, or position, but Christ. He now knows that Christ satisfies all.)*

"My flesh and my heart fails: but God is the strength

of my heart, and my portion forever. *(When Asaph begins to lean on his own strength, which is woefully inadequate, he 'fails.' But now he realizes that 'God is his strength.' Also, he now knows that anything and everything he needs can be provided by God — 'my portion forever.')*

"For, lo, they who are far from You shall perish: You have destroyed all them who go a whoring from You. *(He now fully sees the position of the wicked. They 'shall perish.')*

"But it is good for me to draw near to God: I have put my trust in the Lord GOD, that I may declare all Your Works. *(Some bad things have happened, but some 'good' is coming out of this as well. His perilous situation has caused him to 'draw near to God.' Now, his 'trust' is in the Lord, and not in the things of the world. Asaph vows that he will no longer talk about the prosperity of the wicked, but now will 'declare all Your Works.' This should be a great lesson to us!)***" (Ps. 73:1-28).**

THE WORD OF GOD

And finally, we must understand that our life is not temporal, but eternal. The Psalmist said:

***"For a day in Your Courts is better than a thousand. I had rather be a doorkeeper in the House of my God, than to dwell in the tents of wickedness. For the LORD God is a Sun and Shield: the LORD will give grace and glory: no good thing will He withhold from them who walk uprightly. O LORD of Hosts, blessed is the man who trusts in You"* (Ps. 84:10-12).**

CHAPTER TWENTY-NINE

Is Contemporary Gospel Music Satisfactory To Be Used In Church?

QUESTION:

IS CONTEMPORARY GOSPEL MUSIC SATISFACTORY TO BE USED IN CHURCH?

ANSWER:

No, I don't think it is!

The answer I will give will be predicated on my definition of Contemporary Gospel Music. The truth is, if one would ask ten people what Contemporary Gospel Music is, you would likely get ten different answers. Most of the answers, like mine, would not be cast in concrete and would be somewhat nebulous.

The word *"contemporary"* means *"that which is marked by characteristics of the present."*

Contemporary music, such as Christian alternative, Christian rock, or Christian punk, has a meandering, dislocated melody which means, in everyday terminology, there is no harmony. It is, by and large, discordant, with little or no set pattern; consequently, it is impossible to worship God in a setting of Contemporary Gospel Music.

MUSIC AND SINGING, THE GREATEST FORM OF PRAISE

Gospel or Sacred music, if it is as it should be, is the highest form of praise. We know that, because music that is truly of the Lord contains petition, prayer, prophecy, and praise. Considering that the Holy Spirit dedicated the longest Book in the Bible, to music and singing, we know from that, of the great significance of music and singing as it refers to praise and worship. We must remember that praise is what we do, while worship is what we are. Understanding this, and I continue to speak of the great significance of music and singing, then we should understand how important it is, which is the

reason as well that Satan fights it so hard.

SATAN

The one we now know as Satan was formerly named Lucifer, one of the noted Archangels. He was created by God and, for an undetermined period of time, he served the Lord in beauty and holiness. His name means, *"the morning star,"* or *"son of the morning."*

There is some thought that Lucifer, when he was serving God in Righteousness and Holiness, was in charge of the worship of God. The Scripture says:

"Where were you when I laid the foundations of the Earth? declare, if you have understanding.

"Who has laid the measures thereof, if you know? or who has stretched the line upon it?

"Whereupon are the foundations thereof fashioned? or who laid the corner stone thereof.

***"When the morning stars sang together, and all the sons of God shouted for joy?"* (Job 38:4-7).**

Some think that Lucifer, inasmuch as his name meant *"morning star,"* was in charge of the worship section of Heaven, which was referred to as *"the morning stars."*

As the Prophet Ezekiel said of him, *"The workmanship of your tabrets and of your pipes was prepared in you in the day that you were created"* (Ezek. 28:13). *"Tabrets"* and *"pipes"* have to do with music. It is ironical, any person who has a good singing voice, is referred to by the world as *"having a good set of pipes."*

Knowing of the power of music and singing as it refers to the worship of the Lord, and considering that Satan may have once been in charge of the choirs of Heaven, so to speak, this is at least one of the reasons that he has done his best to corrupt not only the music of the world, but the music of the Church also. In fact, music and singing as it regards the worship of the Lord can be said to be the barometer of the spirituality of

the Church.

AN EXAMPLE

I was preaching a Service in Warsaw, Poland some time back. Individuals had been brought in from other Churches to provide the music. The place was packed. The first two or three songs were Contemporary Gospel Music. I did not recognize any of the melodies. As I could not understand their language, the songs meant nothing. As well, I noticed that even their own people just sat there and stared. They could not worship, also, because there was no spirit of worship there. Such disharmony and meandering of melody (which, in reality, is no melody at all) is offensive to the Holy Spirit, and which characterizes all contemporary music. It impacts, adversely so, the trichotomy of man, of which I will offer more explanation later. Their last song, even though I could not understand the words, was a beautiful hymn. Instantly, the people started praising the Lord. The melody in that particular song (the hymn) was predictable. The harmony blended with the melody, and the result was instantaneous praise. It was like a light had suddenly been turned on in a darkened room.

A MATTER OF TASTE?

Naturally, all of us have our preferences when it comes to music just as we do in clothing, etc. but I am not responding to musical preference here. If anyone thinks that, then it is not understood as to what I'm talking about. And, basically, we are talking about a Moving and Operation of the Holy Spirit.

I will give you the reasons, as I see them, that contemporary music cannot be conducive to worshipping God.

MAN, A TRIPARTITE BEING

"And the very God of Peace Sanctify you wholly; and I pray

God your whole spirit and soul and body be preserved blameless unto the coming of our Lord Jesus Christ" (I Thess. 5:23).

The trichotomy of man is his spirit, soul, and body. Man also is a trichotomy in his senses, which would include melody, harmony, and rhythm. If the melody of a song is not structured, there can be no harmony (and herein is the definition of contemporary music). When the melody is structured, there is automatic harmony. If there is rhythm, there are measures as well. In this musical atmosphere, a person can worship God with his spirit, his soul, his body.

Without the melody, we are left with a discordant song. The Spiritual Senses cannot respond because there is no conduit. The ears hear, but the spirit cannot respond. When the spirit of man is in tune with the Spirit of God, there is harmony.

Contrary to the opinions of some Churches (and individuals) rhythm is not worldly. What these people fail to understand is the trichotomy of man: that man is a melodic being and a harmonic being and a rhythmic being.

Other Churches seem to feel if they eliminate all rhythm (which would be percussion or stringed instruments) and rely solely on an organ, it will produce a *"religious sound."* And they are right. But oftentimes that *"sound"* is filled with depressing spirits.

Man is a rhythmic being, so rhythm in itself is not wrong; however, if rhythm is used wrongly, it then takes on an improper stance. The same is true with melody and harmony.

I'm sure some will disagree with me, but I do not feel it is wrong for people to clap their hands to the music in Church. Neither is it wrong to have percussion or stringed instruments played in Church. Actually, it is Scriptural.

"And Miriam the Prophetess, the sister of Aaron, took a timbrel in her hand; and all the women went out after her with timbrels and with dances" (Ex. 15:20).

It appears obvious that rhythm was employed here, considering especially that timbrels — which are tambourine-type instruments — were used. In Psalm 150, we are again given

an impressive list of instruments that would fall into the category of percussion and stringed instruments, or *"rhythm."*

AN EXPERIENCE

When Frances and I first began in full-time evangelistic ministry (1958), many of our Pentecostal Churches were trying to emulate their Baptist and Methodist counterparts in that their choirs were basically devoid of all rhythmic instruments. As a result, there was precious little *"spirit"* in the Services, at least where the music was concerned. I tried, wherever I could, to change the music to what we now refer to as *"Sacred Gospel Music."* To be frank, I met with little success, at least in the U.S., but had excellent success in other countries where our Telecast was aired. Now, many Churches have incorporated melody, harmony, and rhythm in their worship. So, maybe we had a little more influence than I at first realized!

WHY CONTEMPORARY MUSIC?

The proponents of Contemporary Gospel Music say, *"It draws the unsaved."* I might quickly ask, *"Draw them to what?"* The drunk is not won to the Lord by serving alcohol to him! As well, the gambler is not converted to the Lord by setting up gaming tables in the Church. The truth is, Sacred Music was never actually meant by God to draw the unsaved or to address itself to the unsaved. The truth is, it may most definitely touch the unsaved, and it may be a blessing to them, but that is what might be referred to as the spill over, and not its main purpose. The primary purpose of Sacred Music is to worship God (Ps. 150).

***"Teaching and admonishing one another in Psalms and Hymns and Spiritual Songs, singing with grace in your hearts to the Lord"* (Col. 3:16).**

Paul also said, *"Speaking to yourselves in Psalms and Hymns, and Spiritual Songs, singing and making melody in your heart*

to the Lord" (Eph. 5:19).

The phrase, *"Singing and making melody in your heart to the Lord,"* places the approval of the Holy Spirit on the same forms of music and styles of worship as was begun in the Old Testament. In fact, most of the music and singing that we use today in worship of the Lord was begun by the sweet singer of Israel, David, as he was guided by the Holy Spirit.

"Melody" as it's used here in the Greek is *"psallo,"* which means *"to play a stringed instrument with the fingers; to strike a chord; sing to the music of a harp."*

Actually, the word *"melody"* would have probably been better translated *"music."* Nevertheless, we are told here by the Holy Spirit through the Apostle, that it's perfectly proper to use musical instruments in the Church, or in any type of worship of the Lord. The idea is, that all such worship comes from the heart, which speaks of worshipping in *"spirit and in truth"* (Jn. 4:24).

Music and singing that is truly of God, always glorifies God! Otherwise, it glorifies man.

"Praise you the LORD. Praise God in His Sanctuary: praise Him in the firmament of His Power.

"Praise Him for His mighty Acts: praise Him according to His Excellent Greatness.

"Praise Him with the sound of the trumpet: praise Him with the psaltery and harp.

"Praise Him with the timbrel and dance: praise Him with stringed instruments and organs.

"Praise Him upon the loud cymbals: praise Him upon the high sounding cymbals.

"Let everything that hath breath praise the LORD. Praise you the LORD" (Ps. 150).